The Kaiser, Hitler and the Jewish Department Store

The Kaiser, Hitler and the Jewish Department Store

The Reich's Retailer

John F. Mueller

BLOOMSBURY ACADEMIC
LONDON • NEW YORK • OXFORD • NEW DELHI • SYDNEY

BLOOMSBURY ACADEMIC
Bloomsbury Publishing Plc
50 Bedford Square, London, WC1B 3DP, UK
1385 Broadway, New York, NY 10018, USA
29 Earlsfort Terrace, Dublin 2, Ireland

BLOOMSBURY, BLOOMSBURY ACADEMIC and the Diana logo are
trademarks of Bloomsbury Publishing Plc

First published in Great Britain 2022
Paperback edition first published 2024

Copyright © John F. Mueller, 2022

John F. Mueller has asserted their right under the Copyright, Designs and
Patents Act, 1988, to be identified as Author of this work.

For legal purposes the Acknowledgements on pp. viii–ix constitute an
extension of this copyright page.

Cover image: Works meeting at Wertheim in Leipziger Strasse, Berlin, approx. 1933–1939;
Jewish Museum Berlin, Inv. No. 2007/218/0

All rights reserved. No part of this publication may be reproduced or transmitted in
any form or by any means, electronic or mechanical, including photocopying,
recording, or any information storage or retrieval system, without prior
permission in writing from the publishers.

Bloomsbury Publishing Plc does not have any control over, or responsibility for, any
third-party websites referred to or in this book. All internet addresses given in this
book were correct at the time of going to press. The author and publisher regret any
inconvenience caused if addresses have changed or sites have ceased to exist, but
can accept no responsibility for any such changes.

Every effort has been made to trace copyright holders and to obtain their
permissions for the use of copyright material. The publisher apologizes for any
or omissions and would be grateful if notified of any corrections that should be
incorporated in future reprints or editions of this book.

A catalogue record for this book is available from the British Library.

A catalog record for this book is available from the Library of Congress.

ISBN: HB: 978-1-3501-4177-3
PB: 978-1-3503-0131-3
ePDF: 978-1-3501-4178-0
eBook: 978-1-3501-4179-7

Typeset by Newgen KnowledgeWorks Pvt. Ltd., Chennai, India

To find out more about our authors and books visit www.bloomsbury.com
and sign up for our newsletters.

Contents

List of Illustrations	vi
Acknowledgements	viii
Introduction	1
1 Foundation: 1834–90 – 'Travelling Sons of David'	15
2 Expansion: 1890–1900 – 'Each Sale – A Piece of Renown'	49
3 Labour: 1890–1930 – 'Qualified Young Ladies'	69
4 Apogee: 1900–14 – 'The Kaiser Is Impressed'	87
5 Survival: 1914–29 – 'Dear Corner of Homeland'	115
6 Decline: 1929–32 – 'Voices of Envy'	141
7 Fall: 1933–9 – 'Two Million Hitler Portraits'	161
Conclusion	185
Notes	193
Bibliography	223
Index	237

Illustrations

Figures

1.1	Birthplace of Oscar Tietz	16
1.2	Georg Wertheim	22
1.3	Flora and Leonhard Tietz	24
1.4	Oscar Tietz	26
1.5	Wronker family	28
1.6	Max Knopf	30
1.7	Margarete and Arthur Levis	32
1.8	Jandorf family	34
1.9	Salman Schocken	37
2.1	Cross-section of Hermann Tietz	50
2.2	Sales strategies	55
2.3	Hermann Tietz picture book	57
3.1	Fashion show	70
3.2	Shopgirls of Knopf	78
3.3	Rest home of Leonhard Tietz	81
4.1	The Emperor and Empress	88
4.2	Interior of Leonhard Tietz	90
4.3	Knopf in Karlsruhe	94
4.4	Wertheim flagship store	99
4.5	Schloss Sassleben	102
4.6	Promotional stamp for Jandorf	107
4.7	KaDeWe	108
5.1	Battle cry of the Emperor	116
5.2	*Die Deutsche Mode*	119
5.3	Karstadt in Berlin	125
5.4	Wertheim in Breslau	128
5.5	Knopf in Freiburg	130
5.6	Schocken in Stuttgart	133
6.1	*Der Stürmer* cartoon 1	142
6.2	*Der Stürmer* cartoon 2	144

6.3	*Der Stürmer* cartoon 3	145
6.4	Promotional stamp from Wronker	154
6.5	Wronker shop window	154
7.1	Adolf Hitler	162
7.2	Albert Brosmann	176
7.3	Labour Day celebrations	179
7.4	Shopgirls in uniform	179

Tables

1.1	Interconnections between Retailing Families and Their Companies	29
3.1	Married and Single Women in Employment, Karlsruhe, 1906	72
3.2	Place of Residence and Birth of the Female Workforce, Karlsruhe, 1906	74
3.3	Assistant/Apprentice Ratio and Years of Apprenticeship, Karlsruhe, 1906	76
3.4	Average Pay Per Month of Employees of Three Randomly Selected Department Stores, Baden, 1900	77

Map

1.1	Department stores across Germany	46

Acknowledgements

Long before Wes Anderson used the department store in Görlitz as a set for his film the *Grand Budapest Hotel*, it inspired my research. During the time of the German Democratic Republic, in which building materials were in short supply, the people of that town took it upon themselves to restore this early twentieth-century store to its full grandeur. They did so in their own time and at their own cost. It is to these people, who in a socialist state renovated a seemingly capitalist symbol, that I owe a debt of gratitude. Through their dedication, I got a tantalizing glimpse into the world as it was a hundred years before, and I began asking questions about the purpose of the building, the people who frequented it and the context in which it existed.

This led to a PhD at the University of Cambridge under Professor Sir Richard J. Evans, who has been the most reliable and supportive mentor of my work. I am deeply grateful to him for all he has done for me and in particular for his – to my mind – surprising faith in my abilities. He and Professor Sir Christopher Clark helped me shape the thesis out of which this book was developed. It was, however, Maja Hattesen, from the German public broadcaster who, after filming a documentary on the history of department stores with me, finally got me to expand and adapt the work for a broader audience.

Sir Richard and Dr Helen Bettinson made the biggest impact on what you are about to read, as they share an ability to be bluntly critical and highly constructive at the same time. I am thankful to them as well as to Charlotte Perry and Charles F. M. Wright for reading drafts of this book. My colleagues and friends Dr Oliver Coates, Dr Christine Corton and Dr Matthew Neal have been wonderful in their encouragement and companionship over the years. Samuel R. Burns, also a dear colleague, produced the map for me. I have had the privilege to work together with wonderful people, including almost everyone at St Edmund's College, University of Cambridge, the staff at Bloomsbury Academic, especially Laura Reeves and Rhodri Mogford, and my former employer Helen Cornish. I thank John Barber, Roger Carver, Esme Fay, John Nolan and Paul Coles for their support and friendship.

A lot of the colour in this book was provided by exclusive access to documents provided by Wolfgang Ziefle, who grew up living next to a department store, and the Knopf, Tietz and Wronker families. It is to these families and to Michael Borth as well as to my parents and brother that I dedicate this book.

Introduction

'Let the Jews die' the Nazi brownshirts chanted as they marched down the high streets of Germany on 1 April 1933.[1] They daubed hate-filled slogans on the shop windows of stores with Jewish sounding names. Calls such as 'A beginning has been made against the Jews'[2] went up, and shoppers were harangued by thugs: 'aren't you ashamed to be buying from a Jew? … if it happens again I will lock you up'.[3] It was the largest nationwide protest against Jews in German history. Just thirty years earlier, the Jewish-born department store entrepreneur Georg Wertheim noted in his diary: 'At first the Emperor looked at the grand light courtyard, with the first two bridges and was clearly impressed by the building.'[4] Wilhelm II and his entourage had come to pay a visit to the store. Wertheim's Jewish rivals and colleagues had also been graced with royal and aristocratic shoppers; in some cases they had been given accolades and medals by the German ruling class. What had happened?

It is human nature to consider one's own lifetime to be one of the most intense and disruptive in history. Without any doubt, however, there is a generation of Germans of Jewish origin that experienced one of the most shocking and deadly transformation of any generation. These men and women, whose parents had been travelling Jewish salesmen, were involved in the establishment of small businesses in insignificant towns in the 1880s which grew into some of the most glamorous, feted and iconic department stores in Germany – some of which exist to this day. But these were also the people who lost them through social and economic crisis and brutal anti-Jewish sentiment in the 1920s and 1930s. Some of them were even murdered towards the end of that decade. Their story will be told in a way it has never been done before. This book is not about antisemitism. It is not even about shopping. This is a book about Germans who happened to be of Jewish ancestry, and it will overturn misconceptions about these people by looking at the department stores they owned.

From the very beginning, National Socialists had singled out Jewish businesses in general and department stores in particular as a threat to Germany. The 1920 party programme demanded 'the creation of a healthy class of craftsmen and artisans and its preservation, the immediate nationalization of the great department stores and their leasing at cheap prices to small businesses, strictly favouring of small businesses'.[5] Department stores were even given room in Hitler's *Mein Kampf*, in which they were described as ruining honest German craftsmen.[6] They were emblematic of all that had gone wrong with Germany and the world. Instead of gothic cathedrals and town halls under whose shadows proud artisans and honest merchants had plied their wares for centuries, the next generations would have nothing to look upon fondly but 'the busts of the most cunning profiteers' in the lobbies of department stores.[7] Department stores stood for destruction of the essence of Germany by urbanization, capitalism and Judaism. They were a lightning rod of dissatisfaction, and yet, like lightening, it struck with little warning.

Hitler's view of department stores was not original. He and his party can be seen as continuing a tradition of opposition that reached back to the founding of the first stores. The earliest department stores were established in the French- and English-speaking world. The Bon Marché in Paris, founded in 1838 by Aristide Boucicaut, is usually considered to have been the first.[8] In Britain, Bainbridge's, Fenwick's and the like brought this type of retailing to the provinces, while Harrods, John Lewis and associates transformed shopping in the capital.[9] Whiteleys department store declared itself 'the Universal Provider' – a title so at odds with the theology of one dignitary of the Church of England that he ordered an elephant from them. Promptly depositing the animal on the clergyman's terrace, the department store proudly added the slogan 'Everything from the Elephant to the Needle' to its advertisements.[10] From the outset, these places attracted some unwanted attention, and it is this negative side that most historians emphasize, particularly the agitation from shopkeepers and craftsmen who suffered as a consequence of department stores' success. In 1888, small retailers in Paris formed the League of the Defence of Work, Industry and Commerce against department stores.[11] They accused department stores of destroying traditional structures, selling cheap products, bankrupting local shopkeepers and craftsmen, employing women of dubious background, tempting respectable ones, destroying the towns and generally causing moral standards to drop.[12] While in Britain those against large retailers laid the emphasis on women prostituting themselves as sales clerks or frittering away their hours and money with pointless shopping, in France the stores were seen chiefly as creating a 'broken community of small shopkeepers'.¹³ We are told, most recently by Paul Lerner, that department stores generally felt offensively different because of the goods they sold, their design and style, their business techniques and their advertising.¹⁴ These sentiments were held by business rivals and subsequently used, and blown out of proportion, in popular fiction, where the general public came into contact with it. Myths and legends around department stores developed separately from their actual existence, fuelling dissatisfaction with this form of retailing in reality.

The origins of the Anti-department store rhetoric can be traced back mainly to works of literature, most prominently in Emile Zola's novel *Au Bonheur des Dames*. Zola created a vision of the department store as a temple 'of materialism, of salvation through consumption, of the commercial glorification (and exploitation) of women. At the same time … a giant beast, a vast living organism, gorged with gold.'¹⁵ The title 'Pleasuring Women' would render Zola's intention plainer than the usual translation 'The Ladies' Paradise', underscoring the department stores' seedy character.¹⁶ The image created by Zola was of enduring commercial appeal to publishers, leading Erich Köhler and his literary compatriots to create an entire genre of German fiction declaring the department store to be the end of all morals.¹⁷ These claims were eagerly transliterated out of fiction and into the mouths of those who had most to lose from the existence of department stores.

Lerner believes Jews 'stood at the centre of the raging controversies around consumer culture and the department store in Germany', but has a major problem with sources.¹⁸ He starts with Zola and uses literature, theatre and other forms of popular entertainment as evidence for the widespread disjoint between German society and Jewish stores. He supplements this with reports of psychologists and psychiatrists, spending a great deal of time with the writings of intellectuals. Lerner admits that the problem with these sources is that they do not explain the triumphal arrival and continued success of stores in every provincial town.¹⁹ As many historians have pointed out, some Germans did believe stores were the 'unholy attraction' in which shop girls prostituted themselves to supplement their meagre income.²⁰ The sales clerk and the lady kleptomaniac were seen, by a few, as symptomatic of German society becoming greedy and unrestrained.²¹ Some historians believe their obvious worldliness was at odds with German provinciality.²² The National Socialists' objections to department stores have been seen as originating from these views. This opinion is persistent and popular, not just among historians, but also in Germany itself, where it offers a ready explanation for the expulsion of Jews from business. Yet, it extrapolates the sentiment of an entire nation from a handful of readily available fiction and pseudoscience. The resulting genocide of a people is much too dreadful to be considered on that evidence alone, especially as the vast majority of the population were totally unaffected by these ideas. A closer examination of the success of department stores as they are imbedded in their locality and in non-intellectual society is needed to supplement previous work.

'No history of modern German economic, social, or political development can afford to dispense with artisans or their institutions' who came under the label of 'Mittelstand'.[23] As one boy's father explained to him when he asked why the National Socialists were being so nasty to Jews in 1933, they were currying favour with craftsmen and shopkeepers. For 'owners of a shop or a company belong to the *Mittelstand* and a broad *Mittelstand* is the surest foundation of the state, its economy and its culture. A well-established fact.'[24] Unterstell, Winkler and von Saldern concluded that the *Mittelstand* as a stratum were a significant demographic for the Nazis' rise to power.[25] Members of this group – farmers, craftsmen, and shopkeepers – believed their way of making a living not only made them the creative and creating part of society, but also, with that, the backbone of the economy and the state. When department stores, cooperative societies and mail-order businesses seemingly threatened their existence, we are told they appealed directly to state authorities, demanding, and receiving, protection for their anachronistic economy in return for supporting the German establishment. Although department stores only made 2.5 per cent of the turnover of retailing, even after the First World War, Spiekermann sees the importance of stores in their relationship to the allegedly reactionary *Mittelstand*.[26] Chain stores and the like, selling cheap and shoddy goods to their victims, did – so one believes – no value-producing or creative work for the community and were hence unethical.[27] In Germany, most department stores were founded and run by Jews. For the critics of mass-consumption this made sense, as Jews 'lack the ethical satisfaction that only value-producing, truly creative work provides: work by the sweat of the brow with the goal of ethical elevation of the commonweal' as Lange described it.[28] Mosse describes it as the stereotype of the gentile artisan waiting in his shop to sell solid handmade goods, while the Jewish tradesman lures customers in to sell shoddy wares.[29] However, in the Weimar Republic the state no longer laid its protective hand upon the *Mittelstand*, making them, as Gellately put it, 'harken back to a semi-mythical *ständische Gesellschaft*'.[30] In the foreground, as Spiekermann believes, was the fight of the traders and artisans for their rightful place in society.³¹ The National Socialists' demonizing of department stores was a way of garnering support with this group. The almost exclusive Jewish ownership of stores was particularly emphasized; they were presented as a conspiracy of the shtetl against German society.³² In the nineteenth century, antisemitism flared up particularly when the economy was contracting. Then, as in the 1920s and 1930s, the Jewish element could be blamed for the misery.³³ 'Most historians agree that these new forms of consumption and new kinds of experience remained demographically limited and had yet to extend behind Germany's largest urban centres', Lerner claims.³⁴ Modern cities, mass culture and capitalism were seen as the instruments of Judaization right into the last provincial backwater.³⁵ The department store was the beacon of this development. This view is still held in the German popular historic imagination.³⁶

The idea has been very popular, not least because it presents an easy explanation for the incomprehensible misery of the Holocaust and the Second World War: Germany's failed modernization in 1848 and continued anachronistic government after 1871 failed to produce a healthy modern state and society, we are told.³⁷ As, according to this reading, all Western nations have gone through this process, Germany's development has been characterized as being a special path or *Sonderweg*. Historians have claimed Germans loved militarism, bombast, brutality and had a propensity to admire charismatic, authoritarian leaders.³⁸ Some even go so far as to say they were unlike any other people in the world, fearful of the new.³⁹ Originally grounded in the history of politics and foreign policy, the idea of this special path soon became the subject of social and economic history.⁴⁰ The history of Jews in a sociopolitical context has concentrated on the process of discrimination, suggesting the inevitability of genocide in every aspect of Jewish life in Germany, particularly their role as the nation's retailers.⁴¹

From the earliest foundations in 1881, department stores grew rapidly, reaching the size and sophistication of their French, British and American counterparts within just two decades. In Berlin, Abraham Wertheim, Hermann Tietz and the Jandorfs were described as 'Berlin's uncrowned Emperors' in 1908.⁴² Between 1880 and 1900, Coles reckoned that a department store – mostly under Jewish directorship – was founded in every city and almost every town in Germany, with minor branches appearing even in villages. ⁴³ By the 1910s and 1920s, London stores were copying techniques from German companies. This expansion was remarkable by any standards, but appears even more so if one considers that the emancipation of Jews had only been achieved within the lifetime of the stores' founders in 1871. Their success was unprecedented. So why, if department stores were seen as the harbingers of all things that Germans hated (mass consumption, independent women, a new aesthetic, liberal morals, social upheaval, Jewishness, democratization and commercialization of society), did they expand, establish branches and serve millions of customers a day?[44] Surprisingly no one has asked before: why were department stores so successful in Germany?

Although Blackbourn and Gellately revised the view that small retailers and artisans had entered some sort of pact with the ruling elite of imperial Germany, the study of Jewish entrepreneurs is still stuck in this narrative.[45] One problem has been that in the past the *Mittelstand* has been oversimplified. 'The artisans and small shopkeepers – the heroes of Professor Winkler's book – are not a class' and cannot be treated as such, as Lebovics observes.[46] It would be unwise to translate the term *Mittelstand*. The term is a vague ideological construction of a group of people without clear-cut objectives and with vastly divergent views. They had no central representative body.[47] Their only common denominator is the belief in the creative labour of their own hands being essential to the stability of society. They are located anywhere on the social scale between the working class and affluent patricians or *Bürgertum* and included not just shopkeepers and craftsmen but also farmers, small manufacturing businesses and eventually even sales and administrative clerks. It is almost impossible to generalize about this group.

Latest research has tried to be more specific in examining the relationship between the *Mittelstand* and authority. Oded Heilbronner, on examining the farming communities of the rural Black Forest, noted that a long process of disenchantment with traditional Catholic institutions made them susceptible to National Socialism.[48] Even more recently Hal Hansen concluded that the craft, industry and retailing institutions in the cities of Baden had a complex and often supportive relationship with the authorities.[49] Anthony McElligott points out that due to their social status, many *Mittelstand* families hid their actual economic situation and views from the outside world.[50] Briesen is clear that frequently quoted contemporary pamphleteers were ranting about everything modern in general and may thus have little or no actual consideration for small shopkeepers at all.[51] Contemporaries like Werner Sombart, who believed the honest man fed himself by his own handicraft alone, were rare.[52] The complaints and those voicing them are unspecific, generalized even by historians, often equating anti-department store rhetoric with antisemitism, simply because that is the way the Nazis used it fifty years later.

As Elon poignantly shows, nowhere in Europe were Jewish families better integrated than in Germany.[53] Jews were members of the *Mittelstand*, with their German companies among the most successful in Europe:[54]

> For businessmen who embraced German culture, aspired to a high degree of social integration and, yet remained extremely active in Jewish philanthropy ... being a Jewish cosmopolitan was a worthy goal. Cosmopolitan consumption was not only good business, it was good culture.[55]

This means, they may not have wanted to fit in to overcome prejudice of their religion, but because it made economic sense – in the end this may make little difference to the process or outcome, but it is important to consider. This book will demonstrate that Imperial Germany and the Weimar Republic were neither an Elysium, nor was antisemitism an all-inhibiting element of Jewish life. 'The relative indifference of most Germans towards the "Jewish Question" before 1933 meant that the National Socialists had a job on their hands after the takeover of power to persuade the population of the need for active discrimination and persecution of Jews.'[56] The history of German Jews cannot simply be seen in terms of success or failure.[57] Jews and Jewish companies had very localized experiences and, as Rahden points out, the lifestyle of these Jews became that of archetypal middle-class Germans.[58] This would suggest Jewish life was a continuity of the liberal and commercially advanced Germany.[59]

A simple reason why questions have not been asked of Germany's successful retailing record is the great difficulty of finding material with which to address the issue. Commercial enterprises destroyed records as soon as they were legally permitted to do so, as keeping them was expensive. Everyday occurrences, such as shopping, were not recorded officially. Those whose lives were dominated by hard work in their shops either did not see the need to keep personal memoirs or liked to exaggerate the success achieved.[60] Thus studies of German department stores seldom come with a comprehensive approach, usually focusing on individual entrepreneurs who had left records, on literature, or on the subject of *Mittelstand* politics. There are only a few full studies of department stores in a regional context in the German-speaking world. Konrad Fuchs's work, in which he places the Schocken company in the economic and political setting of Saxony, may be the only serious attempt at doing this.[61] There are scholarly studies of department stores as businesses, but the majority are written by journalists, concentrating on the persona of the management and seldom putting the companies into a wider context.[62] Such works plant the department store firmly within *Sonderweg* theory, laying great emphasis on the Jewish origin of the owners and their persecution during the Third Reich. There are two well-written examples: Simone Ladwig-Winter's PhD, later published as a book, embeds the Wertheim dynasty within the history of successful German Jews and, of course, Fuchs on Schocken. While Anthony David's subsequent biography of Salman Schocken is very enjoyable, painting a vivid picture of an ambitious man, one must read this with a little caution as David clearly admires his subject highly.[63] What almost all monographs share is a certain concentration on the department store as a contemporary symbol of consumer society. The best publications are good cultural histories, but there is, as Spiekermann rightly warns us, the danger of marginalizing its socioeconomic importance.[64]

In the first place, department stores were not interesting social or cultural phenomena to contemporaries; they were businesses, suppliers of goods, employees and taxpayers. Jewish entrepreneurs and their counterparts throughout the world created a business model that is still in practice today: 'Reacting to consumer choice in a cost-effective way, in an accessible location at a convenient time for the customer;'[65] in short – retailing. Modern retail marketing theory has it that products have an 'heraldic' quality.[66] By combining atmosphere, pricing, promotion, display and staff, the entrepreneur gives the product this emblematic status.[67] It is only thus that the purchase of the most mundane item carries significance as a message about the customer to the outside world. Cultural, social and economic levels overlap heavily. How singular was German retailing compared to the rest of the Western world? Did those in authority see how department stores fitted into a broader picture of the economy? How did department stores manage to survive the First World War and the disasters caused by the economic slump during the Weimar Republic?

A problem when studying Germany is the disjointed nature of the country. The Germany that formed in 1871 was a federation of hitherto independent states that would continue to enjoy a great deal of self-government. Not only did each state have its own legislative, executive, judicative, administration and schooling (to name just a few), each also had its own provincial identity. Rooted in centuries of fragmentation, religious strife, aristocratic feuds and economic disasters, the varied geography of Germany had led to several cultural peculiarities existing alongside each other. Studying any geographic area of Germany and extrapolating from that must be done cautiously. Two main aspects held the German lands together: First, the vague adherence to some variant of the German language. Second, the conscious awareness of the Germans of their national collectivity within their local individuality. Thus, the provinces are arguably far more important to German history than the cities (indeed, Jennifer

Jenkins asks whether even the second largest, Hamburg, was not provincial).[68] The latter aspect is therefore key to the German people's sense of self.[69] They are, as Applegate's book title suggests 'A Nation of Provincials'. This book will try to embrace this idea and will show that Jewish businessmen understood it, using it to their own advantage when establishing and growing their retail empires.

Department stores were an international phenomenon, and Berlin, the capital and largest metropolis of the German Empire, attracted more large and elegant stores than anywhere else in Germany. Research heavily favours Berlin, not just because of the many stores one could find there, but also because here 'there was a scene of artists and journalists who commented intensively upon contemporary happenings in a culturally critical way'.[70] Yet a widely disregarded fact is that most department stores were founded in provincial centres and that most Germans would have come into contact with this local Jewish store.[71] The British experience is not unlike the German, where department stores emerged and flourished in county towns.[72] It is surprising that no one has made a comprehensive study of German department stores in the provinces. It is here that a large part of the German identity is formed and here that most department stores – including all the grand ones in Berlin – were founded. Michael John has given a brief overview in a journal article of some stores in Linz and Salzburg, but unfortunately provincial retailing in the German context does not seem to have been the subject of an academic work beyond the confines of a chapter.[73] This study seeks to remedy this by looking at developments in different areas of Germany in parallel.

There have been some good studies of consumer culture in Britain, most notably by Erica Rappaport. English consumers, especially women, have been revealed as a complex conglomerate of individuals, not swept away uncontrollably and senselessly by department store retailing, but empowered by choice, increased wages and more free time.[74] With the exception of Tinda Dingel's excellent thesis on male consumers between the 1920s and 1950s, there have been few studies of German shoppers. Dingel demonstrates quite convincingly that men were engaged in consumer society, but simply in a different way when compared to women.[75] Is the customer the carrier of modern culture, 'revealed in her power, the main arbiter of demand to which the market responds, before whose sovereign judgement the markets stand in awe', as it is put in modern retail marketing theory, or swept away uncontrollably in a shopping frenzy?[76] More succinctly, Lerner asks if shoppers are a 'mob' or if they are 'savvy', without answering the question.[77] Why, if department stores were disliked, did people patronize them? Who would want to be seen frequenting them? Were there gender or class differences in the shopping experience? The study of sales staff has not been so neglected in Germany, but they have in the past been examined only in the context of their membership of the *Mittelstand* and not specifically as employees of department stores.[78] In retailing, the customer comes into contact with the firm through its sales clerks. Are they exploited, as Miller reports of the staff at the Bon Marché in Paris, or are their talents fostered, as Benson reports of their counterparts in the United States?[79] What were the working conditions in a German store? How did they change over time, and how were they regarded during times of mass unemployment?

Addressing some of the questions above will necessarily lead to reassessing the relationship between Jewish stores, their staff, local authorities and consumers during the Third Reich. By 1939, all Jewish influence had been coerced or forced out of department stores, and one must ask if it made any difference to consumers shopping there or whether this improved working conditions for employees. It seems necessary to establish within a wide social, political and economic context how stores were able to flourish in Germany. Germany was a very diverse geographic area in the centre of Europe comprising cosmopolitan cities, industrial towns and rural villages, representing Catholics and Protestants of the academic, middle and working classes. The emphasis of this book is on the Knopf family and their department stores in south-west Germany.[80] Not only have this family – one of the largest and most influential retailers in Germany – never been the subject of any published book, but they also had stores in towns representing every economic and social facet of the Empire. Retailing outlets of the Knopf family, roughly stretching from Frankfurt and into Switzerland and from Strassburg to Stuttgart, could be found in Protestant and Catholic, industrial and academic, rural and urban, and social democratic-loyal and centre party-voting cities and towns. Thus, the Knopfs and their retailing empire stand for the diversity of the German Empire and will allow us, by drawing on new and original research, to take a fresh look at Jewish entrepreneurial families as a whole. Thus, to a degree, this book is also filling a gap and is supported by previous research on other large German department store chains, which is also supplemented by my own on Schocken, Wertheim, Jandorf, Wronker, Karstadt and the Tietz companies.

The type of material hitherto used, pamphlets and *Mittelstand* publications, is easily found in almost any German university library. These and state papers are officially retained, but the transient, everyday processes of running a business, going to work and shopping is not seen as worthy of official record. Even finding the mundane dealings of governing authorities and *Mittelstand* organizations can be tricky: 'The most striking characteristic of modern records is that they are fractured or fragmented, in spite of their creation by a single organisation, common agency or person.'[81] Documents are disbanded, disregarded, lost, scattered across the world and wilfully or accidentally destroyed. In addition, most entrepreneurs were too preoccupied with their business well into their old age to bother with writing memoirs or recording histories. 'Research in the field therefore is tinted with a degree of frustration.'[82]

This fundamental problem needed to be addressed creatively. I published articles in German newspapers on the history of department stores, asking for those who were associated with them, remembered shopping there or had ephemera connected to them to come forward. This resulted in letters and parcels being sent in and a string of interviews – including one over coffee and cake – with over a dozen ladies aged eighty or more who had worked for such companies. Some could provide hard evidence in the shape of staff manuals and photographs, while others enjoyed simply reminiscing about the 'old days'. Most of the people interviewed had worked for the companies in their mid-to-late teens and were now elderly and in some cases frail. The passage of time and the benefit of hindsight must have naturally clouded the information I gathered from them; however, they provide a little colour to the account of the last days of the Jewish ownership of department stores. This period's research is usually dominated by post-war legal documents, in themselves in some ways not free from being heavily influenced by the politics of the time in which they were created. As a result of the newspaper articles, an unofficial archive that had languished in a cellar for seventy years which gave a tantalizing glimpse into the organization of a department store and the lives of their staff was discovered. The descendants of the retailing families, in particular the Knopfs, gave first-hand accounts and ephemera, hitherto unknown, which provided a rounded picture by supplementing official records consulted in six countries. More recently, a well-received feature-length documentary on German national television featuring my work further increased the visibility of my research and not only encouraged more resources to be made available to me, but also inspired this book.

The various archives of the state of Baden-Württemberg were a major source of information when it came to parliamentary records. Police files unfortunately sorely lacked much information on either kleptomania or the involuntary involvement of stores in riots between the First and Second World Wars. Municipal records – as will become apparent – do not provide consistent information from town to town. Vast parts of the archives of the city of Mannheim are lost, Karlsruhe keeps a catalogue of information on all Jewish families who fled or were murdered during the Third Reich, while Freiburg has an excellent collection of papers relating to the organizations of the *Mittelstand*. The archive at Chemnitz was a very valuable source concerning the Schocken business. The Leo Baeck Institute in New York, as the guardian of the German-Jewish heritage, and the Deutsches Tagebucharchiv in Emmendigen, which holds a large collection of German diaries, provided insights into the store owners' and shoppers' private lives.

These sources naturally have their problems, for, on the one hand, one cannot read the promotional literature of department stores or autobiographical accounts without questioning what remains assumed, unsaid or aspirational. Just because some of these sources will not mention antisemitism or anti-department store sentiments, it does not mean they did not exist. However, on the other hand, as rose-tinted or unreliable as private ephemera and personal recollections are, ignoring them would produce 'a one-sided picture in which antisemitic rhetoric, publications and organisations drown out the daily lived experiences of German Jews, a picture that would have been unrecognisable to Jewish contemporaries'.[83] Therefore, this book must be seen in the context of the much larger discussion on vitriolic and murderous antisemitism that existed – and still exists – in Germany.

Given the inconsistency of the sources and the different emphases of collections and archives, comparing department stores in different cities and states is not always possible as equivalent material is usually not available. The stories of the individuals who lived through these extraordinary times are complex and varied. Their origins are obscure; the course of their lives marked by business and hence largely undocumented; their expulsion or murder hushed up by the perpetrators; and their fate made emblematic for different concepts of German history and thus liberally reinterpreted. Yet, the new sources used in this book reveal the symbiotic nature of Jewish-owned department stores and the population of Germany. These stores helped to feed and clothe a growing nation which was – mostly – grateful for it. The development of these businesses hence reflects Germany's society, politics and economy from the middle of the nineteenth century to 1933. They are not only innovative, urban, international and industrial, but also traditional, provincial, familial, class-obsessed and culturally conservative. This book will show that department stores were not the targets of continued open antisemitism to the degree that many previous scholars have suggested. On the contrary, it will try to explain why the sales of department stores grew and how they engendered positive feelings. Further, it will show why department stores took up a significant place in the mental landscape and social life of cities and towns in Germany. It will tragically link locations which Jewish businessmen enriched and in which they were honoured at one time with the violent antisemitic hotspots they became later. To do so, the history of department stores and their Jewish owners will not be read backwards, from their fate under the Nazis. We will have to experience every step of the growth of department stores to fully appreciate how integrated they were in society and the economy. This new account will embed Jewish retailers as much as possible in German provincial towns, where most department stores expanded from and where Germany is, according to some, most German due to its federal constitution and the importance of the local area in the construction of German identity. Wherever possible department stores will be seen in relation to local shoppers, authorities and the general public. Through that, this book will demonstrate, alarmingly, that intense prejudice against a group need not exist universally or for a long time among a population for that group to become subject to violent hatred. It will show how a highly assimilated community, who had got used to ambient prejudice, can face rather sudden dangers they could not have anticipated.

1

Foundation: 1834–90
'Travelling Sons of David'

Before they were 'department store kings', they were 'Travelling Sons of David'.[1] An interconnected group of predominantly Jewish families, who were hawkers of trinkets at the beginning of the nineteenth century, emerged within the course of the century to become the retailers of the German Empire, serving every strata of society – from the labouring woman to the Emperor himself. This chapter will demonstrate how the formation of the German Empire allowed Jewish men and women to establish businesses selling essential goods in every corner of Germany and how in doing so they made themselves indispensable to the burgeoning population by becoming providers and to the growing economy as clients. We will see how the population were dependent on the stores – as the stores were dependent on the consumer – and how the department stores were dependent on manufacturing industry for their goods – as the industry was on the department stores to buy these goods.

Importantly, this chapter will introduce us to the entrepreneurial dynasties and their extraordinary rise. It will show the relationship between the origins of department stores and the religious identities of the proprietors, and thus establish the important link between the nature of Germany's rooted provincial identity and Jewish retailers. By charting the geographic locations and expansion of department stores in their early stages, we can fully appreciate the diversity of the landscape Jewish businesspeople were serving and the way they became embedded in every town and city. We will see how, in these places, business people, customers, local authorities and the public in general worked together to establish these stores as well as the hard work put in by these store owners and their experiences in living among the local communities. The origins of the great department stores of Berlin, Hamburg or Munich lay in the German province, and they remained of primary importance to the nationally operating businesses throughout the period. In the very month Hitler took power in 1933,

Figure 1.1 The humble provincial birthplace of Oscar Tietz, who would have a palace-like store built in Berlin. © Author.

the German Federation of Department Stores (Verband Deutscher Waren- und Kaufhäuser) noted the following in their periodical:

> In small towns the store always needs to feel more personal than in large towns. Of primary importance are the quality of products, the management and the location of the store. In small towns the most important factor is the personality of the owner or branch manager. Trust in the owner ensures custom; it is the fundament of the whole business ... There are still families which have, for generations, purchased their wares from the same department store.[2]

This trust was, as we will see, built in the 1880s.

The rise of these Jewish family businesses was in parallel with that of Germany as a nation and an economy. At the beginning of the nineteenth century, the area roughly sandwiched between France and Russia was a collection of small states, all of which shared German as their language. These states included Prussia, ancient Hanseatic cities and tiny principalities such as Lippe, Oldenburg and Schwarzburg-Sonderhausen. The vast majority of these mainly monarchical states had their own written constitutions, independent judiciary, the right to assemble, some form of freedom of worship and little censorship. Moving people, goods and services across principalities was a nightmare, especially if one was Jewish, and treated very differently in each state.

The first tentative steps towards Germany uniting into one single economic area were made in 1834 when the German Customs Union was established. Since the early nineteenth century, capital markets – the raising and moving of money to invest – had become more mobile. This was driven by the building of the first railway lines, improvements in the postal system and the introduction of the telegraph service. Communication and exchange of money and goods became easier for those willing to agree on shared terms of reference. The Customs Union was a way in which these advances could be enjoyed across a large part of central Europe without being hampered by the bureaucracy of the myriad of German states. The borders of the Customs Union were roughly those the German Empire would have (without Luxembourg and Alsace-Lorraine) until the end of the Second World War. A British traveller in 1839 saw the potential of the Customs Union for Germany and the disadvantages this had for his own country, describing it as 'uncourteous [sic] of the Germans to have united in a convention virtually excluding the manufacturers of a liberal nation which regards them so favourably as England does'.[3] The union was headed by Prussia which took full advantage of the easy access to steel and coal the scheme gave them, leaving the traditional principal state in the German family of nations, Austria, out of this economic innovation.

The German War of 1866 finally established Prussia as the most powerful nation in central Europe, sidelining the Austrians as leaders of the German-speaking world. The loose German Federation under their Austrian headship was dissolved, and Prussia established the North German Federation instead. The southern kingdoms were excluded until they joined forces with the northern Germans against the French in 1871. Baden, willingly, Württemberg, indifferently, and Bavaria, grudgingly, accepted Prussian leadership during the Franco-Prussian War. The headship of Prussia was not just because of 'the political weight which her position and extent naturally give', as our British traveller noted, but also due to 'a strong moral influence, arising from the just and amiable character of her king, as well as the intelligence of her government'.[4] The King of Prussia Wilhelm I was declared the German Emperor.

Although the new capital of the Empire was Berlin and Prussia would dominate politics, considerable power was left with the other German states to regulate most of their internal affairs as they pleased, with their own parliaments, police forces, schooling systems and economic policy. The constitution of the German Empire allowed for a joint parliament, elected by universal male suffrage. The Evangelical Church (a mixture of Lutheranism and Calvinism) was the established church of Prussia, but Jews were granted the same legal rights as non-Jews across the Empire, even if in practice considerable discrimination continued. Real power lay directly with the Emperor, who could appoint ministers at will. In effect, however, as Wilhelm I saw himself foremost as the King of Prussia rather than the German Emperor, it was Prince Otto von Bismarck who as chancellor held the reins of power.

'Concerning what will then happen one feels curious. For the German nation is still young, and its maturity is of importance to the world. They are a good people, a lovable people, who should help much to make the world better', Jerome K. Jerome noted during his visit to the new nation.[5] A powerful state had been formed in the centre of Europe within a relatively short space of time. It had unified borders, laws, currency, weights and measurements, as well as railway and telecommunication systems. The increasingly strong economy of the German states received a huge boost from the single market. By the end of the century, Germany's industrial production rose by 100 per cent, in comparison to only 40 per cent in Britain. While investments reduced in other countries during this period, the new German Empire, bolstered possibly by the optimism of its recent foundation, increased them. The electricity network was expanded, telephone exchanges installed and the railways began reaching even remote areas of the country.

The state could even afford to increase investment in social security, mainly to attempt, unsuccessfully, to halt the rise of the German Social Democratic Party (Sozialdemokratische Partei Deutschlands, SPD), a socialist establishment. The SPD's influence and 'radical views' resulted in many of their members being imprisoned, entirely legally under the German system in which criticism of authority could land you in jail.[6] The SPD was to become one of the most politically powerful forces in Germany as it served the growing working classes. In 1875, the German population was 37 million and by 1910 it was 62.5 million, of which many laboured in the industrial cities that replaced provincial towns. The vague terms 'urbanization' and 'industrialization' are used to explain both the explosion of the population and its successful housing, feeding and clothing. The growth of industrial output and the subsequent expansion of cities would not have been possible without mass-producing food, clothing and hygiene articles and providing these at reasonable cost to the population.

Before mass manufacture, one bought the items one needed for everyday life from the people who produced them. Most wares were made individually and bespoke for the customer. The few things that were manufactured from early on, such as cloth, could be bought from a merchant or directly from the workshop. Pedlars, often Jews as it was a living they were permitted to earn, offered the few things that were made in bulk as door-to-door salesmen. In the mid-nineteenth century, pegs, pins and little practical haberdashery items that the frugal housewife needed and that could easily be transported were the mainstay of their trade. Shops at this time were described as dark dens, above which the family of the retailer lived; the purpose of the enterprise was subsistence of the family, and not profit.[7] 'Entering, for instance, one of the larger butcher's shops ... one finds oneself transported into a patriarchal milieu, as it has been able to survive in the same form for hundreds of years and more.'[8] The private and public spheres overlapped. The serving of customers and the administration of the business were neither separated nor specialized. The office would open straight out into the shop and only stairs would divide the master's sitting room from the courtyard where the apprentices would work. In these dimly lit, poorly designed shops, the retailer, his son or an assistant girl would sell items they had produced on the premises or purchased from a merchant as stock. The price was dependent as much on who was buying as on who was selling. Payment was hardly ever by cash; an account was kept to be settled at intervals[9] – hardly an appealing prospect for the customer.

This type of shop had to rely on suppliers, not just for their wares, but also for the credit they could give them. Independent companies usually had very little capital, so they bought their merchandise with credit, paying it off once the items were sold and then purchasing new ones with yet more credit. In practice, this meant a shopkeeper purchased products off a wholesaler, a middleman between producer and retailer, promising him payment once the goods were sold. Once the retailer had managed to sell them, he paid off the wholesaler, purchasing more items with a fresh credit. The middlemen would naturally mark the items up as they passed through his hands. Hence, small retailers were often utterly dependent on their supplier.[10] The profit margins were very tight for such retailers; they had little ready cash for investments, could not choose their products themselves and could not react quickly to changing trends or needs of the population. There was no spare cash for investment. During the course of the nineteenth century, this form of retailing, practiced by many, became utterly out of step with Germany's development and wholly incapable of supplying the working population with clothing or sustenance. It was also not a secure means of making a living. And yet, shopkeeping was to become the 'success story of the century'.[11] Prepared by the experience of working as lowly door-to-door salesmen, Jews knew this business best.

Before the foundation of the Empire, the individual states and principalities in Germany had their own regulations regarding Jews. Antisemitism was embedded in the law. For example, entering or transiting through German territories was difficult and expensive for Jews, with each place charging fees for their free passage. This made trade expensive. A few Jewish families enjoyed historic semi-aristocratic privileges due to their wealth and contacts. These people were usually bankers who helped fund the small German courts; they were the exception. There had been antisemitic riots in 1819 and around the failed revolutions of 1848, in addition to which, for the vast majority of German Jews in the nineteenth century, life was made primarily and purposefully hard by the state itself.

During the 1870–1 war with France, ordinary Jewish soldiers had distinguished themselves and openly celebrated Yom Kippur during the advance on the city of Metz. With unification as a result of this war, there came free movement and also a significant amount of religious toleration towards Germany's approximately 512,000 Jews. For the first time in history, this segment of the population enjoyed high levels of institutional toleration. Jews were now allowed to travel, settle, worship and trade across a vast area of central Europe without any special permits. Yet, toleration did not come automatically with legal emancipation. The economic slump, soon after the foundation of the Empire, was blamed on Jews. Friedrich Marr, who did a great deal to popularize the term 'antisemitism' with the establishment of the first anti-Jewish organization in the Empire, found blame for the 1873 stock-market crash in his pamphlet 'The Triumph of Jewishness over Germanness'. The title suggests a conspiracy theory that soon gained traction in large parts of the population: there were two ways of making a living. On the one hand, there was financial capitalism, which was the world of Jews. This was selfish in the same way that banking had been a ticket to exclusive privilege for Jewish people at petty German courts in the past. On the other, there was an ethical sort of capitalism, which produced things of value and was German because it, apparently, served the community. So, in the imagination of Marr and those who followed him, there was the greedy and plutocratic Jewish capitalist on the one side and the honest, value-producing German one on the other. The distinction made here is ridiculous. Deeply cynical, one historian describes this way of blaming corruption of any kind on the Jews as the 'comforting explanations for a variety of crises and unfamiliar situations'.[12] It would continue to be a popular way of finding blame notwithstanding religious toleration on paper.

In spite of this negative sentiment against them, Jews grasped the opportunities they had been given. A boom in the building of synagogues ensued as every city, and many towns, received their own Jewish place of worship. However, opportunities were most seized in the commercial sphere, especially by the children of the Jewish pedlars who had to sell buttons and ribbons made by cheap labour, second-hand clothing or, if they had some capital, cattle, horses or linens. Using their skills and contacts as hawkers, they set out across the newly opened borders to feed and clothe the German population. Their own businesses soon developed and expanded to reflect the growth of the fledgling Empire.

The north-east: Wertheim

The transition from hawker to department store proprietor was naturally not one that happened overnight, but developed gradually, over the course of about a generation and a half. Like his father before him, Abraham Wertheim was sent off to travel and make a living as a pedlar. And, also like his father, he sold cheaply produced haberdashery items from the rucksack on his back. Outwardly identifiable as a Jew from his dress, he eked out just enough of a living, travelling from village to village. In some places he would be welcomed with their gossip from neighbouring towns or chased away from others with the cry 'Jud, mach Mores!' ('Jew, get out of here!').[13] A far cry from the semi-aristocratic Jewish banking families with their money, connections and privileges, many other Jewish hawkers would have had similar experiences of grinding hard work, poverty and exclusion.

In 1812, the state of Prussia had introduced some basic citizens' rights for Jews. This meant they had to choose a family surname, rather than use the first name of their fathers, as was tradition. The family surname 'Wertheim' was chosen in consultation with the mayor of Wertheim am Main, where Abraham (soon to be) Wertheim, was at the time. It is, however, unlikely that a Jewish pedlar would have had access to such a man.[14] It may have been convenient at the time to adopt this name as he was passing through. It was however serendipitous: literally translated 'Wertheim' means 'Home of Value' or 'Home of Worth'.

Prussia was gradually loosening its restrictive Jewish legislation, allowing Abraham and his brother to open a shop offering 'manufactured' items in Stralsund, in modern Mecklenburg-Pommerania, in 1852. Initially they would have only sold the sort of things that their father had: small practical things for the

Figure 1.2 Georg Wertheim, who would dine with the Emperor. © Jüdisches Museum Berlin.

household, items of haberdashery, and perhaps some of the more sophisticated mass-produced lines, cloths and ribbons. It seems fitting that a Hanseatic port was the first place such a shop that was to grow into a department store was opened. It was in this city that Abraham Wertheim's second son, Georg, was born. His mother was Ida Wolff who also had retailing in her blood, being the daughter of a Berlin linen merchant.[15]

When he was old enough, Georg was sent off to his mother's family in Berlin for an apprenticeship. Returning in 1875 to Stralsund he began selling products provided to him at wholesale prices by his mother's family. He was only nineteen at the time, but had already brought lucrative innovations into the company. His business model which allowed customers to browse the reasonably priced linen products and purchase them without pressure was incredibly popular. Previously the customer had only been able to look at wares under the mediation of the shopkeeper, which made them feel obliged to purchase. Georg quickly accumulated the capital to open a branch – the Wertheims, like the other Jewish retailers, had no familial links to finance – but, he had little time to enjoy their success as a rival, Leonhard Tietz, offering the same products in a similar setting, opened a store round the corner from them in 1879.

The west: Leonhard Tietz

Leonhard Tietz had been born and raised in the village of Birnbaum an der Warthe, in Poznan (Międzychód, as it is known today). The King of Prussia had offered Jews a degree of protection if they moved there, and Jacob Tietz had been the first member of his family to accept this invitation. Jacob is the collective ancestor of the founders of the Leonhard Tietz, Hermann Tietz, Knopf and Wronker stores.[16] Possibly also of the Joske and Ury families. Thus, the owners of most German department stores had common roots in the Prussian province. Birnbaum, and indeed the entire district, was not a place of great significance. Throughout its history it had been passed on back and forth between great European powers, much like the rest of Poland. It became part of Prussia at the end of the eighteenth century and throughout the 19th had only around 3,000 inhabitants. In the same period, the size of its Jewish population was relatively large, fluctuating between 10 and 25 per cent.

From Birnbaum, Leonhard Tietz and his brother Oscar were apprenticed to a relative in Berlin. Chaskel Tietz had spent some years in America and had fought as an officer on the side of the Unionists during the American Civil War. His wealth was based on having provided the Prussian side with horses during the Franco-Prussian War. He had shipped – one assumes ex-army – horses across the Atlantic and sold them to the German regiments, making a handsome profit.[17] Chaskel was great influence on the Tietz brothers. Later on, Hermann

Figure 1.3 Flora and Leonhard Tietz. Leonhard Tietz, like his fellow department store founders, relied on his wife to build his retailing empire. © Author.

Wronker, and probably many other young Jewish men, were sent to Berlin to learn something useful from their uncle. Leonhard married Flora Baumann, also from Birnbaum, and together they open Wertheim's rival store in Stralsund with a capital of 3,000 *Taler*. While his wife ran the shop on a day-to-day basis, Leonhard travelled around the countryside acting as a wholesaler to smaller businesses. Within a year they had outgrown the premises, and they had a great appetite for establishing branches with the capital they had raised with their first venture.

In the mid-nineteenth century, 'a manufacturing spirit had at length been aroused in the Prussian provinces of the Rhine'[18] and by the 1880s, when Leonhard and Flora were looking for a new market, it exploded. Krupp's steel works at Essen had just employed the inventor of the diesel engine, while in Duisburg, Thyssen was integrating its business by building a foundry almost directly over a coal mine. The area was flourishing, and workers flocked from rural and less-well-off areas of Europe to find employment in the Rhineland. From 1884 onwards, Leonhard Tietz and his family opened dozens of stores in the booming western German industrial towns, finding a ready market there in those labouring in the heavy industry. The store in Elberfeld, for example, was such a success that it had to be closed only two days after their opening to completely restock – an occurrence gleefully used for advertising.[19]

With their achievements in western Germany, Leonhard and Flora moved the headquarters of their business and their family to great cathedral city of Cologne. A branch had been opened there in 1890, and once again it was so successful that the store had to close for a day to restock.[20] More branches in Cologne, Aachen, Mainz and several 'attached stores' under different names, but selling the same products, were established. Soon Leonhard and Flora's geographic expansion reached its limits, with a branch in Amberg, in Bavaria – quite a trip from the central office in Cologne at the end of the nineteenth century. Further expansion towards the east and south was not practical or possible as Leonhard's younger brother, Hermann, had begun opening his own stores there. Encroaching on his territory was not an option.

The south-east: Hermann Tietz

Oscar Tietz was also apprenticed to Uncle Chaskel and subsequently employed by his younger brother Leonhard in Stralsund.[21] In 1882, Oscar hit upon a revolutionary idea for mass-producing lace. Essentially, by burning a pattern

Figure 1.4 Oscar Tietz established Hermann Tietz, which as the brand Hertie is a fixture of German retailing to this day. © Author.

into fabric, he could make vast quantities of intricate decorative material at a fraction of the price. Doubtless his innovation was also sold by the family company Gebrüder Tietz in Birnbaum, but Oscar began marketing this product through his first own shop in Gera, the capital of the tin Principality of Reuss-Gera, in modern-day Thuringia. Here Oscar, his wife Betty, also from Birnbaum, and their Uncle Hermann[22] lived in close proximity to the store. The store was named 'Hermann Tietz', for although Oscar and Betty provided the ideas and the labour, it was Uncle Hermann who had provided the capital for the venture. The enterprise was such a success that they had to employ sixteen staff, all of whom, initially, lived 'above the shop'.

Soon the whole family moved further to open a shop in Munich, the capital of the largest southern German kingdom Bavaria, which according to one British journal, had 'a gay and accessible court … fine picture and sculpture galleries, a library of 500,000 volumes, a good opera, and a considerable variety of promenades'.[23] Thus, apart from being a city of art and culture, Munich was also the administrative centre of the kingdom. Bavaria had been the state most vehemently opposed to the headship of Prussia and presented itself to the tourist as 'the country of travelling broom-girls, gold and silver lace-padded head-dresses, bad German and good beer'.[24] The risk of taking his young wife and infant son Georg to establish a store in the Bavarian capital soon paid off. Oscar had selected a location for the store on the route between the railway station and the centre, allowing for a high foot fall. Although initially only the working classes shopped there, soon the middle and upper classes of Munich came, ostensibly to purchase items for the servants.[25] George Tietz would grow up here, and missed the city very much when his father decided to move to Berlin. It was in also in Munich that the young Hermann Wronker paid a call to his Tietz cousin.

The centre: Wronker

During Hermann Wronker's visit to Munich, Oscar Tietz's encouraged him to develop the idea of cinemas. Wronker would later go on to found the Projektions-Aktiengesellschaft 'Union' company,[26] which eventually become part of the UFA (Universum Film) in 1917. Before all that, however, Hermann Wronker also completed an apprenticeship with Chaskel Tietz. Originally from a Silesian branch of the clan, Hermann married Ida Friedeberg, from Birnbaum, which brought him even closer into the circle of retailing families from there.

Figure 1.5 Hermann and Ida Wronker with their children. Max, the eldest, far left, had to deal with the consequences of his parents' poor investments in the 1930s. © Joski Family Collection.

See Table 1.1, which may be of assistance in understanding the familiar links of the retailers.

Oscar Tietz grew fond of the 'travelling son of David' and as Wronker showed promise and aptitude, Tietz allowed him to establish the branches of Hermann Tietz at Bamberg and Coburg.[27] In 1887, Hermann Wronker joined his sibling Simon in Mannheim, where they opened a store under his brother's name. Four years later, Hermann Wronker opened a branch in Frankfurt am Main on the prestigious Zeil.[28] This store 'flourished immediately' and grew steadily.[29]

The south-west: Knopf

The Knopf family were also related to Hermann Wronker as well as to Hermann and Chaskel Tietz, though the exact familial link is unclear as the term 'cousin' or 'uncle' was used to establish kinship in instances where there were no actual familial bond. In 1881, Max Knopf and his sister Johanna

Table 1.1 Interconnections between Retailing Families and Their Companies

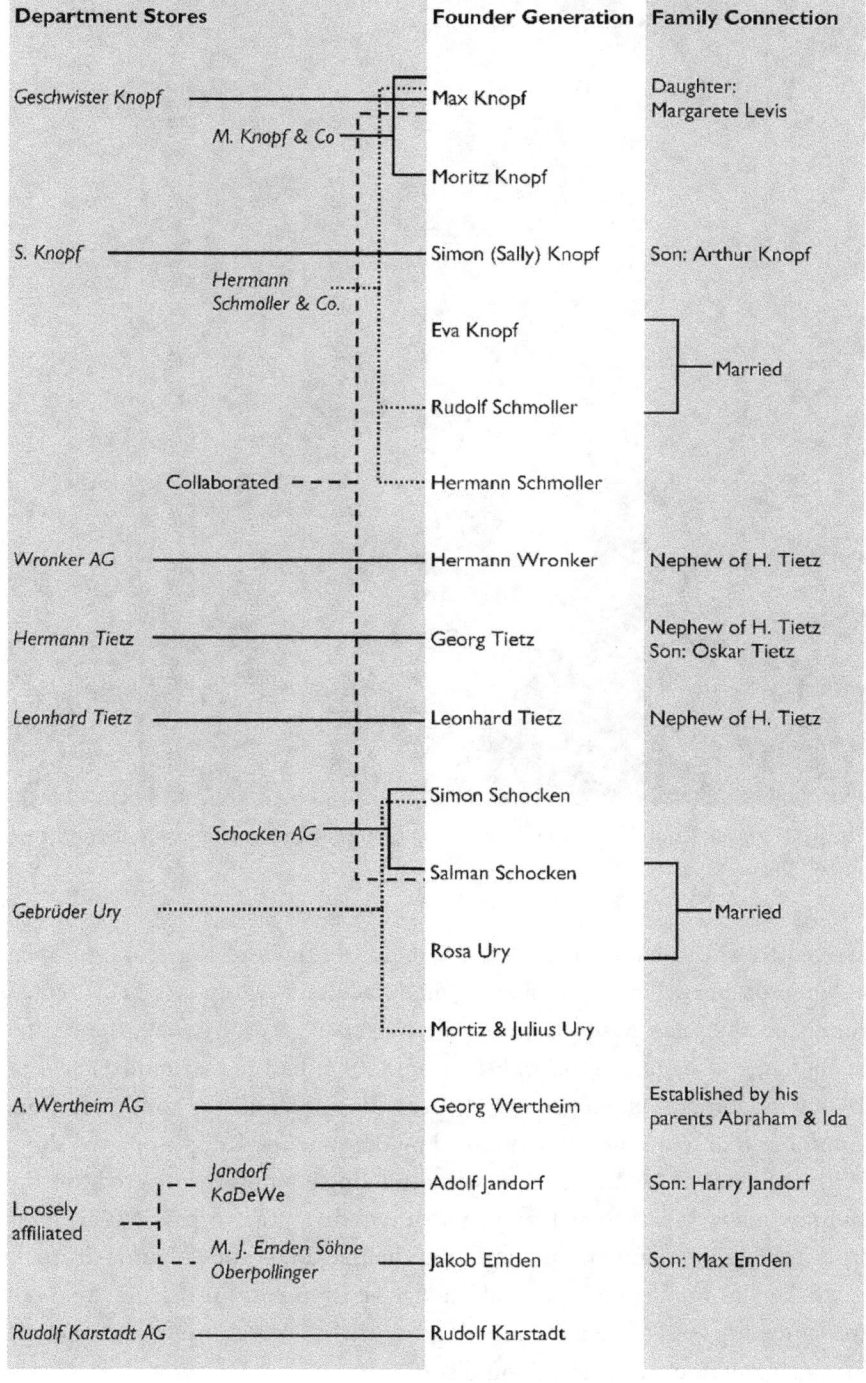

Figure 1.6 Max Knopf established a retailing empire with branches in four countries. © Author.

arrived from Birnbaum in the respectable little town of Karlsruhe to open a 'haberdashery, linen, wool and manufactured wares' shop in rented rooms on the main road known as the Kaiserstrasse. Karlsruhe, the capital of Baden, had begun to expand: In the 1820s it had just around 17,000 to 18,000 inhabitants, employed mainly in civilian and military administration, a number that had more than doubled by the time the Knopfs opened shop. With a capital of 60 *Marks*, and without a single employee or creditor, the siblings made a sufficient turnover in their first year to pay 27.73 *Marks* in tax.[30] Senior members of the family helped Max and Johanna in their early days in Karlsruhe. Life could not have been easy in the first years of the company; only 'iron diligence, great thrift, perseverance and honest management' meant the store could survive.[31]

The exact moment this shop, which sold all types of manufactured goods, especially linens, turned into a veritable department store is not more discernible than for any of its rivals: 'Industry, frugality and perseverance brought the company's success and the ever greater amount of customers, whose gradually growing needs caused the business to expand from a household goods shop to a department store.'[32] Growth was an organic and gradual process visible to every customer and shopkeeper on the same street. Success meant expansion, on the premises – by adding ever more rooms of the former Palais Haber on the Kaiserstrasse to the shop – and by moving to other towns. By 1888, Max had established branches of Geschwister Knopf in Baden-Baden, Metz and Colmar, adding about a branch a year until 1894. In addition, stores at Bruchsal, Rastatt, Bayreuth, Nuremberg and Munich were opened during this time with the aid of several of Max's older siblings.[33] Max also established stores in Luxembourg, Frankfurt and Mannheim as well as a second one in Karlsruhe in 1891 under the Hermann Schmoller & Cie brand.[34]

Mannheim would be the Knopf stores' most lucrative and contended market – with Mannheim being one of the German provincial cities that had grown within a short space of time. Ballooning from just around 20,000 inhabitants in the early nineteenth century, by the time Hermann Schmoller was opened, the city had 90,000 inhabitants, reaching almost a quarter of a million by the beginning of the First World War. This does not, however, include the number of people living and working in the vicinities. Ludwigshafen, an independent industrial city just across the Rhine, was growing at equal speed. Heidelberg and the numerous suburbs and villages on the railway from there to Mannheim also bolstered the potential number of customers. This development was set off in 1828 with the establishment of a port on the Rhine and the first Baden railway to Heidelberg in 1840. The great chemical company BASF (Badische Anilin- und SodaFabrik) was established in the 1860s, as were factories for Carl Benz and the air-ship construction company Schütte-Lanz. Serving this large population was not just the Knopf-Schmoller enterprise, but also Sigmund Kander and Hermann Wronker, which were full-fledged department stores, in addition to a half dozen larger Jewish and Christian retailers operating along similar lines.

The sisters and daughters also played an important role in the family business for all the Jewish department store dynasties, as they were not only useful for establishing dynastic ties with business associates, but were also actively involved in running the stores. Max's sister Eva married a business partner and, like his other sister Johanna, acted as Max's deputy.[35] Another sister Hedwig fell in love

Figure 1.7 Max and Paula's daughter Margarete with Arthur Levis photographed on their engagement. © Schleese Family Collection.

with the linen merchant who had been in Birnbaum on business. Her brother Albert Knopf sang at their wedding: 'Let this button [Knopf meaning button] be for ever fastened to this man.'[36] Family parties must have had the character of business meetings.[37]

It is difficult to say exactly how religious any of the department store-owning families were. They would all support Jewish causes and even establish synagogues when they became wealthier, but we do not know if they were devout or simply performing observance. All of them, if professed Jews, were reformed. This means they did not worship in Hebrew. Many synagogues adopted a gothic design and may well even have had an organ, with the Rabbi donning robes resembling those of a Protestant minister. They no longer prayed for the return to the Promised Land: 'Germany was their beloved home.'[38] This does not mean they abandoned their Jewishness; rather their 'shift demonstrated a continuing effort to retain it even as they amalgamated with the majority by sharing its day of rest'.[39] The prominent role of women in the running of stores especially at a company that called itself 'Knopf *Siblings*' (not Knopf Brothers) may give us an unlikely clue to their piety. Jewish women are given greater flexibility in their observance. While men are usually expected to pray at length at prescribed hours, women can turn up late, especially at the main service on a Saturday – the main trading day for retail even then. In some families, Saturday trading would be done under the sole supervision of the matriarch, possibly meaning the men were at prayers.[40] In some reformed families, the Sabbath was even move to a Sunday.

Max Knopf's brother Moritz was charged with running the concern west of the Rhine. The eldest brother Simon Knopf (known to all as Sally) went on to establish a small chain of department stores in the southern half of Baden. The first S. Knopf & Co. department store was established in Freiburg in 1887 with just three employees along with other members of the family.[41] The municipality of Freiburg had encouraged an economy based on services to clerics, university staff, students and later on to tourists and the many pensioners, especially retired Prussian officials, who moved there. These were the clientele of S. Knopf. Sally opened more branches in small towns in the Black Forest and in Switzerland, which had a similar customer base. In addition, associated firms existed in Switzerland.

Although there seemed to be a dozen different department store chains loosely associated with the Knopf family, essentially Max Knopf could be seen as the head of the entire business – deputized by whatever sister was currently in town.[42] Seemingly without the desire for personal property or aggrandisement,

Max was described as 'puritanically frugal ... free from any drive for externally bestowed honour'.[43] His way of handling customers and staff speak of a mild and pleasant manner, greatly admired by those who came into contact with him: 'Always a joke, well-meaning advice and ever in the interest of the customer, give him the highest popularity among the buying public that adores not just the salesman, but the friend and counsellor.'[44] Yet, in spite of his jovial appearance and pleasant manner, Max, who had been brought up under a strict parental regime, demanded the same self-discipline, conscientious work ethic and sense of duty from his own family and employees. In return, he was the model employer, establishing several socially minded institutions in his firm. His motto was that of Henry Ford: 'Business that makes nothing but money is a poor business.'[45] 'Papa Knopf', as his staff called him, was a benevolent, yet clearly absolute, patriarch. On the contrary, the existing pictures of his brother Sally show a man with the same deep-set eyes, bald and considerably more sickly looking than his younger sibling. With his goatee beard, inoffensive black suit and winged collar, Sally's gilt-framed portrait wouldn't look out of place in a respectable banking establishment.

Figure 1.8 Adolf Jandorf, with his wife Margarete and their son Harry, photographed for the fashionable magazine *Berliner Leben* in 1908 at their home. © Author.

Berlin: Adolf Jandorf

The provincial south-west, where the Knopfs laid down roots, was also the birthplace of the man whose creation is still considered the smartest department store in Germany to this day. The founder of the KaDeWe, Adolf Jandorf was born in 1870 in the village of Hengstenfeld in Württemberg. When he was just fifteen years old, he apprenticed in a shop. Soon he travelled to the other side of Germany, working for M. I. Emden Söhne Hamburger En Gros Lager in Bremerhaven, which had a small chain of stores in and around Hamburg. This former Hanseatic port was 'a great depot for the exportation of the produce of that part of Germany..., as well as for supplying those districts with colonial luxuries and the manufactured productions of foreign countries',[46] and thus a place of domestic and foreign trade extending into local retailing. This was an ideal place for an ambitious man to make his first impression – as Jandorf did so on his boss. When the proprietor Jakob Emden asked Jandorf if he knew the German capital, his reply was 'like my inside pocket', and at the age of twenty-two he was sent to Berlin to do business, though he had never seen the place before.[47] It was this extreme self-confidence, one might say chutzpah, that enabled this 'weedy' young man – who could barely look over the top of a cash register – establish Emden's new branch within six weeks – under his own name: 'A. Jandorf & Co Hamburger En Gros Lager'![48] Naturally Emden was furious, but as everything had been arranged for the opening, right down to the printing of stationery, he had to concede and Jandorf became a business partner without investing a penny of his own capital. This first store was on the Spittelmarkt and served the less well-off customers in that part of Berlin.

Berlin had only just been made the capital of the new German Empire two decades before. Previously Frankfurt or Vienna were arguably more important places for the German-speaking world. Berlin was well suited to be the capital of such a large federation, as described in the mid-nineteenth century by a British traveller as being 'a lead among the capitals of Germany, perhaps even among those in Europe, for elegance: and, being a modern city, it is built on a system of regularity'.[49] By the 1890s, Berlin was a manufacturing centre and also had a large civil service to sustain it. The Empire's principal city was graced with ladies who 'walk with much feminine grace, and are, above all, esteemed the most literary, talented and high-bred of German women'.[50] Jandorf was about to supply them with all they could possibly need to enhance their appearance and lure of their intelligence.

Jandorf cheekily using his own name for the stores in Berlin proved to be fortuitous. An outbreak of Cholera in Hamburg in 1892 meant the association with that city and the Emden name had to be avoided. He dropped 'Hamburger En Gros Lager', which means, in the eyes of the public, the company was not associated with the Emden stores at all. Jandorf's commercial breakthrough was like 'a fairy tale' and was achieved with the words 'Just a quarter of an hour' (').[51] Jandorf had this phrase embroidered on a cushion, inviting the reader to a quarter of an hour's rest on it: 'Not by the hundred, but by the thousand and many thousand, these cushions flooded Germany.'[52] Different sizes, colours, styles, fonts and translations into other languages were sold at home and abroad. All were provided by Jandorf, thus making him a fortune. Soon Jandorf and Emden opened a branch on the Belle-Alliance-Strasse (now the Mehringdamm), even convincing Emden's son Max, who did not like the idea of 'Jewish' department stores, that the venture was a worthy, or at least a lucrative, one.[53] Shops in the Grosse Frankfurter Strasse (now Karl-Marx-Allee), Brunnestrasse and Kottbusser Damm were opened, with all of them serving the working classes of Berlin.

The north: Karstadt

The last department store to establish a flagship store in Berlin, before the Second World War, was also the only significant non-Jewish establishment of the nineteenth century. 'C. Karstadt & Co.', founded in the Hanseatic port of Wismar in May 1881, sold cloths and linens.[54] The Karstadt stores were unusual, not just in having nominally Christian proprietors, but also for purchasing their wares from a middleman initially. It was not until the company began selling gents' and ladies' readymade clothing a few years later, that they went directly to the manufacturer for their products.

The first branch opened in Lübeck in 1884, the city loved by Heinrich and Thomas Mann. Soon they opened stores in Neumünster, Berlin, Braunschweig, Kiel, Mölln, Eutin and Preetz. The founder, Rudolph Karstadt, who had received a formal training as a retail merchant (*Einzelhandelskaufman*), relied on the support of his three sisters and five brothers to run the business, just like his Jewish rival-colleagues who involved their families. Rudolph purchased his bankrupt brother Ernst's stores and additional branches were established, covering most of modern north-east Germany, encompassing the area of Lower Saxony, Mecklenburg-Pommerania and Schleswig-Holstein by 1908.

Figure 1.9 Salman Schocken's penchant for beauty encompassed modernist architecture and blonde women who were not his wife. © Author.

The east: Schocken

Salman Schocken, was, a special case among the department store founders, not opening his first store until the early twentieth century. Short, round and balding from an early age, he believed, according to his grandiose biography, in 'the logic of History; the powers of Reason, Spirit and Will; the virtues of the Common Man; the ethics of self-improvement'.[55] After an apprenticeship in Berlin, Salman joined his elder brother Simon in Zwickau in Saxony, where they set up a store for the Ury brothers in 1901.

Moritz and Julius Ury had opened their first shop in Leipzig in 1896. Leipzig was a key city for German trade, and it was natural that several companies would establish a branch here eventually. Economic unity had proven 'favourable to the commerce of Leipzig which has hitherto been a grand depot of manufacturers for the supply of Germany, Russia, Poland and Turkey'.[56] It was here that the great German trade fairs had always been held for centuries, the first in 1165, and it was at these fairs that many large retailers came into contact with the latest products from around the world. The Urys, Schockens and their colleagues would have visited the city annually to participate in these events.

Simon would later marry one of the Ury brothers' daughters.[57] Apparently, during his time with the Ury company, Salman awakened from a nightmare in which he had turned into the clichéd Jewish clothes hawker. The shock, so we are told, made him resolve to bring smart department stores to the provinces of Saxonia.[58] Salman opened his first own store in 1904 in Oelsnitz, a tiny mining village in Saxony – more than twenty years after his rivals had. Early branches of Schocken traded from very small premises in small settlements under the name I. Schocken Söhne. Salman would sit at the back of the shop running the business, while the genial Simon would be in charge of customer service at the front. An avid reader of literature, Salman chose a quotation from Annette Droste-Hülshoff as his earliest advertising slogan: 'Trade is a delicate structure, and rests greatly on others' columns.'[59] Though it may seem that these pretentious words were chosen only for the purpose of advertising, his director Georg Manasse explained that Salman believed this is what his company was set up to do:

> The chief aim of our company is not earning money ... if we wanted to make a lot there would be the ways of speculation etc., which are avoided by us. The main task of all those who are in responsible positions is to ensure that our company is an absolutely viable and strong organism.[60]

Due to its solid foundations, the company expanded at breakneck speed. Branches at Aue, Planitz, Meissen, Zerbst, Cottbus and Frankenberg were established in less than four years and just before the First World War. The Ury brothers' store was then taken over, and Zwickau became the main seat of the company. It seems that the Knopfs were also involved with the establishment of the store at Zwickau, and both companies continued to be involved with each other in some small way.[61]

Several aspects about the way in which Schocken operated explain its success, in spite of its late start. Their focus on tried and tested popular items made them unusual, as did the stringent organization of the company. Others had a degree of bureaucratic centralization, but none more so than Schocken. Stores were divided into A, B and C size, and every detail of the store according to this classification was guided by head office. The organization, its shortcuts, abbreviations and conventions – apparently so efficient to the insider – were bewildering to the uninitiated. Schocken was so stringently organized that practically anything that was done utilized a pre-printed form.[62] Paramount to the company was the will of the younger Schocken brother. The wide variety of problems Salman handled personally are astonishing: concerns about individual stores, changes in procedure, product range, taxation of department stores, membership of the department store association, items of interest in attached industries, cost of raw materials, minimum price for rose bushes and so on.[63] Salman even believed, later in the twentieth century, that with his system of centralization he could direct an entire economy from Zwickau.[64]

Feeding and clothing a growing population

In the second half of the nineteenth century, and especially in the last quarter, Germany's economy and population developed at an enormous speed. Industrial towns grew, but so did university cites, provincial capitals and regional centres. This meant there was an increasing amount of goods and services that had to be provided to urban areas that, in turn, could be supplied by the very factories and offices that had caused the growth. Traders by tradition, Jewish men and women were particularly suited to act as intermediaries between that which was needed and that which was produced. Able to travel across Germany and settle where they wish, soon there was a store selling 'manufactured wares' in every town and a Jewish name was often displayed above the door. By the very nature of talking about shops that would later turn into department stores, one could be forgiven in thinking that all retailers of this nature flourished and grew. Although one may get that impression, there were countless smaller stores, initially rivals to the 'big names' listed here, that may equally have come to dominate German high streets a few years later. As these examples have shown, what we would recognize as department stores today had all begun as small shops or 'independent retailers' if you will – usually selling linens, haberdashery and so-called fancy goods.

Department stores were hence at the end of a retailing development, most stages of which could still be found existing simultaneously on the high street from the late nineteenth century onwards. The German development is not unusual. When tracing department store history in Britain, a contemporary of the 1950s commented that

> the development of the department store method of retailing is particularly difficult to trace and record, as on the one hand few writers or store owners agreed on the definition of a department store and on the other hand it is not a story of a movement or of the spread of standardised technique but of the progress of a large number of individual shops located in different towns throughout the country.[65]

So, there is no single point at which they become a department store or reach maturity. To understand the difficulty of drawing the lines between different types of retailer, an example may be helpful: The Freiburg outfitter C. Werner-Blust saw itself as part of an old merchant tradition, but turned into a modern retailing venture.

The shop was established in 1848 by Leo Blust, who had to flee into exile briefly because of his involvement with the revolution and the Frankfurt Parliament. Business flourished, according to the founder's grandson Carl Werner, through 'hard work and application'.[66] By the late nineteenth century, the wool shop had expanded to include linens, so-called dowry items and ladies' and gentlemen's clothing in separate departments.[67] The store covered several floors, took up a great deal of space along the high street and sported an impressive frontage. It offered a courier service covering hundreds of miles. By the 1920s, Werner-Blust proclaimed itself as Germany's 'first sportswear house', selling skiing and hiking equipment, tennis, football and athletics gear and, surprisingly successful in Werner's eyes, swimwear.[68] Werner, a Roman Catholic, took great pride in his company: 'There rested on the work of the honourable retailer [*Kaufmann*] the blessing which he could hope for from the fruits of his work.'[69] He managed to combine a belief in traditions with innovation benefiting his store. Werner would later become chairman of the Retail Traders' Association

(Einzelhandelsverband), a member of the chamber of commerce and a special type of justice of the peace for matters of commerce (*Handelsrichter*). C. Werner-Blust, by the 1920s, was noted as a department store-like company by the office of statistics.[70] There were many more firms just like this in towns all over Germany.

It is not easy to define the term 'department store'. The German words '*Kaufhaus*' (literally 'Buy House') and '*Warenhaus*' (literally 'Wares House') are both translated as 'department store'.[71] The lines between these and smaller forms of retail are blurred. Self-definition of these companies is of no help: 'In Mannheim, as in all other cities, one can find many smaller shops which call themselves "department store". This has absolutely nothing to do with the size of the business'.[72] A so-called attached store (*Anschlussgeschäft*) of Leonhard Tietz was Guggenheim & Cie, and this had a very small staff compared to other stores, but was recognized by the German department store association (Verband Deutscher Waren- und Kaufhäuser) as a member.[73] In the 1880s and before, shops which sold a wide variety of only loosely associated products would call themselves a manufactured wares store (*Manufakturwarengeschäft*). However, due to the fact that almost all products were now manufactured, such a title had become obsolete and most would self-define as 'Kaufhaus'. [74] 'Under the term Kaufhaus ... in common parlance, a textile shop is meant, in which a number of different products in different departments are offered for sale together, which has hence not the character of a specialist store.'[75]

Most stores did not even bother self-defining. The tag line 'en gros und en detail' was used by the earliest department stores and continued to appear until the 1920s, usually under the company name. The term was taken from the great stores of Paris and indicated that the company would deal with individual private customers and also act as a wholesaler, applying the duodecimal system to purchasing. It meant the store sold wares in singles or in as much as a dozen times a dozen (one gross = 144). We are usually dealing with a department store whenever this line features with any publicity material, unless a specialization in a certain type of product is indicated alongside. The role of department stores as wholesalers is universally overlooked, as it is even harder to trace than that of the retailer. Others have wasted pages trying to find lexical definitions and failed.[76] Suffice to say, that department stores share a set of retailing principles. A department store, at its most basic level, is 'a collection of shops from all sectors under one roof and under one management' compartmentalized on the premises.[77] The departmental character of the companies was also true behind the scenes. As they grew and had more floor space and branches, the firms had to be run with a strong 'bureaucratic streak'.[78] Each part of the administration of a department store dealt with a certain principle that defined that type of retailing. There were departments for advertising, personnel, accounting, decoration, mail order and so on. Market research, assessment of consumer habits and the like became an aid in decision-making, but did not entirely replace the entrepreneur's intuition.[79] All department store companies had standard methods of operation that applied throughout the firm, but some were more decentralized than others.[80] Wertheim didn't have branch managers, while Schocken and Karstadt were stringently centralized.[81] Wronker and Hermann Tietz would be more were more usual in their practice of allowing their branches a certain independence, whereas Knopf companies were at the extreme end of localized administration. Every company had a different structure and ethos, but there were some common factors.

Consumer societies and cooperatives

Department stores and large retailers were not the only new type of supplier emerging during the course of the nineteenth century. The population was growing too rapidly for it to be served just by private enterprise and especially the poorest industrial workers found it difficult to make ends meet. The cooperative movement was established by labourers to gain easy access to reasonable goods and services. In Britain, there were just four cooperative societies in 1818, but within two years their number had risen to around 300.[82] The cooperative movement in Germany began a little later, in the 1860s, when it was popularized by Herman Schulze-Delitzsch and Wilhelm Raiffeisen. This system not only supported 'traditional village society', but also 'promoted capitalism in the countryside'.[83] Nineteen successful cooperatives were founded each week between 1890 and 1909 in Germany.[84] They included consumer cooperatives (*Konsumvereine*), agricultural self-help groups (*Raiffeisen*) and people's banks (*Volksbank* or *Raiffeisenbank*). For instance, among the five largest food stores in state of Baden in 1927, there were the consumer societies in Mannheim, Karlsruhe and Freiburg.[85] The latter two were founded as early as 1865.[86] The cooperative in Mannheim was founded in 1900 and in 1925 it had a modern bakery, employing twenty-five people, a patisserie, a butcher's shop and even its own vineyard in the Palatine. By 1931, a mineral water plant was added to their portfolio. In all they served fifty-two branches. Mannheim's largely working-class population proved 'a particularly good soil for the development of the consumer society system'.[87] A tenth of the population of Mannheim were members of cooperatives. In Karlsruhe, the so-called every-day needs society (*Lebensbedürfnisverein*) was established in 1865 and sold colonial foodstuffs, bakery goods, patisserie, wine, beer, spirits, shoes and firewood. It was founded to supply not just industrial workers, but also military officers and civil servants in thirty-six stores. It had an annual turnover of 6.3 million *Reichsmarks* in 1925. The industrialist Mez in association with an insurance company for industrial workers founded the thirty outlets of the Freiburg equivalent. It had its own bakery and patisserie, a lemonade factory, a dairy, a textile workshop and a coffee roasting facility with a turnover of 2.5 million *Reichsmarks* in 1925. Sixty such cooperatives with many branches could be found across Baden. There were 396 stores as part of sixty different cooperatives in Baden in 1927. In the same year, 5.4 per cent of the population were members of one food cooperative or another; in Karlsruhe, the number was as high as 15 per cent. Cooperatives were no less popular or innovative than department stores. The Pforzheim society, also in the state of Baden, even had so-called auto-branches, setting up shop in rural locations according to a bus-like timetable.[88] These cooperatives consolidated and collaborated with the aid of technology and communication in the same way that the department stores did, with the only major difference in the way they operated being that they were run for the benefit of their members rather than for the owners.[89]

Role of manufacturing

Modernization of manufacture doubtless aided the set-up of the pre-cursors of department stores and cooperative societies. They were, after all, the first to sell cheap linens that were being made in the Alsace or Saxony at the time. We can probably assume that the development was driven by both increased supply and a simultaneous increase in demand. Early mass-produced wares were considered below the standard norm. Thus, as products became more popular, makers could invest in development, invent more sophisticated machines and use better raw materials to increase the quality of their output. The price of mass-produced items hence fell simultaneously with their rise in quality. More factories started producing similar items giving purchasing departments of stores a choice of suppliers. For instance, since department stores had been established, the production and sale of porcelain had risen steadily. In 1896, the German pottery industry began mechanically manufacturing its products and decorating them with transfer prints rather than hand-painting them, thereby drastically bringing down the prices.⁹⁰ Even Emperor Wilhelm II had a pottery factory of his own in Cadinen, Eastern Prussia. In the second half of the nineteenth century, the manufacturing of men's clothing took off on an unprecedented scale, much aided by the, albeit limited, demand from the department stores.⁹¹ These pioneering manufacturers sold via outlets in large cities or, more usually, participated in a large trade fair like the Leipziger Messe where they came into direct contact with the directors of the purchasing departments of large stores.⁹² By the end of the nineteenth century, prices of consumer goods were drastically reduced. Further overhead reductions could be achieved only by streamlining logistics. Large orders, which could be shipped together, received discounts from the state railways for bulk transport. It was thus in the interest of stores to order as much as they could possibly hope to sell. In some cases, department stores were almost wholly responsible for innovation. Factories needed a great deal of capital to set up, run and modernize. Department stores could invest in such enterprises, thus gaining control over them while making them more efficient.⁹³ The development of canned goods was largely developed by department stores in order to transport and store goods that would otherwise easily spoil.⁹⁴ Mass-produced postcards were also a case in point, giving work to the newly established lithography companies, as department stores sold postcards produced of local landmarks (which naturally always included the department store itself).⁹⁵ It was not just large stores that profited from cheaper and better quality goods; smaller companies could also acquire these goods. They were however usually dependent on a wholesaler, as they had the disadvantage of not having specialist purchasing departments. The smaller store was at a double disadvantage: first because the middleman would add his own profit to whatever he sold and because they could not place large orders which would give them a discount for bulk purchases.⁹⁶

The successful small retailers expanded by way of branches rapidly in order to increase the customer base and – hence – sales. An independent retailer had little chance at negotiating prices with his supplier or manufacturer as they were just too inconsequential. Some stores would produce their own items, usually everyday products that were sure to sell well, thus allowing for a maximum profit. Wares would then be sold in-store or resold to other companies. Schocken would buy some of its products from Karstadt. Another option would be to accessorize standardized wares or upgrade second-rate goods to make them into near-perfect products.⁹⁷ Improving standard goods in-house had the advantage of allowing these stores to quickly keep up with the changing fashion trends.⁹⁸

As we have seen, Germany's political and economic unification coincided with the liberation of its Jews. Stores that had been in the businesses they had been permitted to do before 1871 used their entrepreneurial acumen to provide the growing German population with the goods that traditional forms of retailing could no longer provide and that the new German factories were producing in huge volumes. They were fulfilling the needs of a new class of labourers that without them would not have been clothed or fed. They managed to keep prices low and within reach of their clientele by expanding their branches rapidly to allow them to increase orders and reduce prices. Soon there was a department store-like business in every city and town in Germany.[99] These were not the palace-like structures we imagine them to be, but rather small shops that appeared largely indistinguishable from their neighbours in their outward presentation. They even had branches in small towns serving the rural population. Entrepreneurs concentrated on set areas within Germany where they were familiar with the people's need. Thus each retailing family settled down in a different part of the Empire, thus establishing links with the locality – something that is so important to the German sense of place and patriotism.

It has been said that 'most historians agree that these new forms of consumption and new kinds of experiences remained demographically limited and had yet to extend behind Germany's largest urban centres'.[100] However, this chapter demonstrates that this was not entirely the case. We have also been told that part of the fascination or rejection of department stores was due to their otherworldliness[101] and yet their establishment shows that they were initially and, as we shall see in subsequent chapters, continued to be in small towns and in quite humble shops. Jews were visibly hard-working and serving the community, just like shopkeepers of other faiths. This means many Germans will have experienced the foundation and gradual expansion of department stores close to home and throughout their lives. And hence by the time the Jews were attacked by Nazis in the 1930s, these department stores had almost organically become part of the mental and physical landscape. There is thus no discernible 'origin' of consumer society for the consumer, a point at which this apparently offensive form of retailing suddenly appeared.[102]

Further still, it may be suggested that the founding of department stores in limited geographic areas roots them firmly within the 'Heimat', the almost mythical idea of a homeland that is different wherever one goes in Germany. It is a place that is both comfortable and reassuring, while at the same time 'offered Germans a way to reconcile a heritage of localised political tradition with the idea of a single transcendent nationality'.[103] The feeling of belonging

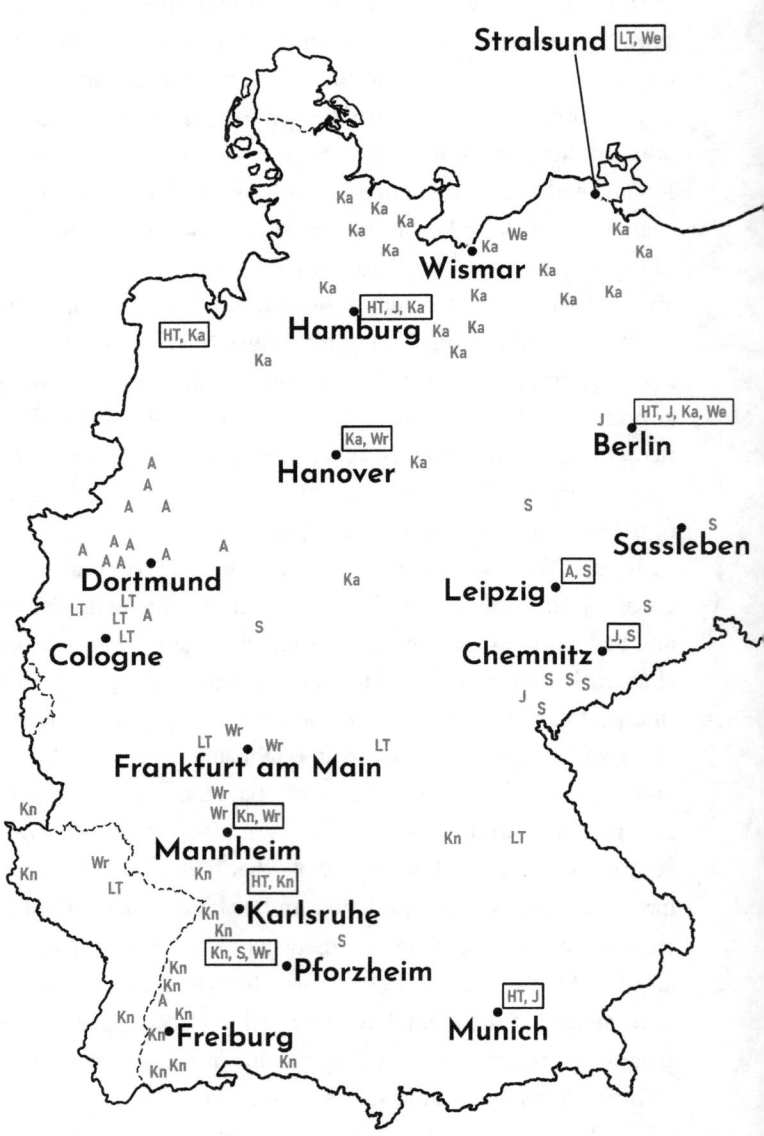

Map 1.1 Department Stores across Germany (only locations mentioned in the text are shown): most Germans would find a branch of a large-scale retailers catering to their specific region close to home.

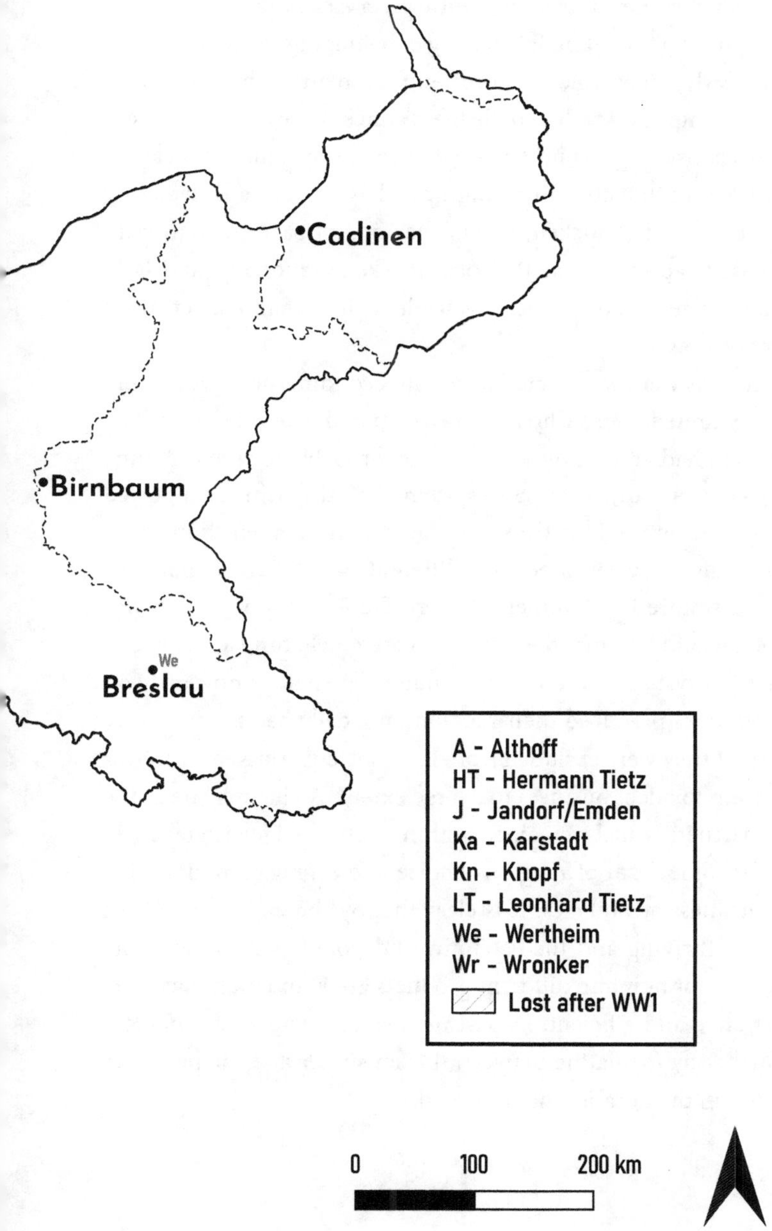

Foundation: 1834–90

•Cadinen

•Birnbaum

•Breslau ᵂᵉ

A - Althoff
HT - Hermann Tietz
J - Jandorf/Emden
Ka - Karstadt
Kn - Knopf
LT - Leonhard Tietz
We - Wertheim
Wr - Wronker
▨ Lost after WW1

0   100   200 km

to the abstract and, in the late nineteenth century very new, but finally real, German nation came from a more tangible feeling of belonging to the provincial community. Thus, early department store entrepreneurs, through their conscious system of kinship-rivalry that made them concentrate on certain areas in Germany, subconsciously tapped into a very German sensibility of localism and nationalism. At Knopf, the customer could purchase a postcard depicting the Grand Duke of Baden, at Schocken, one of the King of Saxony. Both were mass-produced goods adapted to suit the local market. Nationally, and later internationally, standardized products were available within a familiar setting at fledgling department stores.

Due to their faith, Jews were constricted to certain economic activities before 1871. When Germany united, those who had grown up in the families of pedlars and travelling salesmen had an economic advantage, probably for the first time in the history of Jews in Germany. They had a system of kinship which supported economic activity. Wherever the Jews from Birnbaum went to open shops, they would find the Jewish life there developed to a different extent. For example, the family which opened a store in Mannheim, where the Jewish population was large and established, would find that their cousins had to help fund a synagogue in Freiburg in order to crystallize a Jewish community.[104] There is no clarity on how these specific families practiced their religion on a daily basis, nor can we assess as to what extent they were excluded from local society. Antisemitism was rife, but it did not seem to affect business to a large extent. A clue may be in the choice of marriage partners, which remained within established Jewish business networks, suggesting some form of religious choice and segregation alongside the more obvious business advantages. It is clear that by the end of the 1890s these businesses were thriving and the economy and population of Germany were growing. Demand for new and different products grew, and manufacturers became more innovative and efficient. Department stores were set to increase sales and profits further by mediating between the consumer and the producer in more exciting ways in the decades that followed.

2

Expansion: 1890–1900
'Each Sale – A Piece of Renown'

With a less provincial outlook than his grandfather and more reactionary tendencies than his father, Wilhelm II became the German Emperor in 1888. His court chaplain was the Lutheran Adolf Stöcker, a vitriolic antisemite who Wilhelm II likened to Luther. Stöcker's argument drew a direct line from the alleged murder of Christ by Jews in the New Testament of the Bible to contemporary Germans of Jewish origin. We will see, however, in this chapter that this affected our retailers very little. Instead, they gradually grew their businesses into recognizable department stores, by widening the demographic they served, managing to meet the increasingly specific demands of their customers as well as expanding and specializing their levels of service. This chapter will show how successful Jewish retailers were in the early years of Wilhelm II rule, enshrining societal conventions and barriers that were held dear at the time. It will also demonstrate how this attracted – in comparison to the general population – almost negligible resentment among those jealous of their accomplishments.

Some historians, however, give a great deal of space to the critics of department stores, not fully reconciling the stores' success with the vitriol poured upon them. As department stores become more recognizable as such, we will examine how true the complaints of contemporary critics were that the stores were offering cheap and nasty goods to women who, away from the control of their husbands or families, were swept away in a frenzy of consumerism.[1] We will investigate the accusation that Jewish retailers ruined the business of other shopkeepers on the high street with their dumping prices and look into who made these claims.[2] Finally we need to consider how emblematic they were of social upheaval.[3] It will become apparent that previous research, in focusing on those who only saw the perceived negative sides of department stores, have not given us a reasonable explanation for the triumph of these stores.

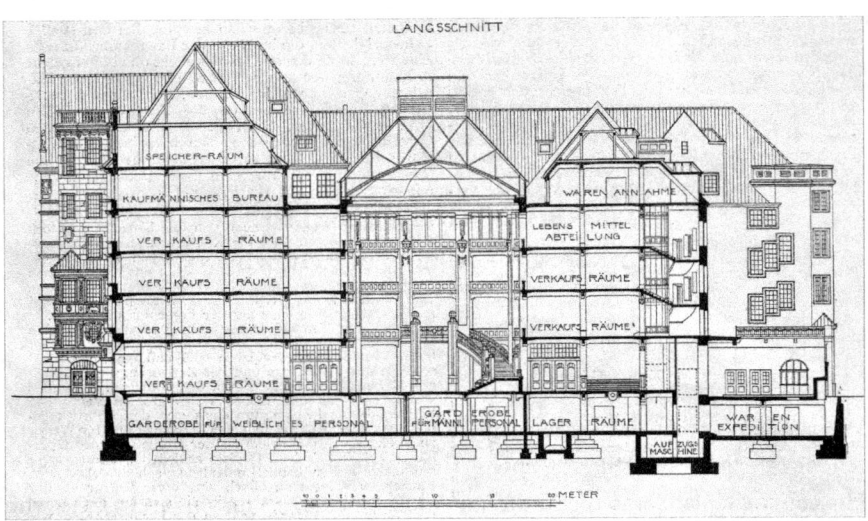

Figure 2.1 Hermann Tietz, Munich, a cross-section. © Author.

In 1890, Bismarck, the architect of German unification, was caused to resign by Wilhelm II. By this point, Germany had slowly come out of the slump which had begun in the early 1870s and emerged into an economic boom. Chemical industry, electronics and mechanical engineering became the drivers of affluence. By 1913, the German economy was almost as powerful as that of the United States or Britain, and was eyed suspiciously by the latter. With this power came an increase in quality of life, fewer working hours, greater social security and general confidence in the Empire's abilities, which tipped towards a growing and fatal arrogance.

The new Emperor's naval ambitions were backed by a strong economy with plenty of ability, raw materials and money. By the end of the nineteenth century, a small section of German society, led by their monarch, were clamouring for their 'place at the sun': namely by establishing colonies, with the aim of boosting international prestige, expressing naval prowess and supplying exotic consumables. The retailers' answer to this was 'colonial wares' (*Kolonialwaren*), a category of food stuff which covered products that could easily be shipped from beyond Europe, under the watchful eyes of the ever-expanding German navy. Not only oranges imported from Italy or Spain, but also bananas and pineapples made their way from fairground prizes to the delicatessen department. The Purchasing Cooperative of Colonial Goods Retailers, later named EDEKA, was established in 1898, which soon brought exotic products even into provincial towns. Coffee and hot chocolate were no longer the preserve of a Sunday afternoon in a bourgeois household, but a part of the workforce's morning ritual, and it would need to be served in a porcelain cup even there. Someone had to provide these modest items of luxury and also the marine-themed jacket for the lady and a toy gunboat for junior to go with the new sense of pride. Department stores were at the centre of this development, supplying expensive foodstuffs at ever lower prices and reacting to the public's demand for products demonstrating Germany's affluence. With the increase in consumption of non-essential goods, it would be hard to call some mass-produced items in the 1890s 'luxury'; department stores began improving their service and choice to attract a wider – and above all more affluent – demographic. This was much to the dislike of some who were not doing as well out of the German economic boom as they would have liked.

A wider demographic

At the turn of the nineteenth to the twentieth century, the homes of the lower to middle segments of society were now becoming, as one early historian of department stores put it, 'simpler, more beautiful and practical' due to mass-produced goods available in department stores.[4] In order to ensure high turnover, a principle of the first department stores was to refuse credit, insisting on cash at point of sale. A credit system required a great deal of control, especially in an era before computerized data, and was of questionable financial reliability.[5] Customer credit would have to be laboriously recorded, accounted for and then – uncomfortably – demanded to be settled. On the one hand, people with very low paid jobs, especially the industrial workers in cities who relied on a credit system to purchase even the most basic products, were unable to buy regularly at a department store. On the other, those with more money and leisure time could afford to purchase bespoke items in a specialist store, where the assistant would know these customers personally and fuss over them. Department stores hence initially served a very middling market.

In this earliest period, up until about 1900, many of the stores used gimmicks to encourage customers to shop there. Free gifts, such as calendars, branded glassware or bags of sugar, were offered to the shopper and aptly named 'lure articles' (*Lockartikel*) – products to entice the customer in.[6] Loyalty schemes bound the customer to the store by encouraging them to collect discount stamps. Single-price days offering all things in store for a fixed sum, usually 95 *Pfennigs*, were advertised.[7] Manufacturers' seconds were sold and promoted as such, which cannot have attracted the higher end of the potential market. Before the turn of the nineteenth to the twentieth century, however, department stores did not advertise much. In comparison, small retailers of men's and lady's fashion, with only one or two branches, were far more prolific publicists. Unlike department stores, smaller retailers were also more sophisticated and elegant in their presentation of newspaper copy. They developed a brand image far sooner, sticking to a specific style of advertisement and the use of a single logo type trademark. The earliest and infrequent department store advertisements were neither eye catching nor well written.

Yet by 1900 – within twenty years of beginning with a small upper- to lower-middle-class customer base – the stores had gained a near-universal appeal.[8] By design, a department store's profit margins were tight and dependent on a high turnover. Hence the customer base had to be widened to increase profits. With more shoppers, the orders multiplied, affording significant discounts, considerably cheaper shipping, more efficient advertising and better use of space in store. If the number of customers could be increased, the store could sell more and better products at lower prices. The less well-off labourers and the well-to-do middle to upper classes were large markets. As it was impossible from a bookkeeping standpoint to offer credit to the poor, by the dawn of the twentieth century, department stores worked especially towards including the affluent middle classes in the customer base. They had a greater disposable income and leisure time, meaning there was a greater inclination to spend money. The department stores did not, however, simply trade up, leaving their original shoppers behind, but retained their customer base and generally broadened their appeal.

A sense of demand

In order not to lose their original customer base – the idea was, after all, to widen it – stores increased the gradients of quality to suit a variety of purses. Mass-produced goods were becoming increasingly indistinguishable from handmade ones due to manufacturers introducing more refined production methods. Without large and lucrative orders from department stores, manufacturers would not have had the incentive or the capital to invest in better means of production. Goods of a higher quality but still of a reasonable price helped attract a more discerning public. Schmoller in Mannheim, which was part of the Knopf business, was one such example of a department store where, as one customer put it, 'we could buy at reasonable prices, especially durable goods that didn't wear out easily'.[9]

From around 1900, catalogues featured the same type of product in a variety of qualities and price categories. Selling a multitude of different wares meant that some others could be used as loss leaders. These products were sold for a price lower than anywhere else, sometimes even lower than that of purchase. This bargain would then be widely advertised, enticing customers to their stores to avail of these offers. Stores calculated that people would then buy other items, where the profit margin was greater. This was done particularly often with branded products as these could easily be compared between stores. This was a highly successful tactic, as Lux pointed out in 1910: 'Maggi remains Maggi and seasons the soup just as exquisitely, wherever one has bought it and however much one might have paid for it.'[10]

Throughout the entire period from 1900 to the mid-1930s, the main feature of advertising was the listing of items on sale with prices. The form was generally referred to as the price index (*Kurszettel*) – an item of ephemera one would usually find on the stock exchange listing the prices of shares. The idea behind the name was that the prudent housewife would inspect the lists of all companies and compare the prices for similar items. Armed with her exchange lists, she could head into town.

A sense of service

Department stores did not create the demand for better products or high-end customer relations; they saw the need to improve their performance in order to increase their own sales over those of their competitors. Offering a greater range of products so as to attract a more discerning public, department stores also had to begin providing better service to their customers, guiding the shoppers through the array of wares. Gradually with the expansion of stores from the 1880s onwards, the customer was increasingly being overwhelmed by choice: 'I never knew what I liked best. The variety was stunning', one consumer noted retrospectively.[11] Over the next decades, a dynamic developed between the customer and the sales clerk that had previously not existed: on the one hand, the customer had a vague idea of what she or he wanted, while on the other, only the sales clerk had sufficient knowledge to guide the shopper to the right item.[12] In the early 1880s, the staff at department stores consisted mainly of members of the founding family, which gradually expanded to include extra, untutored, staff who learnt on the job. The middle classes would only come to department stores if the service equalled that of specialist stores. In smaller and smarter retailers, the customer was used to a great deal of advice from the sales assistant who specialized in selling, possibly even making, the products that were on offer. The advantage of a small shop was the personal touch.

As department stores expanded, training their staff became a major task. As of the 1910s, specialist schooling was compulsory for those entering employment and throughout their career. Staff were reminded that 'with each sale a piece of renown and a piece of the future of the business is engaged'.[13] A sale should be conducted in a calm, simple and matter-of-fact way. After all, not all the items on offer were of outstanding quality; the customer was permitted to decide whether or not the wares were worth the money. In the 1920s, the staff were advised in a training manual: 'In terms of the quality of the presented goods the sales clerk must honestly and openly tell the customer the truth.'[14] Once informed of the options, the customer alone was the best judge of what he or she wanted. Julius Barach, the head salesman at Tietz, is reported to have said: 'If the customer demands iron girders as hat pins, then just sell her iron girders.'[15] If at all possible, the customer should be greeted by name. This gave her the impression of being particularly valued.[16] Some regular patrons would be privileged to find, as one then-young shopper put it, 'in the various departments a clerk who knew my mother's taste and always served well. A personal chat was, if time permitted, also included.'[17] This would, however, seldom be the case as more often than not the transaction would be conducted between strangers, especially with the expansion of business between the 1890s and the 1910s. The atmosphere of intimacy which existed in a specialist shop had to be created by making the customer feel at home in the surroundings of a department store. Studying customer psychology made up for the lack of personal information the assistant possessed about the customer. Ideally the salesperson – often patronizingly referred to as 'girl' – would notice 'by the tip of the nose' of her customer what he or she wanted. 'According to the manner by which the customer greets and expresses his wishes, the sales clerk must recognize how to deal with him', an early-twentieth-century training manual advised.[18]

Sales manuals provided advice on how to analyse the dress and features of customers if their manner alone was not sufficient to gauge them. At Knopf, an undated publication, available from the department store publishers Schoettlander & Co., titled *Verkaufserfolg durch Menschenkenntnis* (Sales Success through Knowledge of Mankind), was kept close at hand for quick reference. Its purpose was to give advice on different types of customers. After a general

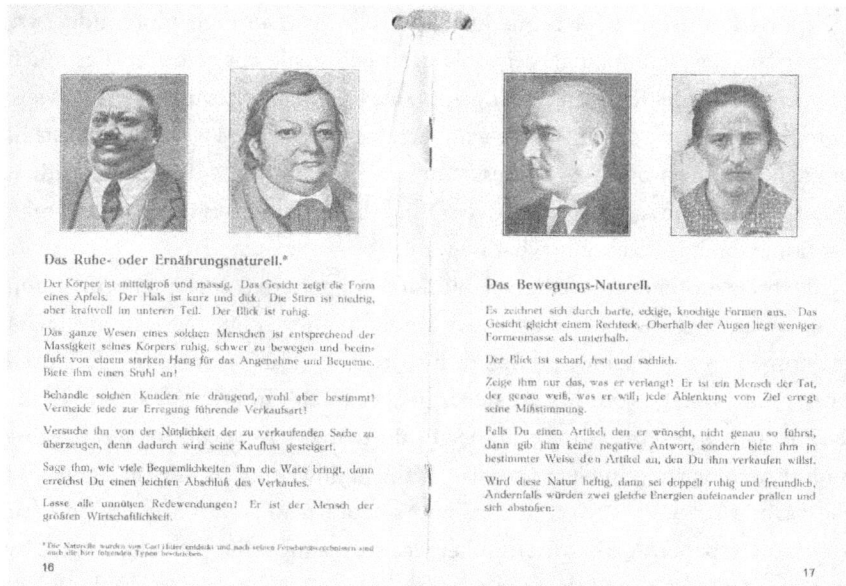

Figure 2.2 Should someone looking like the founding father of Turkey (centre right) visit the shop: 'show him only what he asks for!' Popular pseudoscience advised shop girls how to deal with customers according to the shape of their heads and body type. © Wolfgang Ziefle Collection.

section with pictures of individuals and short captions on what sort of service and goods they would expect, the 'nature' of different types of customers was discussed. Compared to women, men were 'psychologically entirely differently adjusted consumers', the Schoettlander guide advised.[19] Women did most of the shopping, but they also did the shopping for their husbands, fathers and friends. Even if men were not usually physically present in store during shopping, they consumed department store products by proxy.[20] And on the occasion they shopped, they would 'very rarely ... set out to conquer a shoe, but come home with a book', as a nationwide department store publication put it.[21] This did not, however, mean they actively avoided shopping in department stores at any time. We have little data on the enthusiasm of gentlemen for shopping. In Britain, the proportion of men buying clothes in department stores was small in the 1880s and 1890s, but by the turn of the century the figure rose steadily as stores introduced more 'manly' items such as books, stationery, tobacco and toiletries.[22] Throughout the period, wherever in the Western world, men's consumer goods had to conform in style and function to their place in society.[23] In order to be able to sell these, however, men had to be served differently from women. They are reported as being more prone to snap decisions than their more indecisive wives.[24] The German manuals certainly dealt with male customers just as much as female ones. Distinguished octogenarians, looking like country vicars, were not to be questioned during a sale, while weak-chinned ones were likely to steal! On page seventeen of 'Sales Success', under a portrait of the Turkish President Kemal Atatürk, the assistant was advised that the individual of this type 'is a man of action, who knows exactly what he wants'.[25]

Like their mothers and fathers, children were potential customers: 'Children of customers are always to be treated kindly as they might be a future client accustomed to the business'.[26] Before his death in 1907, Hermann Tietz used to distribute sweets from his waistcoat pocket to children in the store.[27] Some advertising was designed to appeal specifically to them. Advertisements targeting children were written in German script – the handwriting most children would first learn at school – so young consumers could read advertisements in their parents' newspaper. A trip to Schmoller was seen almost like a treat, as noted by a customer who shopped there as a child: 'I was never bored with it', doubtless not least because of the enormous toy department.[28] One customer who had been there as a child in the 1930s believed the Christ child or St Nicholas did their shopping at Schmoller![29]

Not being personally acquainted with the proprietor or the staff was not necessarily a disadvantage for department store shoppers. The customer could feel more comfortable browsing a large store, rather than a small one. In a smaller establishment, customers were under unpleasantly close scrutiny from staff and may get the impression that the proprietor knew too much about their private business.[30] At department stores, however, one could 'look and buy', as a slogan above the main entrance of the Freiburg Knopf store proclaimed in 1898. To be simply allowed to look was a great draw to customers. One independent piece of research in 1910 noted that sales assistants were reminded that 'if the customer leaves the department without taking any of the goods presented to him, the salesperson may not show his disapproval of this behaviour with an offended expression'.[31] After all, a customer who left without buying was not always a lost customer. As Georg Manasse advised the new girls at the Schocken department store in 1926, 'while the owner of a normal retail store is fearfully considerate that every customer that enters his shop also buys, we can be generous'.[32]

In the decades after 1881, the stores increasingly became places where many different social classes would meet. With the extension of the customer base, one department store manager told his sales staff that 'whether the customer carries high titles or is a simple working class woman' she was to be given the same

Figure 2.3 A book of fairy tales aimed at children, each featured in one of the nine Berlin stores of Hermann Tietz. The purpose may have been to get young shoppers to pressure their parents to visit each one during the Christmas shopping season. © Author.

service.³³ By the 1920s, accounting techniques were sufficiently advanced to keep track of credit schemes, placing high-quality wares within reach of the working class. In particular, the stores in Mannheim had to serve a large and less affluent labouring demographic. At Schmoller, a customer who was unable to afford a winter coat had it reduced in price by the manager and 'the rest was charged to "expenses" on his orders. Overjoyed, her mother thanked Herr Schmoller for the extremely generous gesture.'³⁴ By contrast, Schocken took exception to 'bartering and borrowing' as there was 'for every customer the same price and the same sale conditions'.³⁵

Some lady customers might well be 'not always amiable, sometimes even sharp and niggly', as one manager's tongue-in-cheek observation was noted in a manual, but the salesgirl had to remain polite, calm and attentive.³⁶ A well-served customer was quite simply the best, and cheapest, form of advertisement. When a member of the Bavarian royal household came to visit Hermann Tietz before the First World War, Oscar instructed: 'If she buys and pays in cash, treat her just like everyone else. If she does not buy, see to it that she inconspicuous and quickly leaves the house again.'³⁷ This attitude did not change in thirty years: Schocken's 'basic principle is not to take advantage of anyone. Every customer should be aware that they have bought at a fair price.'³⁸ The stores had a universal appeal, serving everyone – in their own way – equally, but specifically according to what they were used to, each within their own social category.³⁹ With their success and their broad appeal across classes – while enforcing the boundaries through segmenting customers by type – Jewish department stores were becoming increasingly respectable members of the *Mittelstand*.

Success and jealousy

There are very few examples of direct physical action against department stores. When the new Hermann Tietz in Munich was opened in 1905, there was an instance of students smashing windows because the owner was Jewish. This was however the most radical recorded reaction. Student fraternities had been plied with drink and whipped up into a frenzy by some shopkeepers beforehand.⁴⁰ At the beginning of the twentieth century, the opening of the first branches of I. Schocken Söhne (Zwickau Saxony), later Salman Schocken AG, resulted in nothing more than a couple of newspaper articles questioning the effect of the company on local businesses – but there was no Jewish angle to them.⁴¹

There were less-public ways of attacking department stores: In 1906, Ludwig Kain, the manager of the Hermann Schmoller department store in Mannheim, Baden, was called before the local magistrates. The company had run a whole page advertisement on 14 November 1905 in the *Mannheimer Neue Zeitung* with a special offer: gentlemen's boots of the Goodyear variety were to be sold at 7.50 *Marks* a pair. The local association of shoe sellers (Verein der Schuhwarenhändler von Mannheim e.V.) sent one of their apprentices to Schmoller to inspect the sensationally low-priced items. The apprentice was specially attended to by the head of the shoe department and was offered a boot where the three components of the shoe had been sown into one by a machine. The members of the retail association in court asserted that 'a machine-made boot is of decidedly less quality than a Goodyear boot ... even the layman knows that he will receive a first class boot under the brand Goodyear'.[42] The term 'Goodyear', they claimed, described any sturdy boot where the inner and outer shoe were sown together separately and then stitched to the sole. A cheap shoe would cost 5.50 to 6 *Marks* to make according to their calculations. A Goodyear boot could not be bought from the manufacturers for less than 8.50, let alone sold for 7.50. The shoe sellers were calculating the cost of making the shoe according to the prices the wholesalers gave them. The very fact that the department store could sell a shoe for 7.50, which the smaller shops could not purchase for 8.50, was seen as a point of contention. The lawyers acting for the prosecution demand a high penalty 'as this is a department store operating with great amounts of money'.[43] Kain's defence for Schmoller's store was that it was not the type of manufacturing that gave the shoe its name, but the machine itself. He was right; Goodyear shoes were always machine-sown. Precisely because he was in charge of a branch of a chain of department stores (they were part of the Knopf family's empire), they could buy items cheaper in bulk. The court sided with the shoemakers and Ludwig Kain, being personally responsible for his company's advertisements, was required to pay a fine of 300 *Marks*.[44]

This is an example of how the way department stores worked was, possibly wilfully, misunderstood by some retailers and officials. Yet, other contemporaries understood the matter better. One member of the Reichstag told the story of the manufacturer who sold his products to a department store for 30 *Marks* each, only for the department store to resell them for 25 *Marks*, explaining that it was the way capitalism simply worked and one could not legislate against that without changing the way the German economy worked. The man noting this was a socialist who naturally felt that the only solution lay in a fundamental change in society and politics. As it stood, so this parliamentarian believed, the ways department stores operated was legitimate.[45] Yet, at the turn of the nineteenth to the twentieth century, various organizations throughout Germany were petitioning for a special tax to be imposed on department stores – all self-proclaimed members of the so-called *Mittelstand*. The Mannheim association of shoe sellers was just such an organization. The term *Mittelstand* is almost impossible to translate as it is a unique concept to German society. The problem of trying to define them is exacerbated when we realize that those proclaiming themselves part of the *Mittelstand* could not define what they were themselves. They usually chose to explain what they were by saying what they were not. First, most believed that a member of the *Mittelstand* could not have certain occupations: an employee, a civil servant or an industrial worker was not a *Mittelständler* (although even this changed in the course of the twentieth century). Some of them might have considered themselves *Bürger* (part of the bourgeoisie or *Bürgertum*), but they certainly were not proletarians.

Individuals considering themselves part of the *Mittelstand* held a corporatist view of society and established organizations propagating their opinion. Many of those who met under the label of *Mittelstand* believed their way of making a living made them the independent, hardworking and above all the 'creative' part of society. Retailers, traders, craftsmen, artisans and farmers and the variants thereof united into organizations which differed according to how its members made their living, the location they were in and the time at which they existed. Not until the forced amalgamation by the National Socialists did there exist a national umbrella organization or even conventions on the structuring of these organizations. They would include anything from a national chamber of commerce to a rural butchers' guild and would be founded, amalgamated and disbanded at various times. The most powerful, long-standing institutionalized ones were the chambers of commerce and craft of which every town would have one. These particular chambers not only played the role of internal regulators, but they also represented their members to the outside world. They acted as lobbying organizations to influence politics and society. They claimed the right to comment on laws before they were passed and corresponded with figures in politics and prominent members of society to gain influence over them. As the creative part of society (the *schaffende Stände*), the different organizations were clear on only one thing when influencing politics: their existence was essential for the well-being of the country. The fruits of their labour and the ideals by which they lived made them the backbone not only of the German economy but also of the German society. The term is hence a very vague ideological construction for a group of people without clear-cut objectives and with vastly divergent views.[46]

A typical radical self-styled supporter of the *Mittelstand* in the Reichstag was Member of Parliament for Giessen Ferdinand Werner. Voicing a the litany of complaints typical of extreme right-wing parties in Germany, Werner brought up several loosely connected topics during his speeches: large banks, the German aristocrats who sit on the boards of these banks, civil servants owning shares in businesses, large milling companies, cooperative societies, sensationalist newspapers, lack of funding for the Roman-Germanic Museum in Mainz, advertising in public spaces, the lack of import duties on sugar beet and the existence in public of 'coloured people'.[47] He also claimed that department stores were ruining the businesses of small shops and hence needed to be taxed. Other members of the Reichstag had suggested this before:

> If you go into a department store, not to buy, but just to see the business, one can be horrified ... In my opinion it is the duty of the governments of the German states ... to do something against them... it is not too late to do something against this cancer. This can be achieved best of all through immense taxation.[48]

The favoured solution proposed by *Mittelstand* companies was to ask for a special tax to be levied on their rivals, and department stores were no exception. Department store taxation had first been introduced in Bavaria in 1899 and was set at between 0.5 and 3 per cent of their turnover. Württemberg followed in 1903, with Saxony raising the tax for the benefit of local government soon after.[49] In Prussia, a complicated system of assessment was set up and stores were taxed up to 20 per cent of their annual profit.[50] In all cases, taxation had been introduced as a result of pressure being put on the state governments by *Mittelstand* organizations.[51]

In Baden, in the state of which there were several branches of Hermann Tietz, Wronker and almost all Knopf stores, department store tax was a very minor parliamentary issue for the legislators. Between the 1899–1900 and 1900–1902, parliamentary years the lower chamber received two petitions requesting an extra levy to be placed on department stores. These were filed by the right-wing and overtly antisemitic German Nationalist Association of Commercial Assistants (Deutsch-Nationaler Handlungsgehilfenverband).[52] The internal logic of these petitions is jumbled and hard to unravel. Macro- and microeconomics levels are indiscriminately mixed with politics, hysteria and hearsay. No arguments were made or data presented; statements were simply listed as facts. What they stated did not always make sense, and the members of parliament were well aware of that. The Nationalist Association of Commercial Assistants believed that staff at department stores were 'at the mercy' of their employers and a levy for the benefit of local authorities would compensate for the low wages that sales clerks received. The tax would compensate councils for the loss of revenue caused by the tax advantages that department stores allegedly enjoyed and would cut the losses that small shops incurred due to the existence of such stores by acting as a disincentive for department store expansion. Finally, the association claimed that the presence of department stores devalued property prices in their vicinity, which could be prevented by increased taxation. Parliament was warned that if nothing was done against department stores, they would 'turn against the hitherto well treated consumers and dictate these prices of their own convenience'.[53] As if to disprove their own claims, the Nationalist Association of Commercial Assistants demanded a tax on the turnover of stores as they made very little taxable profit. The Union of Independent Merchants and Tradesmen of Baden (Verband selbständiger Kaufleute und Gewerbetreibende Badens) also petitioned the Ministry of the Interior – rather than the parliament, showing their ignorance of the system – claiming that taxation would be a measure against the 'dishonesty' of department stores, whose mode of operation was considered to be corrupting the morals and customs of the 'lower classes'. Unlike department stores, they claimed that smaller shopkeepers, companies with branches and cooperative societies served the community better and hence taxation would compensate for the loss of so-called community work which smaller retailers did.[54]

In answer to the claims of the Nationalist Association of Commercial Assistants, employees of the department stores in Baden – in whose interest they were allegedly speaking – petitioned the parliament themselves in 1904.[55] The signatories (the list ran to many pages) vehemently denied that 'the staff are excessively exploited, moreover they benefit from above average pay and treatment than in other companies'.[56] They gave statistical evidence that the number of small shops in Baden had risen (from 133,600 in 1882 to 231,300 in 1895) and not fallen since department stores emerged. They proved that property prices in their vicinity had on the contrary increased – in fact in Hesse, statistics show that those living in inner cities dropped by 60 per cent reflecting the conversion of dwelling places to retail spaces. Finally, they demonstrated that they were offering a service to society by providing the population with consumer goods at moderate prices.[57]

The Baden Parliament was slow to act upon the petitions received and the subject was not broached until the 1903–1904 term. One delegate, Dr van der Borgh, summed up the sentiment of the parliamentary majority when he asserted that department stores had their place in the economy. They were, after all, nothing more than a market place – the most ancient form of retailing. Even if they were a completely new phenomenon, he asked, had only small and old businesses the right to exist? The parliament was fully aware that no existing laws were being broken by department stores. It had been established that there was no instance of legally proven unfair competition.[58] Borgh claimed a dangerous complacency was going round the pressure groups of small- to medium-sized businesses; he pointed out: 'It is a fact that some time ago in Offenburg the small mills made demands against the larger mill.' This was symptomatic of the lack of readiness to tackle rivalry like any business should.[59] Even if such a tax were to be introduced, Borgh asked, what would this achieve? Only a very small percentage of shops might profit and department stores themselves would not worry at all. In Paris, the Bon Marché absorbed its 2 per cent tax easily, passing on the price to the consumer. It was found that those petitioning against department stores and for extra taxation could not 'support their claims by no actual material evidence' and in some cases were simply lying or were misinformed. Department stores did not, for instance, receive tax breaks. The government decided to do nothing until the chambers of commerce had commented upon the matter.[60]

The chambers of commerce in Mannheim and Karlsruhe, representing the largest commercial cities and the industrial north of the duchy, failed to respond within four years. The statistical evidence provided by Freiburg and by Lahr was completely inaccurate and hence petitions were disregarded. Only Heidelberg's chamber of commerce sent a full and detailed reply, deciding to sit on the fence: even if some department stores might sell substandard wares and employ unusual means to attract customers, on the whole the accusations made against stores were 'gross exaggerations'. Although the chamber in Heidelberg lamented the loss of small entrepreneurial businesses, 'it seems to us more than doubtful that smaller shops will be helped in the long term with this; we don't promise ourselves the least success from a higher taxation'.[61] If department stores really were found to be a problem, only the most crippling tax would curtail their trade – something the chamber most vehemently advised against. As these department stores had emerged from small beginnings about two decades earlier, taxing them out of existence would have amounted to 'setting a penalty on hard work, thrift and enterprise', the chamber of commerce in Heidelberg asserted in 1904.[62] Those with a mandate to represent the *Mittelstand* – which small shopkeepers considered themselves to be – and regulate trade in the duchy either provided inaccurate information, ignored the debate or advised against taxation. The response from Heidelberg was the only one noted verbatim in the printed parliamentary records.

The tax commission's head Dr Johan Gustav Weiss was to consult on this matter. Weiss was the mayor of the town of Eberbach and a member of the ruling National Liberal Party. In 1895, he had established an association for mid-sized towns. As its president, he moved from being a member of the lower chamber to the upper house. Weiss noted that all petitions in favour of taxation basically made the same claim: department stores had unreasonable operational practices which drove some people out of business. It was thus reasonable for the state to help those at a disadvantage. Conversely, he presented the department stores as meeting a need in society, their goods being cheaper owing to mass production and not of inferior quality, and their practices, as part of a wider retailing trend, understood and accepted by the public.[63] Weiss thus advised setting up an extra department store taxation rate as a gesture towards the perceived plight of small shops. 'But', Weiss warned, 'government intervention will not be the all-healing medicine for the trials and tribulations of the *Mittelstand*'.[64] Another member of the Landtag Dr Rümelin expressed the general consensus of both Houses of Parliament when he 'doubted that the public is going to be fooled by unfair business practices in the long run'.[65] Only time would tell whether this would be of any help. On 18 June 1904, the law for the taxation of department stores was passed through the upper chamber and presented to the Grand Duke for signature. Baden department stores were, from then on, to pay a surtax of 0.2 per cent on all turnover if it exceeded 200,000 *Marks*. The tax was not to be more than 8 per cent of the income.

In Bavaria, Saxony, Prussia and Baden, the tax remained ineffectual. In the case of Hermann Tietz, the Prussian Minister for Agriculture Victor von Podbielski encouraged Oscar Tietz to allow him to supply his department stores with milk – in return for preventing effectual taxes.[66] Unsurprisingly, Podbielski had to resign in 1906 due to allegations of corruption. Oscar Tietz recalls the introduction of the tax and its effect in Bavaria. It had been rejected by the Social Democratic Party (SPD) in the lower chamber of parliament, as they saw the advantages of department stores to the working classes, as well as by the upper (aristocratic) chamber, but eventually forced through in order to placate the *Mittelstand*. What had been planned as a restriction on the family's Hermann Tietz branches in Bavaria ended up being hardly noticed by the consumer. In Prussia, Georg Tietz believed it allowed the store to have a near-monopoly as there was an incentive to cooperate with manufacturers to reduce the price of wares by the paltry amount required to mitigate the tax.[67] Smaller stores could not hope to negotiate with their supplies like that. All over Germany, department store taxation failed to hem in the operations of large retailers and in some cases proved detrimental to smaller ones that suddenly saw themselves categorized as department stores.[68]

One member of the Reichstag, the SPD parliamentarian Heinrich Pëus, endeavoured to explain that however clever the laws were made to protect the *Mittelstand*, it was in the nature of business to find ways to flourish – large ones just as much as small ones. The latter in particular as they need the flexibility to survive by being innovative. He believed the vast population was reliant on such retail outlets to purchase the basics of life at a reasonable price. The many rules to allegedly protect business were, according to Pëus, simply used by business rivals sending 'police men with spiked helmets' into each other's shops in the hope of spoiling a day's worth of trade.[69] People claiming to be the *Mittelstand* also complained about the purchasing cooperatives and many other indiscriminate activities of civil servants and military officers. The only point of the debate regarding the curtailment of department store trading, he believed, was for politicians to gain favour with those who lacked sufficient business acumen. His words turned true when the National Socialists found new ways of gaining a following.

Around the time that Wilhelm II ascended the German throne, the small haberdashery stores that had been founded by Jews under his grandfather's rule started developing into enterprises more recognizable as department stores. Critics of viewed these as a projection of all things modern and bad: mass consumption, independent women, changes in morale, social upheaval and commercialization of society.[70] Some historians have emphasized on these factors to help explain the fate of Jews after 1933. Department stores were credited with bringing about too much change. They were swamping markets with cheaply produced goods.[71] They were tempting respectable women –even those, one believed, were prone to irrational behaviour – into stealing things they did not need.[72] They were propagating values and lifestyles of the upper classes to the lower ones as 'a medium for the creation of a national middle-class culture'.[73]

Yet, we have seen that department stores, far from breaking down class structures, have enforced them by serving each customer as was suitable – and comfortable – to the shopper. The population was growing and diversifying independently of what any individual company could influence, and it was much better for retailers to follow societal trends. Simultaneously improved production techniques in particular meant not only the quantity, but also the quality, of wares increased. The working classes and the upper middle classes were attracted by the stores introducing practices and products that suited their lifestyles. This meant each shopper was offered the same courtesy they were used to in public, the same discretion they liked in private and directed towards products suitable to their station. Shopping may have been a particularly feminine pastime, but German class, gender and age barriers were upheld regardless.[74] Tearing them down would risk upsetting customers and be bad for business. Store proprietors knew this and that is why they continued to be so prosperous in this period. As Rappaport points out in Britain, shops became safe and pleasurable places that became central to civic improvement and women's emancipation, within the framework of established society.[75] This was change, but change that cemented an established order within the boundaries set before the unification of Germany.

We should see department stores as a mediator in a world that was gradually changing, at once holding onto the structures of a societal order, while manifesting them through the new ways of organizing the economy. Further, I would suggest, stores allowed everyone to be part, to the degree that they were able to afford, of the affluence that Germany was enjoying. Thus Jewish-run department stores were contributing to a shared experience of the new Empire where the wives of civil servants in Berlin and workers from the Ruhr could see, touch and purchase wares that outwardly demonstrated a unity and prosperity Germany had never had before. A communal experience, for instance, of imported coffee and clothes that reveal naval ambitions helped create a national pride while keeping everyone in their place through products and services graded by class.

Department stores were thus, ironically, very successful and respectable members of the *Mittelstand* and pillars of society even if others who counted themselves among that *Mittelstand* claimed the opposite.[76] The fact that the *Mittelstand* was an amorphous concept that lacked definition or central organization explains how these two views could exist simultaneously.[77] Their economic success and the acceptance by the population brought about a good deal of envy not just from the shopkeepers of the less popular businesses, but also from the new class of sales assistants who were employed in these shops. In spite of the combined efforts of various organizations, in particular the Nationalist Association of Commercial Assistants, the German states did not curtail fledgling department stores by issuing a punitive tax. The lawmakers in Wilhelmine Germany understood that the population was growing fast and needed to be supplied with reasonably priced goods and services and that small businesses could not do this on their own. They also recognized that smaller or older businesses were not worthy of more protection due to their size or age. Yet, the political establishment also wished to be seen as doing something to calm their hysterics. Thus department store taxes were introduced which were completely ineffectual. The Nationalist Association of Commercial Assistants had been particularly vocal about the apparent shortcomings of department stores as employers. As staff in larger stores were usually female or Jewish or both, the openly chauvinistic and antisemitic membership of the association could, in fact, have had no experience of what it was like to work there. Although the petitions of the association against department stores did not have antisemitic content, they were written by a deeply antisemitic group concerning a form of retailing dominated by Jews; hence this veiled antisemitism. Thus the members of the association may have been dissatisfied simply because they were jealous of the working conditions. The association, like so many organizations claiming to represent the *Mittelstand*, were not just fighting for a place in the economy, but primarily for recognition in society and the status that was necessary in Wilhelmine Germany. The next chapter will show that those who worked at department stores were not only treated better than most other wage earners, but also that they grew to serve as ambassadors of their employers. The shop girl of department stores went on to become the epitome of fresh-faced and respectable German ladies and thus one of the biggest assets of a department store.

3

Labour: 1890–1930
'Qualified Young Ladies'

On the face of it, the main problems the Nationalist Association of Commercial Assistants and other organizations had with department stores was not their 'Jewishness', but the alleged 'oppression' of staff. We have certainly been told that employees were just tiny cogs in huge machines, for whom life was a continual struggle.[1] Historians believe that not only were department store staff taken advantage of by their employers,[2] but the employers in turn – all being Jewish – were treated like 'lumpen' by their staff.[3] This juxtaposition raises questions. Female sales clerks put up with the hard and unhealthy working conditions – so it has been reported – because people believed they were depraved women who were money-mad.[4] On the other contrary, research in the United States has shown that a healthy paternalism existed in which department store owners were respectful towards their staff, instituting welfare systems and rewards for good work.[5] In addition, department stores in the United States fostered the skills of young women, especially at a time when most other forms of female employment tended to undermine them. Central to this support for staff was the sure knowledge that an overworked shop girl was incredibly easy to spot and extremely off-putting to the customer.[6]

The overwhelming majority of these employees in Germany would have been young working-class or lower-middle-class women. At the end of the nineteenth century, opportunities for women to find self-fulfilment and independence were very hard to come by, especially for those who came from a poor or rural milieu. Due to this, shop girls remain relatively mute in archival sources. When we do hear them, we only hear *of them* through the mediation of men who falsify the female experience. Thus, the Nationalist Association of Commercial Assistants were not speaking for these women, who they actually exclude from their ranks; they claimed something in order to further their own ends. Equally, claims that women who worked in department stores were one step away from prostitution

Figure 3.1 Staff at Geschwister Knopf in Karlsruhe modelling the latest fashion. The most successful girls could win a short-term modelling contract and go travelling. © Author.

were fictitious and were made to fuel the writer's own sexual fantasies. Also women who did take up the cause of the shop girl did so from the lofty heights of their comfortable upper-middle class lives. They had no idea what it was like to work all day in plain sight.

Fortunately the social activist Marie Baum, although the daughter of a surgeon, took a sympathetic and scientific approach to women in the workforce, ensuring that her work was not stained by possible prejudice of her class. She researched and presented an official assessment of the background, working conditions and health of wage-earning women in Karlsruhe. Published in 1906, this statistical volume gives us a woman's systematic perspective on female employment. This is supplemented by first-hand accounts from women in the employ of department stores in the 1920s and 1930s, showing a continuity in the way staff were treated here, reaching back to the late nineteenth century.

Quite contrary to what was propagated by some at the time and is still reported as fact in history, this chapter shows that department stores provided women a near-unique opportunity to work independently and respectably away from the home. It will also reveal why department stores offered these chances. In fact, we will see that a key to the success of department stores was their pioneering working conditions. Thus female employees and large-scale retailers had a symbiotic relationship illuminating much broader themes in female emancipation.

Professionalizing women's work

In 1904, Karlsruhe had 210 registered shops, of which three were department stores, sixty-eight were clothes shops and eighty-two were delicatessen and provision stores. Baum's research found that of these only ten shops employed more than twenty people.[7] Hermann Tietz was the largest retail employee in Karlsruhe with approximately 500 people working there by 1914. Across all their branches, Knopf had more employees in Baden and throughout the complicatedly organized company they must have given work to upwards of a thousand people.[8] Before 1914, the Schocken department store company employed 400 people, and by April 1932, the number rose to 6,000, of which 500 to 600 of them worked at the headquarters alone. Zwickau was solely responsible for employing 1,200 people – in Zwickau, approximately 5,000 of the total population of 85,000 were in one way or another involved with the company.[9] At whatever time and in whatever store the workforce was mostly female.[10] Women's work had increasingly shifted from the household to the public sphere in the course of the nineteenth century. Originally there had been only a limited number of jobs a woman could do. Employment in manufacturing could be found, but working in a shop was favourable as it would allow a woman to continue to dress and act like a lady.[11] As one contemporary put it: 'So now the girl who used to make socks and sausages at home stands behind the counter and sells the same items to her mother.'[12] The great advantage to their employers was the low rate of pay they commanded, mainly due to the lack of an established lobby – in other words, women were pricing their male colleagues out of the market with their involuntary low wages.[13]

By around 1904, in Karlsruhe, 231 female retail assistants worked in the three large department stores, 316 worked in clothes shops and 155 sold food. More than a quarter of females in Karlsruhe retail were employed in department stores. Most of these were single. Out of 231 girls assessed by Marie Baum to be working in department stores in 1904, only three were married or widowed. In food shops, the ratio was seven single to one married (Table 3.1). A total of 9,037 people were registered as working in general retailing in Karlsruhe in 1925. Of those 2,158 were single women working as employees.[14] In 1910, 62.2 per cent of the employees in an average department store in Karlsruhe were sales personnel,

Table 3.1 Married and Single Women in Employment, Karlsruhe, 1906

Place of employment	Single	Married/widowed	Under 14	14–16	16–20	20–25	25–30	30–40	Over 40
Department store	228	3	1	20	99	75	29	7	–
Women's clothing	113	2	–	5	50	24	19	15	2
Boots and shoes	17	7	–	1	10	5	3	–	–
Food	66	10	–	2	18	18	13	16	9

	Single	Married/widowed	Under 14	14–16	16–21	21–50			Over 50
Factory workers	–	–	9	351	949	767			23

Source: Baum, *Drei Klassen von Lohnarbeiterinnen*, p. 134.

less than 1 per cent were or had been married. Just as young unmarried women would be the mainstay of the workforce before the First World War, widows would be after it.[15] It was the rule, throughout Germany, that a woman gave up working when she got married, or did so only in private, and hence single young women aged between fourteen and thirty constituted the body of the workforce in retailing from the 1880s to 1940s.

With the increase in clerical jobs, associations were established representing interests of the workforce. The staff were keen to increase their own respectability and improve their working conditions; societies naturally formed to support these intentions.[16] They ranged from those groups emphasizing their membership of the *Mittelstand* to quasi-trade unions. The extreme ends of the spectrum were the socialist Central Association of Male and Female Commercial Assistants on the left and the very vocal German Nationalist Association of Commercial Assistants (which we encountered previously), excluding Jews, women and foreigners on the right-wing end of politics.[17] Before 1900, these societies campaigned for anything from Sunday as a day of rest to more occasional seating for sales clerks. Their conditions cannot have been perfect and they would have wielded considerable power as 'a labour dispute in a department store could, through expressions of sympathy, especially through a boycott by working-class customers, get quite different support than one in the mining or paint industry', as one observer had it.[18] However, there are no detailed records to be found of labour disputes in department stores. We know of only three cases in which there seem to have been bad labour relations before 1910. The events in Berlin, Breslau and Kiel could not be retrospectively reconstructed as no archival sources have been preserved to inform us. We can thus not say what the dispute was about or judge how severe they were. The lack of sources and the hearsay of only three cases of labour action do indicate that it cannot have been a very frequent or serious occurrence. Want of concerted action on the part of sales clerks might have to do with the absence of a national umbrella organization. Yet, over the decades, working conditions improved. By 1928, the well-being and respectability of staff was encouraged by employees: 'We want to show that department stores promote with all their power the establishment of a solid *Mittelstand* of private officials', the department store association stated.[19] Some members went so far as to call their assistants as sales officials (*Verkaufsbeamte*). There was a shift in the way staff, in particular female, were seen by their employers between the 1880s when the early stores were established and the turn of the nineteenth to the twentieth century.

Salman Schocken believed no one was better qualified to serve customers in a department store than women: 'young girls and women bring a natural gift for the sellers' profession. Therefore this profession is one of the happiest for the female sex. What could be more appropriate than advising buyers the right way in a well-ordered store?'[20] The job of a sales clerk in a department store could only be taken by 'a qualified, practically predisposed, young lady', Fritz Richter, the manager of a Knopf store, wrote in a training manual.[21] Most retail jobs did not require 'dexterity', hence it was easy to recruit girls to do the work. However, the job of an assistant in a department store was different from that in a clothing shop. Here, as Baum recorded in her study, 'pleasant manners [and] knowledge of foreign languages is desired and conducive to advancement; here one strives to see the world, here through frequent changes in dwelling and working place one expands ones horizon and in such a way that it enables better paid professional positions'.[22] In order to vouchsafe the quality of employees, stores did not acquire their staff exclusively from the immediate vicinity, but accepted applicants from a variety of social backgrounds and places of origin. Of the 549 retail assistants in the city of Karlsruhe in 1904, 205 came from craftsmen or artisan families, 68 from civil servants' families, 65 were born into retailing and 43 girls' fathers were farmers.[23] A total of 56.3 per cent of female employees in Karlsruhe had been born in another town, with 27.2 per cent of girls not coming from the same state, while 9 per cent weren't even German (Table 3.2). Instead of joining a department store, most girls from the surrounding villages or from agricultural backgrounds would usually take up work in a bakery or a butcher's shop where 'their fresh, healthy appearance suggests a good diet', but were considered too coarse, not just by Baum, to work for a department store.[24]

Before 1900, the employees of department stores had not been of the best calibre. Potential employees with good prospects had avoided working in these stores, according to Baum, mainly because 'in comparison to fine specialist

Table 3.2 Place of Residence and Birth of the Female Workforce, Karlsruhe, 1906

	Living in town	Living out of town	Born in town	Born out of town
Department store	217	14	107	124
Women's clothing	114	1	64	54
Boots and shoes	17	2	8	11
Delicatessen	76	–	26	50
Factory workers	680	941	–	–

Source: Baum, *Drei Klassen von Lohnarbeiterinnen*, p. 136.

shops the relatively unskilled work of the department stores could be performed by less practiced workers'.[25] In the first two decades of their existence, many department stores were little more than glorified haberdashery shops, where very little external help supplemented the work of the family. In the early stages of their development, department stores were not distinguishable from other shops, and neither was their staff. Once stores expanded physically and widened their customer appeal, and especially climbed up the social scale, higher qualifications were required to work there. Department stores introduced the division of labour as soon as the number of staff was large enough. Specialization would lead to greater productivity; efficiencies of this kind brought great savings and became a cornerstone of department stores' retailing principles. In a small shop, advertising, decorating, accounts, packing and so on would all be handled by the same people. Tietz, Knopf and Wronker all started in this way in the 1880s, with the family providing an untrained workforce. In a fully fledged department store, the staff would concentrate on performing a single task to a high standard: haberdashery sales clerks, furniture sales clerks, painters, decorators, bell boys and chauffeurs had unique job descriptions. Specialized male individuals were assigned to work in personnel, accounts, purchasing, and advertising, and usually dealt with the administrative side. Stores had an absolute minimum of administrative staff, and most of the workforce was front of house and female. In 1910, over 62 per cent of the staff in an average department store were sales personnel, just under 20 per cent were males employed as painters, bell boys and chauffeurs, 10.8 per cent were pure administrative clerical staff and just 7.2 per cent were employed in managerial administration and in the purchasing department.[26]

Baum could show that the calibre of the workforce improved drastically with professionalization: 'Today, however, the entrepreneurs of the largest enterprises make planned endeavours to supply a well-trained, proficient and reliable staff.'[27] Rigorous selection, extensive testing and continuous training achieved this.[28] By the first years of the twentieth century, only the very best would be called for an interview. We catch a glimpse of the types of character one could find at an average department store during the search for new staff at a Schocken store in 1930–1: There was the 34-year-'old Fräulein' Weingärtner, who worked as a cashier at Wronker for 180 *Reichsmarks* a week. She had made a good impression with the interview board, but they were reluctant to employ her as her father worked for a rival company. Then the cashier's aid and packer, 29-year-old Frau Nordwig, was considered. She too had been positively received. It was noted particularly favourably that she was supporting both her blind father and a six-year-old son.[29]

Herr Willmann and Herr Kling were recorded as talking too much, Herr Kückel as looking younger in years than he was, Fräulein Wagner as making a better impression on paper than in the flesh, Fräulein Weikelmann as being a bit of an old spinster and Herr Grocholsky as showing a dry sense of humour. Frau Hellstern was considered rather clumsy – which must have been unfortunate as she was hoping to get a job as a waitress.[30] Similar characters are playfully chided almost twenty-five years before, in a song from a staff party at Schmoller in 1906; from Herr Kain the grumpy accountant to Herr Hermann whose constant demonstration of the newest 'Edison' phonograph was driving his colleagues mad.[31]

The selection had to be rigorous as the staff were the public face of the company. If an individual had the basic aptitude, the company could mould him or her into a competent employee. In smaller and more traditional establishments, new apprentices were not necessarily trained properly.[32] At the Karlsruhe stores, from the turn of the nineteenth to the twentieth century onwards, there were significantly more trained staff per apprentice and more guidance than at specialized retail outlets. In a department store in 1904, there were 6.5 sales assistants per apprentice, while in a women's outfitters there were only 3.6, less than the Karlsruhe average of 4.6 (Table 3.3).[33] The training of an assistant at Knopf took at least three years; only after completing this was one considered for permanent employment. Training at department stores included reading of literature provided by the company and visits to the commercial school (*Handelschule*). Oscar Tietz was instrumental in founding some of these schools. Outside of department stores, few retailers provided institutionalized training until it was made compulsory by law. Department stores pioneered in training of shop girls, making them an ally of the female clerks' lobbying associations in the late nineteenth century.[34] By the 1920s, staff at Schocken would 'participate in a course in which teaching staff from the company's organization department introduced them to business and

Table 3.3 Assistant/Apprentice Ratio and Years of Apprenticeship, Karlsruhe, 1906

	Apprentices	Assistants per apprentice	Years of apprenticeship
Karlsruhe average		4.6	
Department Store	31	6.5	1 (rising to 3 by 1919)
Women's clothing	25	3.6	1–2
Boots and shoes	4	3.8	1
Food	15	4.1	1–2

Source: Baum, *Drei Klassen von Lohnarbeiterinnen*, p. 140.

sales expertise and in particular the unique facilities of our house'.[35] Even though training was more rigorous and by the 1910s better than at ordinary shops, it would remain hard for a trainee from a department store to get employment in a smaller specialist retail establishment until well after the Second World War.[36] Yet swapping between different department store companies was relatively easy and one of the reasons ambitious girls would join.

The heads departments were often men of Jewish origin, but it was not unheard of to have a female in charge, especially from the beginning of the First World War when male staff became scarce. He or she had far-reaching rights and duties as the head of a department. Among other things, they advised the company on what items to purchase and then fixed the price for them when they arrived. It was usual for the head of department to be individually accountable for the department's performance. Departments would be charged with the cost of lighting, heating, transport wages and goods purchased, which would be weighed against what profit had been made there.[37] In some stores, it was the practice from 1900 for a selection of goods to be presented to heads of departments and let them select from those. Further still, they were to advise on the best means of advertisement (for which the department would be charged) and to design and pay for the window display out of the department's account. They commanded considerably higher wages than other people working in store and had more secure incomes than if they were running their own shop (Table 3.4). All this means that the head of a department was like the owner or manager of a specialist retail outlet, where he or she would be responsible for his

Table 3.4 Average Pay Per Month of Employees of Three Randomly Selected Department Stores, Baden, 1900

Employee	Number of employees			Average pay		
	Store I	Store II	Store III	Store I	Store II	I Store II
Female salesperson	34	63	30	831.00	785.50	832.00
Porter, liftboy etc.	2	8	3	1,050.00	1,215.00	1,100.00
Cashier	3	4	2	1,160.00	1,065.00	1,380.00
Male salesperson	4	5	2	1,470.00	1,464.00	1,140.00
Storekeeper	4	10	–	1,695.00	1,626.00	–
Manager	2	4	1	4,902.00	4,005.00	2,340.00
TOTAL	69	135	49	19,295.00	20,656.50	14,812.00

Source: GLAK 231 5016.

or her own actions, only, in this case, embedded into a larger structure and with less financial risk.[38]

As early as 1906, the workplace of shop assistants was believed to play a significant part in advertising, as Baum puts it in her study: 'through that which large powerful companies have to offer in this regard, the audience has become gradually with time so spoilt, that a narrow gloomy shop would remain without customers'.[39] Departments were to be kept in 'meticulous order' and had to be ordered even before the lunch break.[40] Personal belongings required while on the shop floor could be kept only in the special drawers intended for that purpose. Sandwiches or snacks were not allowed on the shop floor for fear of mice. The cleanliness, air and space that were provided for the customers meant the staff had better working conditions 'than one could ever ask for, on sanitary grounds', as Baum's state-sponsored survey concluded approvingly in 1906.[41]

There was a positive side effect to the crossover between workplace and public space. Order and cleanliness, dictated by the handbooks, as well as light, space and ventilation, provided by the purpose-built store, did not just attract customers; it benefited those working there too. In smaller shops in the early twentieth century, staff did not have the advantages of central heating, electric

Figure 3.2 Work as a familial sphere: shop girls of Knopf in Freiburg pose for a photograph featured in a family album and captioned 'my world'. Some staff had exceptionally warm feelings towards their employers. © Wolfgang Ziefle Collection.

lighting and double doors and porches preventing drafts. Small shops were stuffy and claustrophobic in the summer and were poorly heated (or not at all) and badly lit in the winter.[42] Initially, department stores had similar problems. But, as soon as the first female clerks' associations were founded in the early 1890s, they campaigned for better working conditions, such as provision of seating for the staff in retailing.[43] Legislation was passed in 1900 and added to various codes of practice; yet the best provisions were rendered without effect, as most girls were too busy to afford even a moment's respite on a chair.[44] Good working spaces and regular breaks for shopworkers and women were institutionalized only in firms where employees realized the negative effects the sight of exhausted staff had on sales. Department stores were hence the first in the field of retailing to improve their working conditions. Disgruntled and unhealthy staff were a commercial threat, so department stores provided conditions improved way beyond legislation.[45]

Perks of the job

'Built on the achievements of the individual, the achievement of the entire workforce is crucial for the overall economic success of the company', Knopf told its staff in 1934, which is why exceptionally hard and good work was rewarded with a bonus and long service with additional perks.[46] These practices were in line with other department stores, but not usual in other sectors of employment.[47] After the initial period between 1880 and 1890, the basic advantage of working for a department store was higher wages than normal.[48] At any given time, the better payment of staff and the more regulated working hours was two of the major problems smaller retailers faced when competing with department stores to recruit good staff.[49] In the early twentieth century, a salesgirl until about the age of thirty, if unmarried, tended to place her wages in the parental purse. In the 1910s, if frugal, a girl could live independently on 61.50 *Marks* a month, 65.70 if she wanted a good room, while 75 *Marks* were required if she wanted a little more space. The average female factory worker at the time earned only 10.37 *Marks* a week, with the girl doing manual work and forced to live either with her family or in the cheapest lodging available.[50] A total of 47.24 per cent of employees in branches of retail establishments other than department stores earned just 50–100 *Marks*. In department stores, however, 61 per cent earned that much. The average pay at a department store in Karlsruhe was around 97.25 *Marks*, allowing most assistants to lead independent lives, even allowing for small luxuries and recreational activities.[51] Female shop assistants were, however, not the only people getting better pay. Across Germany, work was being rewarded to a greater extent, and, in particular, the working-class population benefitted by having more free time and more cash in their pockets – more opportunities to spend leisure time and money.[52]

From around 1900, heads of departments received considerably higher wages than if they had been running their own company while branch managers received even higher wages. This practice continued in stores even during the worst times of unemployment; Schocken paid at least the minimum wage plus up to 50 per cent above market rates for good to exceptional work in 1932.[53] Wronker paid even better wages, especially in the lower wage brackets of under 50 *Marks*, and also gave bonuses to sales clerks who performed well.[54] Throughout the period, wages of shop girls would rise steadily until the 1930s when they were about double what they would have been before the First World War.[55] Compared to wages across Germany, in 1906–10, female staff at a department store earned considerably more.[56] In addition to this, regular wages we paid during apprenticeship, rather than after training. As most employees were female, their wages were lower, but they were still higher than average at department stores. Men earned more than women everywhere in Germany, and department stores were no exception. While women working in stores in the first years of the twentieth century did not earn more than 300 *Marks*, 7.7 per cent of the males did.[57]

Women would have to leave the company once they got married, usually with an extra two months' salary. By 1934, female employees received 100 *Marks* upon marriage, if they had been part of the company for more than five years, with the sum rising to 200 if they had served for ten years or more.[58] Besides above average pay and staff discounts for purchases in-store, regular holidays were contractually cemented at a time when most people did not get any time off at all. Knopf did not just guarantee staff up to eighteen days leave, but also paid for them in as early as 1904. At Schocken, girls who had only just begun their apprenticeship were given twelve days of holiday a year, as opposed to the six required by law.[59] Only eleven of the forty food shops gave holidays in Karlsruhe. Most shops at the turn of the century would not give their staff any vacation. Regular holidays were the norm only for those working in department stores and in the clothing industry. It was not until later that the minimum leave owed to the employee as per the law would be accepted by other proprietors. Schocken and Leonhard Tietz even owned vacation homes where their staff could enjoy their holidays at discounted rates. Directors of stores were concerned with

Figure 3.3 Rest home for the staff of Leonhard Tietz. © Author.

the health of their younger female employees. After having enjoyed so many holidays during their schooling, the constant work was a shock to their system, and they were given a priority at in-house hotels.[60] Germany was pioneering in Europe in social reform, mainly in a failed attempt to curb the power of left-wing parties. Public sickness funds (*Krankenkassen*) had been instituted for a few decades, and yet a quarter of German department stores paid more health insurance than was legally required of them. Before the First World War, Knopf had a special fund with which staff were sent on holiday to the Black Forest. Unfortunately, the war and inflation completely annihilated it.[61] Other socially responsible practices were continued after 1918. Should a member of staff die, their dependents would receive the full salary for a whole extra month at Knopf, while for their longest serving employees, two months' salary was given.[62]

Working hours too improved gradually owing to professionalization of department stores. At the end of the nineteenth century, work in a department store would start at 7.30 am in the morning and not finish until 8 pm; 38.5 per cent of workers had to tolerate more than twelve hours of work a day, some up to thirteen and a half.[63] In the two decades after 1880, working hours of sales and office clerks were long and irregular with little respite.[64] In department stores, the working day could be longer than in average shops. Late shifts had become the norm; as Baum puts it, when the store began to be lit 'in an extravagant manner', it meant that some retailing staff had longer hours than factory workers.[65] Small establishments could not afford the expense of electric lighting and had to close early. Under pressure from sales clerks' associations, by the beginning of the twentieth century, the German department store association pledged to bring working hours down to 48 a week and institute a day of rest. Both were achieved by 1908.[66] As was usual at the time, between 1900 and 1933, Sundays were not shut entirely as a day of rest. Knopf's policy on public holidays would vary according to the location, as the store would open on Sunday during local festivities and trade fairs, and according to the local laws regarding Sunday trading. Usually the three Sundays before Christmas were open days in any large German town, but even when the rules were totally relaxed, no worker at Knopf would have to spend more than three to four hours in store on a Sunday. At Wertheim, however, Sunday was a day of rest on principle.

In 1921, a Wronker store employee had a forty-eight-hour work week, excluding mealtimes and breaks. For lunch, each member of staff had an unpaid two-hour break, in addition to a further half hour at another point of the day. The working day for salespersons began at eight o'clock and for other staff at quarter past eight. Lunch was taken in two shifts, between 10.55 am and 12.55 pm or between 1 pm and 3 pm. Other quarter-hour breaks could be taken between 3.15 pm and 4.30 pm for those having a midday meal, and between 9.15 am and 10.15 am for those lunching in the afternoon. If personnel did not return from their break within five minutes of it ending, it was the department manager's duty to find them. No one's breaks were to be shortened due to other colleagues' slackness.[67] Persistent lateness was grounds for dismissal. The opening of the store at 8.00 am and its closing at 6 pm on weekdays and 6.30 pm on a Saturday was marked by the sounding of a bell.[68] In 1910, the law required all workers to have at least eleven hours of rest in any twenty-four-hour period, and one and a half hours of break spaced throughout the day. On the contrary, in small shops, staff often had to forgo their breaks, meaning lunch or other meals had to be taken on the job. In Wronker in 1921, staff were allowed a two-hour break for lunch, taken in two shifts, in addition to another half-hour break at another point in the day. At Knopf, a system of flashing coloured lights which could be viewed from the counter was used to herald the beginning and end of breaks. Either the top floor or the cellar of a store would accommodate the staff canteen, traditionally known as the 'casino', where a meal was provided for the staff.[69] Employees were supposed to take their lunch here out of sight of customers, even if they brought their own food. In Karlsruhe, the cellar of Knopf's flagship store also housed 212 lockers and twelve sinks together with wash- and changing rooms.[70] In 1902, when the plans for the new flagship store were drawn up, most dwellings did not have running water at all, making this a luxury for the staff and a way of ensuring cleanliness.

There were good reasons for this benevolent paternalism. The structure of the family business was kept in most companies, even after the death of the founder-owner. Not just because the first stores were run only by family members, but also because it was the only way loyalty in such a large company could be ensured in an age before establishments had large personnel departments and CCTV surveillance.[71] Employees were expected to behave in an exemplary way, integrate into the hierarchy and 'have good manners towards their superiors, inferiors and fellow workers'.[72] Benevolent patriarchy was supplemented by motherly guidance and control, as set out in handy rulebooks. New girls were to look upon the older ladies as wise counsellors. Whether the familiar system of control was cemented by continual spying on each other, as was the rule elsewhere, is hard to say.[73] Honour was encouraged to such an extent that most rule-breaking did not even have set penalties. This was not considered because, at Knopf in the 1920s, 'it is expected that every employee sees it as a matter of honour to do his duty without such enforced rules'.[74] A good ticking off by a senior member of the company (as usual a member of the family) would usually do the trick. If anything, this was seen as part of the training: 'Fear no strict boss or superior, from a lenient one you can learn nothing', one manual urged.[75]

Before beginning work, employees were to enter through the staff entrance. They were not permitted to use the main doors at any time or walk through the store in their overcoats and hats. The reason for using the staff entrance was because the commissionaire checked their clothing, bags and parcels before entering and leaving. Trying to avoid the checks could lead to dismissal.[76] If a member of staff wished to leave, they needed permission from their head of department and the reason was recorded in the commissionaire's book. In special circumstances, a head of department could give someone the day off, staying away without his permission would, however, result in a penalty being deducted from her or his wages.[77] Illness had to be reported to the personnel office as soon as possible.

George Tietz relates the jovial and patriarchal style with which his Uncle Hermann dealt with his staff.[78] Yet upon his death in 1907 there was no one to replace him and Oscar, his mind more on the account books than on his staff, introduced a set of written regulations regarding staff interactions with customers and the company. Any employee in need was helped personally, by Hermann himself until his death. 'Support banks for employees at the expense of the company' were introduced as a proper channel to access extra financial help.[79]

Far from retail assistants in department stores being poor suppressed shop girls from the villages, these were intelligent and ambitious women with many abilities. Good wages, perks, greater respect for the individual and better working conditions meant this type of job attracted bright women who could thrive and grow if they wanted. If in the 1880s, the department store employee was a poor untutored servile girl of working-class parentage, by the 1910s she was a respectable sales clerk of independent means and good prospects. Ambitious men could earn more money and have more of a career running a department of a large store, than if they owned a shop selling the same items. In 1904, department store employees, in a petition to the Baden Parliament, denied 'that staff is excessively exploited by department stores, the same enjoy moreover better than average pay and working conditions than in other companies'.[80] Small companies were less scrutinized by the public, inspectors and unions. Schocken knew that his staff would be more prepared to work and work well for their employer if he used his financial power and emotional support in their favour.[81] The staff also knew that they in turn would be treated better if they demonstrated their loyalty to their employer. During the annual staff party at Schmoller in Mannheim in 1906, the staff sang a song about their loyalty to the company and gratitude to their employer – followed by 'colossal applause'.[82] At Wronker in 1916, on the occasion of the silver anniversary of the store's foundation, one staff member recited a poem on his 'love and devotion' to the firm.[83] Similar sentiments can be found at Knopf and Tietz.

The tactics of the department store companies to attract better workers clearly paid off. In 1931, there were members of staff at Knopf that had been with the company for over forty years, and it was not unusual to have served for longer than twenty, even among the unmarried women.[84] Schocken was so proud of this fact that it advertised that half its employees had begun their career within the company.[85] The kernel of social and economic life, according to Schocken's director Manasse, was the company people worked for: the manager or 'leader' of the company had to care for his employees or 'followers', while they in turn must remain loyal to him. This has been the vision of the company, so we are told, for the past thirty-three years, proof of which were the 500 employees that had been with the company for more than ten years and the 60 per cent that had been with Schocken since their apprenticeship.[86] This was a trend which could be discerned in Baum's statistics: as early as 1904, there were already twenty-seven people employed in department stores that had been there between five and twenty years. Staying with the company for so long did not mean a standstill; the hierarchical structure and the size of the business allowed for advancement within the company, both financially and socially, over the years. Salman Schocken realized that the department store's own system of employment was unusual, to such an extent that he doubted people who came from outside would be of much use to the company. This meant executives could only be recruited from within, and any person entering Schocken's employment was a potential candidate for a managerial position in the future.[87]

It is clear that department stores in Germany offered model working conditions to their employees, which especially benefitted women who would be treated with a lot less respect in their position elsewhere. Considering the good work environments, the perks of the job and the prospects of personal development female employees had at department stores, one would be forgiven for suspecting that the real issue all-male groups, such as the German Nationalist Association of Commercial Employees/Assistants, had with department stores was neither their 'Jewish' character nor their supposedly poor working conditions. Instead, one wonders if the superior terms of employment – in all but pay – for women raised jealousy among the men. The German Nationalist Association of Commercial Employees/Assistants, and those like them were not just being antisemitic and anticapitalistic, but also envious of women's limited liberation. It is important, however, to note why department stores offered such exceptional benefits. It was not out of some sense of altruism; it was good business. A happy workforce was attractive to the customer and encouraged good sales. That it offered an environment in which women could enjoy a certain degree of freedom and independence was simply an added bonus for the shop girls. Making a living independently, earning a little more than was needed and having prospects of travel and promotion were not things many women could experience at the time. Yet, as department stores were organized into a structure that was paternal yet strict, it gave these women both job security and respectability. Thus, the new and emancipatory work for a department store was neither threatening to those who worked for them nor for society as a whole. Given the respectability of their staff and customers, a wide range of products on display, some of which could even be luxurious, and the expansion and beautification of the stores, it is little wonder that the German Emperor himself would become not only interested but get personally involved in the success of department stores.

4

Apogee: 1900–14
'The Kaiser Is Impressed'

This chapter is key in understanding the relationship between Jews and German society after the First World War as it shows us the pinnacle of the development of department stores before the conflict. We see a positive progression, a veritable trend towards financial and societal success. Berlin, as the capital, was unusual in having several department stores in one place, but the rise of their importance is exemplary for the entire Empire. As one contemporary put it:

> There are four rulers in Berlin, uncrowned emperors, whose strict regimes are everywhere acknowledged… they are Wertheim, Tietz, Jandorf, and – for a year now – Kaufhaus des Westens. The transformation of Berlin into a major metropolis, a world-class city, is closely tied to the arrival of theses shopping palaces … When one shopping palace after another lines the thoroughfares of the Imperial capital today, when light-infused display windows not only tempt with the most amazing manufactured goods from around the civilized world, but also appeal to our aesthetic senses, when even today's little man is in a position to come into possession of luxury items at trinket prices – then it is the sole doing of the modern department store.[1]

By 1900, the inhabitants of every German city and town had not just become accustomed to the sight of a department store on their high street, but relied on it and similar retail outlets to furnish them with the essential and beautiful things they needed in life. As one historian observed, the German middle class believed that their little luxuries were a reward for success.[2] Simultaneously department stores were physical manifestations of a relative tolerance of Jews in German society.

This chapter will show that, as art historians have already demonstrated, department store buildings combined a vernacular architectural language with the advantages of modern construction techniques.[3] This combination – of cloaking the innovative in traditional shapes – proved to be very successful with customers, and in turn it was advantageous to German Jews to thrive in their

Figure 4.1 Emperor Wilhelm II, who supplied the Wertheim stores with pottery from his own factory, and Empress Augusta, who joined her husband on an official visit to his business partner's flagship store. © Author.

business and private lives. Jewish entrepreneurs 'who embraced German culture, aspired to a high degree of social integration ... cosmopolitan consumption was not only good business, it was good culture'.[4] In this period, Jews integrated with the core of the German middle class by way of economic security and a certain lifestyle.[5] While the zenith of the companies and their owners coincided, the first serious signs of animosity against department stores in this period are levelled at the business only. We will see the height of social mixing between Jews and gentiles, revealing, as other authors have noted, 'an extremely complex picture of inclusions and exclusions – sometimes at the very same point in time'.[6] This shows that there was ample room for optimism, on the Jewish side, for full inclusion at some point, even if there was no precise discernible moment for that.

Fundamental to the department store's raison d'etre was the idea of it being a part of an 'organic' change in the economy. Contemporaries believed that only an organic business – evolved from humble beginnings and grown through hard work – was a legitimate addition to the economy.[7] Department stores had naturally developed from small shops into large stores. German cities had grown considerably since the unification of Germany, and the people living here needed to be fed, clothed and their dwellings furnished. The small shop on the corner was incapable of doing this, and so they grew into ever larger and more sophisticated establishments. As an economist of the time recorded: 'The needs of the consumer have created the department store, i.e. the department store is not a capricious invention of their creators or an invention of their owners, but have according to the gradual demands of the consumer evolved from small beginnings'.[8] Yet, after servicing this basic need of the population, retailers extended their remit, providing products beyond those of necessity. So demand and creation of demand went hand in hand not to introduce 'artificial and alien institutions into the economy', but to establish 'institutions which grew out of the tendency to concentrate retailing and out of the need of modern living conditions'.[9] Even if there were instances of department stores breaking some kind of unwritten code, this was no more than 'occasional degeneracies and teething problems of an only recently developed type' of retailing, as a member of the Knopf family stated in his doctoral dissertation at the University of Heidelberg.[10] It was accepted that stores had grown 'organically' out of the hard work of those who had founded them and were an absolutely necessary element in providing goods to the growing population. The emergence of more demand – both by creation through clever sales techniques and the growth of the population – did not just serve one type of retailing: 'Department stores

Figure 4.2 The swansong of Vienna Secession founder Joseph Maria Olbrich was the designer of the Leonhard Tietz store in Düsseldorf, which was erected between 1907 and 1909. As the award-winning architect Olbrich died before the building was completed, a plaque in his memory was installed on the first-floor landing. Note the elaborate chandeliers set with cut and coloured glass reminiscent of the dome of the Secession Building in Vienna. © Author.

themselves have encouraged sale and increased consumption. They have also provided many impulses for an efficient management of goods and for an extension in the field of goods sold by mid-sized and small retailers.'[11] Germany needed these mediators in the economy – but stores went a step further from being a logistical tool in serving the nation. Through their architecture, their design and chosen locations, they put themselves at the heart of the German high street, elevating their mundane trade to a symbol of a sophisticated mercantilism literally rooted in the soil of the fatherland.

A sense of place

It was usual for the first department stores to start in rented rooms, often above an existing shop, and then expand. The Knopf store in Karlsruhe began business in a corner of a residential property; in Freiburg, the store opened above a butcher's shop. Georg Tietz, Hermann Wronker and Salman Schocken set out in a similar way. Yet all these businesses rapidly expanded, taking over adjacent shops and buildings, using upstairs rooms and creating larger shop windows. Within just a couple of years, most premises were far too small for the amount of trade that was going on in them. The results were ugly and replaced with new premises in the 1890s. Wronker's first purpose-built branch in Pforzheim, replacing a townhouse the firm had rented previously, was erected in that period. However, it was abandoned just ten years after its construction. It had originally been a 'new modern department store, which even at that time represented an attraction in the town of Pforzheim. One had believed that the building was far too large and beyond the proportions of Pforzheim'.[12] The city's population had however grown at great speed in the past years, bolstered by the jewellery and cutlery industry, and so had Wronker's clientele – the store had to be further expanded. The branch was relocated to the main road by 1915, allowing the rival Knopf store to dominate the market square. They had been neighbours for a while and a popular joke in Pforzheim went: 'Who is the greatest whore in town? Wronker – he's got Knopf on his back.'[13] It took a long time for the municipality and the state authorities to be clear as to what they wanted from the new Wronker building. The department store company indulged the authorities' every whim, allowing the plans to go through dozens of changes. In accordance with their wishes, Hermann Wronker generously sacrificed retailing space to allow for the road to be widened. The county medical officer praised the proposal saying it was of 'significant hygienic benefit'.[14] In the end, the design in Pforzheim strongly resembled the widely admired Leonhard Tietz store in Cologne, which was designed by Joseph Maria Olbrich. Thus, the Wronker company, through this ground-breaking piece of architecture, claimed itself to be the town's premier department store. The result was heralded as 'one of the most beautiful buildings of the town', by a local newspaper, when it opened in 1915.[15] Not only was the building splendid in appearance, it was also built to the newest standards: the displays could be set up in the basement and then hoisted into position in the windows above, and hence would never appear empty at any given point of time. The store brought 'light and air' into the town, not least due to Hermann Wronker's granting part of the property as public space. 'That this district only gains by such a redevelopment is self-evident', the press praised.[16]

Meanwhile, on the market square in Pforzheim, Knopf also expanded. The hotel in which the company had started out in Pforzheim with just ten employees had to make way for a purpose-built department store in 1911. The new premises – a 'pleasing, modern building' – were opened just in time for Christmas. The town's newspaper believed the new store of the Knopf company equalled the town hall's grandeur: it made an 'imposing impression, it is a magnificent functional building'.[17] Local craftsmen had done all the work.[18] Even before the official opening, a huge crowd assembled on the square in front of the store to admire the window displays.[19] The building was extended a second time in 1913, 'in red sandstone and kept in an elegant style', as the press noted.[20] A new food hall was installed, featuring an ornamental pool with live fish.[21] Despite this expansion, the business outgrew the premises, and a second addition was completed in 1931 in spite of the worldwide economic depression following the Wall Street crash. The firm's expansion was seen as a confidence boost to the local economy in times of extreme hardship. One local newspaper wrote: 'What the company has done with their current remodelling is another massive milestone in the history of the Pforzheim business world.'[22] On the day of opening, an immense crowd watched as a thousand balloons with gift vouchers were released into the sky. The local press believed the market square had changed its appearance significantly for the better in the past decades, not least because of the splendid new Knopf building. The paper went further, saying that the Knopf company

> had once again proven its generosity with this refurbishment. One can justly say that the company has done its part to revive the labour market and created a living for many. This is all the more remarkable as the renovation occurred in the hard times of bankruptcies and bank closures in which some wanted to give

up hope. Yet Max Knopf, that solid business man, did not let this daunt him; he trusted his lucky star and his German capability.[23]

This rivalry in architecture, size and grandeur between stores in the same town can be seen everywhere in Germany. From the late 1890s, when different companies started encroaching on each other's geographic territory, architecture was a means of outdoing your rival. It was by no means confined to the capital, where for instance Hermann Tietz and Wertheim sprawled across opposing sides of the same road. This phenomenon could be observed even in relatively modest cities such as Pforzheim.

The first Knopf store had been one-shop unit, located in the Palais Haber, a grand town house, in Karlsruhe. It rapidly outgrew the small space, taking over the entire building and frontage in gradual stages. In 1911, a large plot along the Kaiserstrasse was acquired and a group of architects asked to submit ideas for a new store. The decision was made to give the commission to prominent architect Wilhelm Kreis who was already engaged in building the Leonhard Tietz branch in Düsseldorf.[24] In order to avoid looking out of place in any of the three roads onto which the building backed, each façade was built in a slightly different design and to a slightly different height. Towards the Kaiserstrasse, the edifice had five stories; on the Zähringer Strasse, it consisted of only three. Echoing the façade of the original house, its main feature was a frieze with large oval windows topped by a massive gable. The site of the new building was, after all, the Palais Haber, built by a pupil of Friedrich Weinbrenner (a great deal of the city was dominated by the classical buildings and decorations by the court architect Weinbrenner). While adhering to the established German characteristics of department store architecture, both the interior and exterior of Knopf would remain true to this historic precursor and present itself in a twentieth-century version of the neoclassical style favoured by institutional architecture throughout Baden. The design of the Karlsruhe store ensured that it would be a significant feature of the main road and yet not look out of place in the city.

Knopf, while using a construction method pioneered by department stores in Berlin, chose to have the reinforced concrete structure built by a local company. The store's vertical window bands were part of what had become the model for German department stores. Alfred Messel pioneered in this sort of façade structure with Wertheim in Berlin from 1896 to 1906. It has been claimed that the great era of Berlin stores began with this building, and it was copied several times for other Wertheim stores.[25] The construction of the Wertheim flagship store however drew some criticism, even from as far as the Reichstag, where one Member of

Figure 4.3 The crowning glory of the Knopf siblings' retailing empire: the flagship store designed by Wilhelm Kreis. Though larger, it closely resembled the building it replaced; the nineteenth-century town house constructed for the Jewish court bankers Haber. The combination of a leading architect and traditional design was an extremely successful marketing ploy. © Author.

Parliament complained that the 'Leipziger Platz is to be defiled with a department store'. The sort which 'ruins the *Mittelstand* in town and country!'[26] Yet, the sense of height, the narrow windows, the heavy pillars, in conjunction with large entrances topped by slender sculpted figures, gave it a sacral feel, just like the Knopf flagship store, which silenced all but the most vitriolic critics. For Knopf, the local sculptor Hermann Binz was commissioned to provide figures and vases for the façade, which remotely resembled the statues in the public royal park in Karlsruhe.[27] These, and the references to Weinbrenner in the architecture, intended to appeal to the civil servants of Baden, whose own offices and departments had been designed according to the ubiquitous architectural style of the duchy. According to Max Knopf's wishes, a building was constructed that was not just part of the national context of retailing architecture, but also unique to Karlsruhe: 'a building which fits perfectly into the cityscape despite its individual design', as his deputy put it. [28] Max's sense of style paid off. The largest newspaper in Baden commented when the store opened in April 1914: 'With real joy and inner satisfaction you look up to the department store presenting itself in monumental simplicity and consistent style', while the interiors 'bear the stamp of high artistic culture'.[29] The mayor and several members of the council were present for the opening alongside deputies from the chamber of commerce, who were greeted personally by Max and thanked for their 'neutral standpoint' regarding department stores.[30]

Centrally located on the main axis of the capital of Baden, this 'construction of the greatest style and first order', as the paper put it, was easily accessible and identifiable.[31] Armed with an exchange list advertisement, one could set out from the suburbs or the countryside to the store that was illustrated on it. From the station in Karlsruhe, a tram went right to the front doors of Knopf and – their main rival across the road – Tietz. The town hall, courts, parliament and royal palace were minutes away. The doors to Knopf were manned by black-uniformed, silver-buttoned commissionaires who held open the double doors. On entering the store, the eyes would first have to become accustomed to the dimness inside. Walking a few steps across the marbled floor that covered 3,000 square metres of ground, one suddenly burst into the light of the grand central hall. The eye, travelling upwards, would pass the marquetry balustrades of the first floor and the iron ones of the second and third, to reach the barrelled glass ceiling from which four enormous chandeliers were suspended. No walls divided the floors, and slender pillars allowed for a light and spacious arrangement of the interiors that could easily be navigated; this dramatic centrepiece gave the entire building its grand and formal character.[32] Little would change structurally between 1914 and the end of the Second World War.

Having reached the department store, the customer's second journey began. Architectural plans always paid attention to the layout and circulation of the spaces, and most stores followed similar patterns. At Knopf, accessories for men and women, linens, stationery, books and leather goods occupied the ground floor. Here there was also a desk at which foreign visitors could pay for their wares in whatever currency they wished. If customers do not find the items they wanted on this floor, they could walk through the hall and take the green marble stairs or the lift to the first floor, where this department extended. Ladies' clothing, shoes and hosiery were also displayed. The top floor was dedicated to porcelain, glassware and delicatessen. Even if one took the lift, he or she could visualize the array of products on offer passed by in the mind's eye of the customer. A once-young shopper recalls:

> The ride in this monster, as this vehicle appeared to me, was always exciting. Inside the lift a man with a hat, usually a disabled veteran of the First World War with only one arm, would call out with a loud voice: 'Up' or 'down' depending on where you got in. At each floor the lift operator announced what could be purchased there. For example 'Women's and men's clothing, hats', 'leather goods, beds and linens', etc. My heart beat faster when we reached 'toys and refreshments'.[33]

Either on foot or by way of the lift, customers had pass through most departments before getting to the food hall and the bargain tea sets on the top floor; this meant that there was a chance the shopper would stop and look at other items. The psychology was simple: people would travel far to save a *Pfennig* or two on food 'while experience has shown that the price is less carefully checked when purchasing any fashion item'.[34] There were several benefits to having so many departments under one roof. For the customer it meant a high density of services and goods in a single convenient setting. The advantage for the entrepreneur was that customers stayed there for longer and saw more products, hopefully buying items on the spur of the moment. 'The longer the department store entrepreneur holds a person in his store, the greater are the chances that he will consume. So he does not arrange the internal stairs in the atrium uninterruptedly, but places the continuation of each on the floor's opposite side',[35] thus ensuring that the customer traverses through every department before reaching the desired top floor. Sales assistants were taught to make positive use of the store's multifaceted offers. Manasse at Schocken advised: 'Anyone who needs clothes fabric needs ingredients [meaning other haberdashery items]; anyone who buys a gramophone needs records and pins. It's a lack of talent if no suggestion in this direction is made.'[36]

Hermann Tietz, Knopf's main rival in Karlsruhe, opened a new store practically opposite the stores premises in March 1901. Hermann Tietz had built on the site of the Hotel Zum Erbprinzen, on the Kaiserstrasse.[37] The hotel was replaced with a five-and-a-half-storied building. Like all houses which backed onto the two major roads in Karlsruhe, the corner was rounded off, but instead of copying the accepted formula of a quarter of a rotunda to fill the curved space (which was the main architectural feature of the Baden Parliament), a six and a half-storied tower was erected, topped by an onion dome and lantern. Usually such architectural design aspects were reserved for use by Catholic churches across Southern Germany and were certainly no feature of any institutional building in Protestant Karlsruhe at the time. Indeed the entire building featured architectural elements which were hitherto more the preserve of the new villas springing up in the suburbs, rather than the established neoclassical style of the city centre. On the ground and first floors, large shop windows were installed. Such windows were fashionable at the time, but soon abandoned; not for any particular aesthetic reasons, but simply because they let in the cold in winter and too much heat and light in the summer, bleaching the expensive items displayed in the windows. The top floors had narrow gothic windows in sets of three, similar to that of a medieval building. The use of buttresses to separate window sets also made it look rather fortified. The sculptural elements in the art nouveau style were restricted to a few areas underlining the overall structure of the building. The main decorative feature was a representation of an armed woman on the tower. As a nod to design of the former hotel, the main entrance to the department store bore the legend '*Erbprinz*' above it. However, in less than ten years this building became inadequate for Tietz's purpose. This first attempt at a purpose-built store was replaced, almost simultaneously with that of the Knopf, by a building far more attuned to Karlsruhe's classical architecture. In Berlin, too, Hermann Tietz had initially struggled to fit its store into the urban context, and it was imperative that this be remedied. Hence, Wertheim commissioned Alfred Messel to build a new store opposite the Hermann Tietz branch on the Leipziger Strasse.

A sense of occasion

'If today one hears in a family: We are going to Wertheim, that does not primarily mean, that one needs something especially urgent for the household, but instead, one speaks of a trip, one which one would make to a beautiful spot on the outskirts', the foreign secretary and future Nobel Laureate Gustav Stresemann ponderously noted.³⁸ Exhibitions, attractions and beautiful interiors were important features created to entice the customers into the store and getting them to linger. Jandorf provided, like many others, a photography studio offering portraits at a fraction of the cost of his rivals, thereby getting people into his store, ostensibly for reasons other than shopping. In Cologne, one of Leonhard Tietz's stores was a passage house (*Passagenhaus*), which means it incorporated covered walk-ways connecting one road with another, which allowed the shopper to browse countless shop windows while not getting wet and crossing from one side of town to the other.³⁹ Leonhard Tietz was so popular among the general population of the Rhineland that they referred to him in the local dialect at 'Tietz Leienard'.⁴⁰ Wronker in Frankfurt boasted its own art gallery where the high-quality furniture of the Deutsche Werkstätten were exhibited.⁴¹ If one was feeling a little tired, a 'reading room and ladies' salon invite you to linger at Knopf in Karlsruhe. The buffet offered refreshments after the rigours of shopping and a promenade concert sometimes provided for diversion, all on the second floor of the same store.⁴² All department stores were well aware of the potential stress of shopping, so the refreshment rooms had their name for good reason: 'From all the looking I was quite enchanted and got red cheeks and hungry too. The finishing touch was the visit to the refreshment room, where I got my beloved apricot cake with whipped cream.'⁴³ The restaurants themselves were attractions and would sometimes feature as the sole subject of the store's advertising campaigns, like in 1912: 'Schmoller's refreshment room is a place of rest for the ladies of Mannheim. Magnificent views of the parade grounds resplendent with the most beautiful flower arrangements.'⁴⁴ Cafeterias, ice cream parlours, hairdressers and photography studios may seem like peripheral activities to department stores but together with the ornamental fish tanks, stained glass and choice interiors, they gave the stores and the mundane purposes they served a sense of ceremonial occasion.

Across the English Channel, the American who revolutionized the dowdy shopping experience in London, Harry Gordon Selfridge, professed these new public spaces to be emancipatory for women. Women indulging in shopping in the London West End at the turn of the century could pursue 'personal exploration, self-fulfilment, and independence' in a safe environment, while being 'indulged, excited, and repaired'.⁴⁵ Outside of department store-fiction and small shopkeeper's complaints, one rarely comes across instances of department stores being described as honey traps. On the contrary, as the press stated in 1914, Knopf of Karlsruhe presented 'a clear overview which is simply a model, for all modern department stores'.⁴⁶ Did people shoplift

(a)

(b)

Figure 4.4 The enormous and elegantly appointed flagship store of the Wertheim on the Leipziger Strasse featured many open-air courtyards and several themed cafes and restaurants. The tiles for the fountain (a) were provided by the Emperor's pottery factory in Cadinen. Apart from a patisserie and a café dedicated only to items made with fruit, the store had a large refreshment room (b) serving hundreds of meals a day. © Author.

nonetheless? Of course, they did. Yet, there are very few recorded instances of this outside of fiction and only a handful of psychiatrist reports. The obsession historians have with the 'hysterical' women who stole from department stores was not one that those running them shared.[47] It may be that department stores kept quiet about kleptomaniacs to prevent any criticism, but internal documentation of the stores never mentions it, nor do sales manuals provide advice on how to handle a customer suspected of shoplifting. The *Zeitschrift für Waren- und Kaufhäuser*, the official publication of the umbrella organization of department stores, was a forum for these problems to be discussed among those running such stores; however, they were more concerned with pickpockets than kleptomaniacs.[48]

The Emperor pays a visit

Georg Wertheim received an endorsement to end them all: the imperial family came to visit his store in 1910.[49] Three limousines pulled up outside the flagship store on the Leipziger Strasse on 23 January: Emperor Wilhelm II and his wife Empress Auguste Viktoria had come to inspect an art exhibition in the carpet department – just the type of location and display intended to attract customers. 'At first the Emperor looked at the grand light courtyard, with the first two bridges and was clearly impressed by the building', Georg noted with some pride in his diary. He then showed them, doubtless followed by a suitably large courtly entourage decanted from the royal cars, the rest of the store, including the palm house and the huge main hall lined with onyx.[50] They must also have passed the fountain constructed from tiles supplied by the Emperor's own factory.

A representative of the self-styled League of Protection of German Quality Work was upset enough about the imperial visit at Wertheim to complain about it. The fact that Georg Wertheim had been christened and married a Christian, did not, in the reporter's eye, make him anything less than a Jew.[51] The visit was even mentioned in the Reichstag, when the antisemitic nationalist Ferdinand Werner raised an objection, in a long-winded and garbled speech, to Wertheim being permitted to sell the Emperor's faience. In this context, Werner noted how deeply resented the number of Jewish people who had been ennobled, as 'the German nobility has given us some of our greatest men, a Prince of Bismarck and a Baron of Zeppelin'.[52] His implication was that the Emperor himself was compliant in the undermining of the German society, for which Werner was reprimanded by the president of the Reichstag.

Antisemitic though these views are, coupled with a reference to the aristocracy, these lead one to the issue of class. Germany had a firm class system in which it was near impossible to move between the different social strata. To call it 'rigid' would be an underestimation – being disrespectful to 'superiors' was a punishable offence. Offers of ennoblement were not necessarily turned down for the sake of modesty, but for the possibility of being considered a traitor to one's own class and being looked down upon by 'real' aristocrats. Middle-class people, be they Jewish or of any other faith, were uncomfortable in the company of social inferiors and superiors, and it was the same for other classes.[53] This is why the stores that had a higher class clientele clung to the hierarchy of service patterns according to status. That the son of a door-to-door salesman was hobnobbing with the Emperor was seen as ridiculous, and his Jewishness made it just worse.[54] Georg Wertheim, as all department store-owing Jews, could not even look back onto a distinguished family tree like the Rothschilds, making them quite firmly members of the new German entrepreneurial class.

The Emperor was, by all accounts, unimpressed by those criticizing his visit to the department store; Wertheim was a good business partner and a very generous donor to charities endorsed by the royal household. The visit was a courtesy call. The relationship between the Emperor and the entrepreneur had begun when Alfred Messel, Wertheim's architect, had arranged for the department store to sell the pottery produced by Wilhelm II's own business in Eastern Prussia. The deal was sealed, in October 1909, after an inspection of the products at the manor house-cum-factory at Cadinen, with only the Emperor, Georg Wertheim and Privy Councillor Etzdorf forming an intimate group involved in the discussions. Ursula and Georg Wertheim had been invited to dine at the manor house afterwards as a couple, but as the Empress was indisposed at the last minute, the convention dictated that Mrs Wertheim could not come to dinner.

That both the Wertheims had been invited to dinner was unusual and probably down not only to Ursula's Protestant religion, but also due to her class. She had impeccable Junker heritage. As a rule, the wives of the Emperor's favoured Jews, referred disparagingly as Emperor's Jews (*Kaiserjuden*), were not included. Wilhelm II's relationship with the Germans of Jewish origin and Jews in general was, like so much in his life, erratic. While the antisemitic court chaplain Stöcker still carried favour with him at the time, he also paid personal calls on and made return invitations to Jewish acquaintances – especially if they were wealthy. German Jews had an equally difficult relationship with him; those that cosied up to the Emperor were seen as traitors. Of note is the fact that, at the time, the father of modern Zionism, Theodore Herzl, hoped to establish a Jewish state in Palestine under the protectorate of the German monarch.[55]

Wertheim noted every detail of the evening at Cadinen with the Kaiser in his diary, from the guests – there were fourteen – to the conversation, verbatim, that he had with the Emperor during dinner – the Emperor preferred apple wine, for reasons of economy one assumes, to champagne – and later, in private and at length, on the terrace afterwards.[56] Hence, the visit at the Wertheim store, much as the imperial couple were impressed by the architecture and interior of the building, was a return courtesy visit of business partners: an survey of the premises, just as Georg Wertheim had inspected the Emperors in East Prussia a few months before. With Wertheim, at least, Wilhelm II showed unusual consistency: during his later encounters, he not only made a point of waving at Georg Wertheim specifically in public, but also sent him personal messages, and eventually decorated him with the Order of the Red Eagle – albeit only Third Class. Oscar Tietz had received the same accolade.[57]

Ursula Wertheim, who had to forgo the privilege of dining with the Empress as the latter was not present, came from a Protestant, almost-Junker, family. Her father, Emil Gilka, owned a small noble estate in Brandenburg and was

Figure 4.5 Georg gifted Schloss Sassleben in rural Brandenburg to his wife Ursula Wertheim. They renovated the house and improved the estate. © Bilderarchiv Heimatverein Calau E.V.

a successful businessman in his own right. Considerably younger than her husband, Ursula married Georg in May 1906 in a Lutheran ceremony in the village in which her family owned the manor house. Intermarriage, between those who were cultural or previously practicing Jews and nominal Christians became increasingly common during this period. Intermarriage increased from over 8 per cent in 1901 to almost 30 per cent in 1915.[58] Baptisms were also on the rise, and shortly before his wedding, Georg had followed his brothers Wilhelm and Franz to the font to be baptized a Christian. Only Wolf and Gertrude Wertheim remained Jewish.

Ursula and Georg's first son, Albrecht, was born in 1910. Georg, overwhelmed with joy, gave his wife the 1,500-acre estate of Sassleben, near Cottbus, complete with a grand stately home, woods and lakes.[59] The Schloss and its environs were ideally situated: close to Ursula's ancestral home and a reasonable distance to Berlin by car. The Wertheims began improving their property through renovation, restoration and addition in the form of a jetty in the lake, complete with an ornamental Sphinx. The orchards are said to have yielded enormous quantities of perfect apples which Georg – ever the entrepreneur – sold in his stores. It would prove fortuitous that this considerable estate was in Ursula's bona fide Protestant, Prussian semi-aristocratic hands.

Becoming middle class

The Wertheims were not the only entrepreneurial family enjoying prestige and gentile comforts. Upon moving his head office to Zwickau, Salman Schocken and his wife Lilly had settled in a modern upper-middle class area there.[60] Apparently, Salman was overly fond of 'blonde gentiles', something his domesticated and rotund wife Lilly pretended not to notice. The couple had very little but the children in common, so we are told, apart from the 'fashionable hypochondria' of the time, brought to full fruition on expensive spa holidays.[61] Like his fellow department store patriarchs, Salman seemed incapable of separating work from pleasure. Business seems to have been made during rest cures, and his assistant George Manasse's letters are full of meetings at spa resorts and their hotels. The first conversation between Manasse and Hermann Wronker concerning a possible cooperation between the companies was held on a train journey from the spa town Bad Nauheim.[62]

The deep involvement Salman had with every aspect of the firm is astonishing, but his private life was equally varied and busy. Hannah Arendt, who had been friends with Salman for a great part of his life, called him the Jewish Bismarck.[63] He concerned himself with international retailing, owning shares in British Homestores, Woolworths and Marks & Spencer.[64] Simon, Salman's brother, had introduced him to the Zionist movement, and Salman would dedicate many hours to the organization. His reading would consist of just about anything sufficiently highbrow; from literature and poetry to economics, politics and philosophy; Goethe was a personal favourite. The Schocken art collection included paintings by Rembrandt, Dürer, van Gogh, Renoir, Chagall, Paul Klee, Paul Gauguin and Käthe Kollwitz.[65] He also collected ancient Jewish scripture. Simon's tastes were less sophisticated. He bought an estate near Berlin and a sports car when he entered semi-retirement in 1928.[66] Just a year later, Simon had a fatal accident in this vehicle. Thus Salman lost his beloved, if less Machiavellian, brother and the company its good-natured managerial core.

The Knopf family's success manifested itself in less aristocratic ways than that of the Schockens. Max, from Karlsruhe, and Sally Knopf, from Freiburg, expanded the business, gradually adding more branches and consolidating their flagship stores into large and beautiful premises. They, their siblings and their children moved into comfortable homes on leafy avenues with respectable neighbours. The Knopfs and their children moved up to being part of the comfortable middle classes within just twenty years of starting out. Not just physically, but spiritually too. They became members of various bourgeois institutions like the freemasons' Carl-Friedrich-Lodge (which had started as an exclusively Jewish lodge[67]) and the ramblers club the Black Forest Society (Schwarzwaldverein). They supported Jewish, Christian and non-denominational charities, even receiving high honours from the hands of the Grand Duke of Baden for supporting the war effort during the First World War.[68] Both Max and Sally were prominent members of their local Jewish communities. From 1919 to 1934, Max was a member of the Jewish council of Baden, and Sally was the founder of the synagogue in Freiburg.[69] They became members of the local *Mittelstand* organizations, such as the chamber of commerce and the retail traders' association, in their respective new home towns. The second generation of Knopfs was brought up to take over from their parents. They had privileged childhoods as offspring of successful German families, attended grammar schools (*Gymnasium*) and enjoyed bourgeois pastimes, such as playing musical instruments and recreational sports. Margarete, Max's daughter, received an expensive education at a Swiss finishing school. She made the acquaintance of a barrister from the state high court in Karlsruhe (*Oberlandesgericht*) on a visit to Helgoland. Dr Arthur

Aron Levis had spent the afternoon smoking heavily and feeling rather ill as a consequence, while Margarete became seasick from a boating trip; to cheer them both Arthur baked a cake. Though she was singularly unimpressed by the gesture, things changed once they returned to Karlsruhe. At a time when increasing conversions to Christianity or intermarriages were diluting the Jewish community, in this case the well-situated couple cemented it: their wedding was celebrated at the Hotel Germania with an extremely opulent menu and an orchestra entertained the guests with tunes from musical theatre, including – rather aptly – a waltz from *The Dollar Princess*![70] Arthur Levis, by marrying into the wealthy family, was expected to join the company, which he duly did. The inventory of the Levis-Knopf household in the late 1930s, written after they had needed to leave most of their possessions behind while fleeing to Lisbon, included an extensive collection of pictures, mostly oils of rural scenes alongside a copy of *Portrait of a Rabbi* by Rembrandt, a set of crystal tableware, a silver service, gold and jewellery (worth in excess of 23,000 *Marks*) and all the trappings of a bourgeois lifestyle.[71] Their rented apartments were, however, not ostentatious; they had just two bedrooms.[72] Arthur Knopf, Sally's son, would marry twice, the second time to a widowed Protestant, Maria, who brought a daughter to the marriage. Arthur's villa, in the traditional style of south Baden, was to be found in the posh area of Freiburg and close to the house of the eminent Catholic publishing family Herder. The family was serviced by a small staff, which included a chauffeur who would not only bring Arthur to work each day, but also drive the family for coffee and gateaux into the Black Forest on Sundays.

Like their cousins the Knopfs, the Wronkers settled down to lead a suitably affluent and bourgeois – yet never ostentatious – lifestyle: a large house in a vaguely Tyrolean chalet style was purchased in a smart Frankfurt suburb. Here, at the Villa Romberg, high above Königstein, the Wronkers would entertain. Pencil sketches of dinner parties in their guest book and handwritten programmes of amateur plays performed for their friends' amusement bear witness of a gregarious company.[73] Yet, the Wronkers used their new-found wealth for more than amusement. Well known for his good community work, Hermann Wronker's 'name is always mentioned there where it is necessary to practice charity', as the press extolled.[74] 'The personal nature of Hermann Wronker is characterized by a winning amiability in dealing with everyone and an *especially charitable streak*. Just as he collaborates in numerous philanthropic associations, he also has a truly open hand for those in need who come to him privately, a Frankfurt newspaper noted.[75]

The Tietz family, which was related to the Wronkers, had also been able to establish themselves. After successfully opening their store in Munich, the next step for Oscar Tietz was opening a branch in the capital city of Berlin. For a long time, Berlin had just three stores selling manufactured products – N. Israel, Rudolph Hertzog and Gebr. Gersons – none of which would develop quite as well as those that had originated elsewhere in Germany. However, Adolf Jandorf's department stores were growing in popularity, and Abraham Wertheim's first purpose-built store went up in 1893 with more buildings to follow soon, including the almost iconic flagship store on the Leipziger Strasse. Oscar Tietz saw the possibility of a third large store in the capital.

His son, Georg, resented the move. He missed Munich with its more liberal attitudes where, as a schoolboy, he encountered teachers who remembered the 1848 revolutions and where the Catholic boys had joined them in the Synagogue and, in turn, invited to play 'tag' during mass on Sundays. A few decades later no one could have called Munich a particularly 'liberal' place. Berlin, on the other contrary, during the same period was still dominated by the old Prussian order and was one of the larger urban areas that would end up having more than one department store chain representation. Mannheim, Leipzig and Hamburg are similar instances, but in all these locations, each chain had a clientele they tried to serve primarily so as to have a secure customer base. In Berlin, Wertheim, which had erected a purpose-built store in 1897 on the Leipziger Strasse, served the 'good society'; Tietz the 'comfortable *Mittelstand*'; and Jandorf that of the 'better Berlin labourer'.[76] Hermann Tietz opened their own store directly opposite that of Wertheim and, like their rivals, rapidly took over the entire block. The Tietz store's architecture, at first, jarred with that of the elegant Wertheim across the road. When Oscar Tietz decided to have his store rebuilt, he was keen to pull down an old people's home to form a coherent plot. The relocation of the institution proved difficult as it needed the Emperor's permission to do so, and his assent was not forthcoming. Eventually it was suggested that Oscar Tietz should donate the fixtures and fitting for a new lung clinic the Emperor was keen to establish – one that could double as a hospital for wounded soldiers 'if necessary'. Oscar followed the 'suggestion', also donating the money for a children's wing. Royal permission for the purchase of the old people's home was granted, and Oscar was even offered a title from the German Emperor, which he declined.[77]

Adolf Jandorf was less reticent in accepting honours than Oscar Tietz, who had turned down the offer of a title not only from the Emperor, but also from the Bavarian King previously. Upon his untimely death in 1926, Jandorf had been

Figure 4.6 A rather bleary-eyed Hermes, god of commerce, on a promotional stamp for A. Jandorf & Co., a chain aimed at the working classes of Berlin. © Author.

Figure 4.7 The Kaufhaus des Westens, or KaDeWe, Adolf Jandorf's second venture was to attract a very different clientele in the west of Berlin and thus, prudently, given a name to differentiate itself from the rest of the company. The store was to host the upper echelons of German society and even foreign royalty. © Author.

decorated not only by the monarchs of Württemberg and Bavaria, the latter for helping to establish the zoo at Munich, but also of Japan, Montenegro, Persia, Bulgaria, Serbia, Spain, Siam and many others.[78] The man whose shops served mainly the working class had opened a store in the west of Berlin in 1907 – the 'wild west' as contemporaries called it as the affluent area did not seem suitable for commercial development. Jandorf proved them wrong by establishing the Kaufhaus des Westens, or KaDeWe, which was designed to be the premium department store of the capital. Around the Kurfürstendamm, a very different clientele existed to the one Jandorf usually served, and so he wisely decided to give this new store a different name. The building's elegance, the exquisite products and the smartness of its customers attracted royalty from across the world. The King of Siam allegedly spent two days shopping at the KaDeWe, spending 250,000 *Goldmark*.[79]

Continued troubles

We can see that a lot of the negative things that have traditionally been said about department stores were not true. Often claims made against them, such as luring and trapping women, were so ludicrously false that the comical rumour acted as a positive advertisement.[80] For a start, although women were the primary customer, as we have seen, men and children were equally considered as part of the clientele, and sales staff were trained accordingly. Also the idea that goods on offer were substandard, luring the gullible working class, was not one shared by the Social Democratic Party (SPD).

Increasingly, from the first elections to the Reichstag to the outbreak of the First World War, the SPD became the most significant political party. They were vested with very little power in a system in which the Emperor appointed aristocrats to govern. Catalysed by the attempted assassination of the new Emperor in 1878, the Bismarck government had introduced a series of acts known as the 'Socialist Laws' to curb the growth of left-wing parties. The new Empire introduced general healthcare, accident insurance and pensions for all – measures many department stores had introduced for their staff long before. The laws were, however, ultimately unsuccessful in curbing the growth of the SPD.

Not just socialists but also Jews were seen as threats to the established order. In Berlin, the three-class electoral system of Prussia meant that Oscar Tietz had one-third of the voting power in the entire district.[81] So, on the one hand, Oscar was – on his own admission – a far too influential Jew, but on the other his son Georg Tietz recalls having to leave his regiment when he refused to be christened. Max Wronker, Hermann Wronker's son, would join the army with fewer issues in Hesse and was even awarded the Iron Cross for merit. The intense nationalism the Tietz encountered in Berlin felt very different to the atmosphere they were used to in Munich; yet there was no proof of antisemitic attacks on them or family's store before the First World War in either the Prussian or the Bavarian capital.[82]

Most serious challenges to department stores were not the overtly antisemitic sentiments, which continued to be voiced by organizations in the *Mittelstand*. It is hardly surprising, given how ineffectual the original department store tax was, that within a few years calls were made to increase the levy. In the parliament of the Grand Duchy of Baden, the idea was first brought up by Otto Schmidt, a member of the Agrarian League (Bund der Landwirte) during the 1911–12 session. He repeated the arguments parliamentarians had heard in various forms across Germany previously: suppliers and manufacturers were crippled by dumping prices, employees had to work more hours for less pay, qualified merchants were unable to open their own shops, taxpayers had to suffer and all because department stores were not just taxed poorly, but because they, apparently, enjoyed a tax advantage. No evidence was provided to support these claims, which sound a lot like the sort of things that featured in racy tales of department stores corrupting women. If the bad business dealings of department stores continued, the 'rule of the proletariat', so Schmidt claimed, was but a revolution away. Preventing such a radical societal and political change could be achieved by raising the tax for turnovers above a million *Marks* to 0.6 per cent.[83] Schmidt was in favour of taxing department stores with less than 200,000 *Marks* turnover in small towns and suggested introducing a surtax payable by all individuals who ran businesses outside their home town.[84] That the Agrarian League's arguments were not unlike those of the Nationalist Association of Commercial Assistants is probably due to the fact that they had links to each other.[85]

The managers of the Grand Duchy of Baden's department stores petitioned the state parliament in April 1910 in response to the Craftsmen. Craftsmen, they said, had no reason to complain as department stores gave lucrative building and manufacturing commissions. As department stores did not exist in most small towns, the majority of retailers were not affected by them either. In cities, there was little support from retailers as many had large businesses that operated similarly to department stores. Department stores ensured people shopped locally instead of in Paris, which benefited smaller retailers by keeping trade on the high streets of Baden.[86] Retailing was indeed burgeoning: in 1895, there had been 24,241 retailers in Baden; this had increased to 30,606 by 1907. Of the entire retailing turnover, approximately 400 million *Marks*, just 1.6 per cent was made by department stores. The people purporting to represent the *Mittelstand* were not taking this into consideration. Neither were they worried about department store employees: 'This new *Mittelstand* of service employees is extraordinarily supported by the stores.' The managers concluded that those claiming to represent the *Mittelstand* were engaging in nothing more than pointless sociopolitical 'fanatical agitation'. Members of nationalist commercial associations, the farmers union and the like were not representative.[87] This statement was supported by a further petition from the department store employees, emphasizing the great social responsibility their employers had, and adding 'do we not also belong to the *Mittelstand*? Are we not in need of protection before anyone else?'[88] The flexible term *Mittelstand* was becoming even more pliant.

In the lower chamber, the SPD and the Progressive Party (Fortschrittliche Partei) elected not to pursue the matter further.[89] The SPD, which had an agreement with the Progressive Party for mutual support, was fearful that department stores would pass on the levy to the consumer, making everyday goods too expensive for labourers to purchase.[90] The parliament made the decision to hand the matter to government and the upper house for resolution as it was sceptical about raising taxes further. One Member of Parliament had been on a fact-finding mission to Berlin: in the Prussian capital, he had endeavoured to establish 'how certain goods are presented to the public, for instance, in the Wertheim department store ... and I have found that ... sometimes the price difference was very small, occasionally even that the price in certain shops is lower than that in a department store'. He could see no evidence for stores using dumping prices against their competitors. The reason people preferred shopping there, he believed, was because all wares could be found under one roof. He also investigated the allegations of poor treatment of employees in comparison to those of smaller stores and reported that 'I have rather found on the contrary that the staff are treated comparatively well in department stores.'[91] Smaller companies could easily improve their lot if they were 'even just a little organized' – implying they were not.[92]

In spite of this, the parliamentarian suggested an increase of the levy, not because the tax commission believed what was claimed of department stores, but because they were aware of the urgency of the loaded rhetoric of those railing against it. He advised an amendment to the taxation rate simply because he believed department stores were able to shoulder it and that it might appease some *Mittelstand* organizations. It would take another two years before the legislation passed through the lower chamber. More authorities were consulted. Although the Chambers of Crafts (*Handwerkskammer*) of the state supported the proposition, the Chambers of Commerce (*Handelskammer*) were not presenting a unified front. Although Freiburg, Lahr, Pforzheim and Villingen were favourable to this idea, partially with reference to similar laws in other German states, the remaining five chambers (Mannheim, Heidelberg, Karlsruhe, Schopfheim and Konstanz) did not consider the increasing of taxes as a good idea. This was because they felt it might lead department stores to expand further or put price pressure onto the manufacturers, while, at the same time, providing little protection to the smaller companies in their cities.[93]

The text of the legislation that was passed in 1912 is set out in complicated language, suggesting that Baden had pulled alongside Prussia and Bavaria. The taxation rates of all three states are noted, but are not set out in the same manner, making it hard to compare. Converting all taxation rates into percentages is revealing. Whereas small department store-like companies with a turnover of under 1 million *Marks* were taxed at 1 per cent, the rate dropped drastically from then downwards. From a 1 to 2 million turnover, only 0.55 per cent tax needed to be paid, up to 3 million only 0.4 per cent and from an income above 8 million

Marks, the tax was less than the original. Baden's tax was considerably lower than those of other states. In comparison, the Bavarian tax rate rose steadily, while the Prussian percentage remained roughly the same no matter how high the turnover. The rationale for the tax stated that government authority was not going to decide if the success of department stores was due to 'the business acumen of their directors' or caused by 'reprehensible business and sales practices'.[94] Thus the imposition of tax remained no more than a fairly empty gesture towards pacifying the more hysterical members of the *Mittelstand*. After the First World War, so the state parliament claimed, only the Reichstag had the power to raise a similar levy. With this erroneous statement, the state parliament dropped the special tax. No further petitions from those purporting to represent shopkeepers and employees exist until 1932.

The German states also introduced fire regulations specific to department stores. These went beyond any rules set up for other public buildings and may be interpreted as discriminatory.[95] In the light of several department store fires before 1914 and the terrible damage they could do to business, these, however, could be seen as having a long-term positive effect. This was actually sensible and understandable – not discriminatory!

After 1900, it was obvious which retailers had managed to take the step from being a successful entrepreneur to an establishment businessman. The stores and their owners had become part of Germany's economy and society as much as the class system would allow. Beautiful and grand buildings which were also practical finally replaced amalgamated and poorly designed premises in major cities. They set in stone that department stores and similar forms of retailing were essential to the nation. The wares they offered were of good quality and tailored to meet customer needs. Their role in the economy was recognized – sometimes begrudgingly and at other times with grand official gestures. Serious attempts at infringing their operations or smearing their owners were not a feature in Germany before the outbreak of the First World War. By 1900, the German consumer of every class, from the highest to the lowest, was 'sold'. The relative luxuries for sale in a department store could be seen as unproductive and creating idleness. But also classed, as one historian put it, as 'good' luxury – for instance, decorative wares a diligent wife would need to beautify her home for the benefit of her family.[96] We can almost see a crossover between the opulence of imperial pomp and department stores when the Emperor visited Wertheim.

Around the time the Emperor inspected Wertheim, religion-based antisemitism had begun to ebb away; it was symbolic that Adolf Stöcker had been sacked as court chaplain – drawing a direct line from the Jews of the Bible to contemporary businessmen was positively medieval and recognized as such. However, in its place, the idea that Jewish people as a race were undermining certain parts of German society was gradually on the rise. However, the people who were part of this thought process believing it to be important in politics and society, were not a coherent group. Jews remained excluded from important institutions, such as the officer corps of the German army, but antisemites were not organized and had little, if anything, in common other than their hatred of Jews. Thus their impact was not large.

Prejudice, such as the Emperor's, was inconsistent and one cannot blame Germans of Jewish origin for believing that it would eventually be overcome.[97] A lack of cultural hegemony in the Reich meant antisemitism could exist only at the periphery. German law-making was considerably 'anti-Catholic, anti-socialist, anti-feminine and anti-Polish', but there was 'not a single law that is specifically anti-Jewish', as one historian observed correctly.[98] Jewish success and acclamation in academia, the economy, culture and society seemed to affirm that hope. Being a good German was being a better Jew – so much so, that the concept was worth exporting into a Palestine under a German protectorate. Jews fleeing the pogroms in Russia were deeply disliked by German Jews, and they needed to be introduced to the more refined ways of a reformed, mercantile, academic and altogether more middle-class life.[99] So, although Jews were still excluded politically and socially in some circles, and the character of antisemitism had morphed in some quarters, on the whole, there was every reason for the German Jewish entrepreneurial families to look to the future with confidence. Mostly they were comfortable in their positions and were recognized as good German citizens. Jewish life in Germany and the department stores were parallelly at their zenith. With the outbreak of war in August 1914, it was entirely natural for the Jewish businessmen to fling themselves, their families and their companies behind the war effort, patriotically fighting the German cause on all fronts.

5

Survival: 1914–29
'Dear Corner of Homeland'

'Hitherto, the German has had the blessed fortune to be exceptionally well governed; if this continues, it will go well with him. When his troubles will begin will be when by any chance something goes wrong with the governing machine', Jerome K. Jerome wondered in 1900. He was soon to find out. War was declared in July 1914. This chapter will recount how, from then to 1919, the German Jewish entrepreneurs acted patriotically, in conspicuous and private ways, throwing their lives behind the war effort with pride. As the increasing wealth of the German Empire was reflected in department stores before the First World War, so was its economic depression during and after the conflict. Valiantly and with increasing financial difficulty, department store owners continued to try to provide essential goods to Germans during war, inflation and depression. Their ability to put ordinary items, which had become luxuries in some cases, into the hands of the population ensured their continued popularity. Especially in hard times, people went to places where they knew they got value for money and trusted the salespeople.[1] This made modernization of stores, once easy credit was available in the second half of the 1920s, the next logical step and a boost of confidence to the new German Republic and its economy. This chapter will show that, during this period, the building and expansion of department stores were heralded as positive developments even by the public.[2] Stores and their owners were determined to continue on the path of economic success and social integration through these hard times.

This chapter will show that Jews, even if they were eyed with suspicion by some during the First World War, were still very much accepted locally after the collapse of the German monarchy. Yet, the perceived threat of Judaism as a religion grew. In the 1920s, as one historian put it, Jews were 'de-personalised'.[3] People would differentiate between their friendly Jewish neighbour and the evil Jewish capitalist or communist. The department store – although traditionally

Figure 5.1 Jewish-born Germans followed the call of their Emperor into battle on the field and the home front. The ability to deal with large-scale logistic operations made department store owners the unofficial quartermasters of the Empire. © Author.

and on the face of it a scapegoat – was too much the neighbour, the provider of essential and lovely things, to fall into the evil category. With the loss of imperial stability, frequently changing governments, food shortages, job losses and financial crises from 1919, far-right groups began gaining traction out of protest.[4] In the meantime, the fascist movement was on the rise all over Europe . In Germany, the National Socialist would go on to harness all such dissatisfied groups into one extremely dangerous group, especially for the Jewish population.

The Emperor had declared that 'he knew no parties anymore, only Germans', – a truce between opposing political, social and religious factions that gave hope for Germany's future, not just in military terms, but a hope for Jews to finally overcome the last vestiges of antisemitism. Yet, the war did not prevent anti-Jewish sentiments and in the army, especially, they deepened. August 1914 was filled with tumultuous joy as men signed up to fight, more or less firm in the belief that they would be in Paris before they knew it and back home in time for Christmas. Germans of Jewish origin were no exception, acting as patriotically as their nominally Christian countrymen. However, the German military command was already discussing the role of Jews in the army. The officer corps, in particular would remain closed to them.[5] Although in the first days of the war the shops remained devoid of customers, business continued largely as usual. Several companies had only just opened new branches or had expensively rebuilt. Although operations remained largely as they had initially, gradually the home front, and with it retailing, got caught up in the conflict. At first, Knopf in Karlsruhe proudly displayed diorama of battles and captured French artillery in their shop windows, but their advert 'Die Deutsche Mode' (The German Fashion), gave an indication that fashion from Paris or London was no longer available: a commercial necessity turned into patriotism.

By the beginning of 1915 it was becoming clear that the war would not end swiftly. Bread was rationed, with all foodstuffs becoming hard to acquire due to an effective British naval blockade. Stores of goods were requisitioned. The state dictated prices, so often – for instance, in the case of tinned beans at Tietz, they were sold for a much higher price than was necessary – due to regulations inflating prices without economic necessity. In the winter of 1916–17, it became difficult to cover even half of the minimum number of calories needed daily. George Tietz managed to get his hand on American cooking fat for the German army, via Sweden. Where businesses could not help directly, the families turned to charitable work. Oscar Tietz was made a 'delegate' of the Red Cross, with the rank and uniform of a major. The Knopfs provided soup kitchens and were thanked and decorated by the Grand Duke in return for their efforts. Wertheim's new meat canning factory, with 1,500 employees, produced only for the front, while the old canning plant was repurposed and became an exemplary supplier to the artillery. In 1914, Wertheim even established a new factory producing up to a thousand 15 cm grenades a day.[6]

The German high command was dependent on the ability of department stores to procure, handle and ship huge quantities of products. The German army quite simply did not have the necessary logistical know-how to deal with the volumes necessary to feed and clothe troops. Such was the power of department stores chains when negotiating with suppliers that the manufacturers formed syndicates or cartels to protect themselves from dumping prices. Although a few cartels had formed before the First World War, producers increasingly joined forces during the conflict. Their main purpose was for manufacturers within a cartel to sell items at the price of production plus a small profit instead of according to what the market provided. The department stores would represent the consumer market. Rudolf Knopf, the son of Max Knopf, wrote his doctoral dissertation on cartels, at the same time giving us much detail of how his father's company was run. Rudolf Knopf believed the cartel to be the 'optimum' of capitalism as these groups could more easily adjust production to suit demand and survey the entire industry.[7] Yet, prices were kept artificially high or raised pre-emptively to maximize the profit of the manufacturer; in effect creating something close to a monopoly, dictating prices to suit the producer rather than the consumer. In the end, it was usually the smaller retail firms who suffered under these cartels having absolutely nothing in hand against them.[8]

Germans of Jewish origin threw themselves enthusiastically into the war effort. Rabbis even preached patriotic sermons celebrating German military victories. However, what may be seen as supporting the war effort with goods and services could also be interpreted as profiteering, especially if things went wrong, fuelling Jewish hatred if the supplies came from department stores. The KaDeWe had been commissioned to supply the Austrian army with 30,000 boots in late 1914. The first 3,000 were severely below standard. That a store which considered itself the best in Berlin supplied a German ally with faulty goods was bad enough. Yet, when the same boots were repackaged by the KaDeWe and sent back to Austria a second time, a scandal broke loose involving the Austrian envoy and the German police. Two members of Adolf Jandorf's staff and employees at the bank which had financed the transaction were found to blame and convicted.

Jandorf's in his personal notes mentions the police record as an annoyance, and that nothing could be proven against him is evident.[9] Whoever was to blame, this event increased the sentiment that Jews were either profiteering, or even worse, actively undermining the war effort.

As the war progressed, and allegiances between nations shifted frequently, enemies within German ranks were increasingly sought out.[10] The German high command commissioned a Jewish census (*Judenzählung*) to support the antisemitic claim that too few Jews were fighting and at the front. The publicized reason for the assessment was that it was supposed to show the opposite. Almost 3,000 Jews had sacrificed their lives for the Empire, as per census that began in October 1916, and yet the figures were not published in the end. Officially it was said that this was to spare Jewish feelings, implying that they did not pull their weight. This meant, the census simply fuelled Jewish hatred.[11] Had the census been made publicly available, it would have shown that 100,000 men of Jewish origin fought for the Empire, approximately the same proportion of, if not even a little higher than, men of other faiths. Adolf Jandorf's son joined his regiment of dragoons.[12] Max Wronker, Hermann Wronker's son, also joined up and was eventually decorated with the Iron Cross, which was a considerably rarer honour in the First World War than it was in the Second World War. By the end of the war, 17,000 Jews had been awarded the Iron cross; 12.000 fell for the Kaiser by the time peace was declared.

Figure 5.2 Necessity turned to virtue: *Die Deutsche Mode*, 'The German Fashion', available at Knopf, because there was no other couture available. © Author.

Defeat

With the defeat of Germany in the First World War came not only humiliation, but also the dismemberment of the German Empire. As a result of this, retailers lost their branches in Alsace, Lorraine, parts of Silesia and West Prussia. Particularly heart-wrenching for many department store proprietors and many other Germans must have been the integration of Posen into the newly reformed Republic of Poland. Birnbaum, the small town that so many Jewish men and women had left to start businesses across Germany, was no longer part of their country. As the geographic area of the German Empire diminished, so did the sphere of influence of German-run department stores and an official connection with the places the Jewish entrepreneurs came from. The Emperor fled to Holland and into relative obscurity. The diplomat and diarist Harry Graf Kessler, present at the plundering of the imperial palace, noted the sheer tastelessness and kitsch of the Empress' private rooms, stuffed with knick-knacks of mediocre quality.[13] Viewed in the context of department stores being accused of selling substandard products to the untutored masses, this shows that the imperial family themselves would have had to be included in that group by the apparent arbiters of taste.

Just a few weeks after the inglorious end of the First World War, the president of a south-west German retail traders association, Carl Werner, a cultural Christian and proprietor of C. Werner-Blust, a small department store-like retailers, expressed his incredulity at Germany's defeat:

> All the wonderful achievements of our army our navy and our people during the four years of war, all the sacrifices of property and blood have been for naught, naught through the fault of our blinded military leaders, naught through the fault of powerless political leaders but also through the premature failure of our people … We will swear, even in this time of trouble to remain true to [Germany], to ever prove ourselves as good Germans, come what may. In the strong belief that our people is called to great tasks amongst the peoples, no matter what. *Deutschland über alles*.[14]

Werner noted in 1918 that Germans would have a brighter future if only they learnt to be more democratic.[15] Yet, we can already discern the anger raging in his words: the 'powerless political leaders' were to be increasingly blamed for Germany's defeat over the coming years.

What followed after the armistice can only be described as chaos. Two republics were declared on 9 November 1918, first a bourgeois republic by the

SPD politician Philipp Scheidemann, and later in the afternoon, a socialist republic by Karl Liebknecht. The representatives of the former prevailed, but had to flee Berlin due to the civil unrest and rioting that was taking place. As Berlin was too unsafe, the opera house in the provincial Saxon town of Weimar served as the meeting place for the constituting assembly of the German Empire that was to be a Republic. Largely those who had sat in the Reichstag before the First World War were part of this gathering. The new constitution included the phrase 'all state authority comes from the people', and women were given the right to vote. The Reichstag was now elected by universal and equal suffrage and a seemingly democratic system of 1 per cent votes equalling 1 per cent of the seats in parliament introduced. This, together with fractured nature of German society at the time, along class, religious and regional lines, meant Germany had, on average, no government lasting for more than eight months.[16] While some ministries could be held by the same politician over several governments, important ones changed almost with every new cabinet. The role of the Emperor was filled by a president, the first one being the social democrat Friedrich Ebert. Through Article 48 of the Weimar Constitution, the first head of state to be elected by the people was given significant power in times of crisis, allowing him to circumvent the parliamentary process and suspend basic rights in order to guarantee peace. Thus, the Weimar Republic had more than one design flaw at its inception.

The new constitution did not help to calm the heated atmosphere in Germany. The military chose not to cooperate with the new government when a group tried to overthrow it in the so-called right-wing coup Kapp Putsch on 13 March 1920 in the hope of preventing the Republic from establishing itself. The democratic government had to flee Berlin again. The city was in a near civil war-like state. Department stores were badly damaged and plundered during the fighting on the streets.[17] Managers had to close and shutter their stores to prevent their destruction; essential supplies to the population were suddenly cut off. Georg Tietz, Oscar Tietz's son, was threatened with his life, by an officer if the stores did not reopen. The complete lack of staff – due to the fact that no one could travel across Berlin – made the demand useless.[18] The government was ultimately restored, but the German population was tense with the heavy burden of a lost war and the lack of decent food: rioting, demonstrations and smashed windows became a feature of life in some inner cities, even in the provinces. In Karlsruhe, the trade unions had organized a rally to protest against the heightened price of food. The department stores of Tietz and Knopf were stormed in spite of the police's best efforts to prevent it.[19]

Knopf could be saved from being ransacked only because managers drastically reduced the prices.

Since the outbreak of war, the German government had partially financed the conflict by printing money. Inflation was rife and increased rapidly when the production of money was hiked further. By July 1923, 1 US dollar cost 1 million *Marks*. Wertheim and Hermann Tietz vouchers and coins – initially only exchangeable in their stores became – first unofficial among the people of Berlin and then with the sanction of the Reichsbank – currency. The cost of a loaf of ordinary bread rocketed from 163 *Marks* in January to 233 billion by the end of November. Later in her life, the department store cashier Berta Klotz's recorded how she was recalled from her holidays to witness 'the rush on the most impossible items because money had no value'. At intervals a manager would announce by which multiple prices were to be calculated, as cash registers did not have sufficient counters to accommodate all the zeros. At the end of the day, one employee complained, 'the money that had once been brought in a bag to the main office was then brought in large suitcases'.[20]

Hyperinflation dealt one of many blows to the economy of the young democracy. Even though some mortgages were paid off practically overnight, savings and bonds were obliterated. The previously better-off were now in a disorientated or even precarious situation. Individuals' purchasing power had slowly dropped since the outbreak of war, but even if one was in the rare position of having disposable income in the early 1920s, there was little they would be inclined to buy. Retailers were overstocked with unwanted, out-of-date goods. Manufacturers were unable to supply new, let alone innovative, products. Raw materials were unavailable, machinery requisitioned and the designing or optimizing of new consumables turned costly. Advertising can hardly be found in the newspapers from 1915 onwards. Only very few reappeared in 1922, mostly in the shape of make-do-and-mend tips.[21] The abolition of the department store tax levied by cities and states in favour of a single Empire-wide value-added tax created a new – if more just – burden for all retailers.[22]

Essential foodstuffs were in short supply. Petty pilfering in department stores was on the rise, not due to the thrill some middle-class housewives got from stealing, but because people could not afford basic foodstuffs.[23] Tempers frayed when even potatoes became scarce. Although the police in Mannheim forbade demonstrations at the beginning of October 1923, the unemployed took to the streets on the 15th of that month.[24] The police attempted to keep them away from the town hall forcing them towards the old palace where the French soldiers keeping guard there repelled the protestors. The situation escalated into brawling and looting across the town, which lasted until the 17 October. Shop windows were smashed, department stores were ransacked and shots were fired. Protesters and police were hurt, with one officer getting killed.[25] The grievance being expressed by the crowds on those three days in October 1923 had nothing to do with antisemitism or international capitalism. The press reported that local shopkeepers and farmers were accused of creating an artificial shortage of produce, in particular potatoes, in order to keep the price high.[26] The unemployed of Mannheim took out their anger on anyone who looked like they may be better off. A variety of reasons motivated riots up and down the country at the time. At the end of September 1923 the French occupation of the Ruhr had spiralled out of control, resulting in separatist violence in Bavaria and the Rhenish provinces. The occupation of the Ruhr caused an energy crisis and, among other things, the requisitioning of railway rolling stock by the victorious allies resulted in a breakdown of transport. Germany was in a state of emergency. Later in October and November, there was a communist uprising in Hamburg and the right-wing-motivated Beer Hall Putsch in Munich.

Across Germany, after the First World War, there were countless antisemitic groups: from clubs and societies who would simply not accept Jewish members to organizations whose primary reason for existence was promoting antisemitism; from elitist student fencing societies to the drinkers at the pub around the corner. By 1923, the National Socialist German Workers' Party (NSDAP) had gained considerable momentum under the leadership of Adolf Hitler. The schizophrenic name was intended to indicate a uniting of the extreme right and extreme left, into which Germany had been purposefully split by the Jews.[27] Although Hitler and his supporters attempted the coup in Munich in 1923, for which he was imprisoned, the party did not gain national importance until late in the 1920s, and was even being banned at one point. However, violence by political parties became the norm during this time. Across the political spectrum, groups were formed ostensibly to keep order at rallies and meetings, but actually functioned more like paramilitary troops, rounding up voters and beating up opponents.

During his imprisonment, Hitler wrote *Mein Kampf*, a quasi-autobiographical tirade against anything he saw as having wronged him in his life. The lack of open conflict between peoples, which Hitler lamented, was ascribed to nations becoming more and more like department stores, vying for vulgar profit, rather than racial superiority.[28] Should the German Empire collapse, he notes – and at the time he believed it would – there would be no monuments to Germanic greatness, such as town halls, cathedrals or defence towers, to bear witness to what had passed, and only the hotels and department stores of Jews would remain.[29] By 1933, *Mein Kampf* had made Hitler a considerable fortune and by the end of the Second World War around 10 million copies had been sold. It is a matter of speculation how many of them were actually read.

In certain areas of Germany between 1890 and the late 1920s, some shopkeepers, tradesmen and farmers would simply vote for whatever was the current protest movement: Socialists, Catholics, antisemites, liberals, farmers' associations, the National Socialists or whoever else railed against what they believed to be the current cause of their plight.[30] Even those who would have consistently voted for right-wing parties would have had to frequently changed allegiances, as they were all short-lived. A typical example of this is Ferdinand Werner, member of the Reichstag, whose tirades of hatred included department stores and complaints about Georg Wertheim receiving a medal by the Emperor before the First World War. He had belonged, in succession, to the Verein Deutscher Studenten, the Deutschsoziale Partei, the Deutschvölkische Partei, then the Deutschnationale Volkspartei which merged later with the Deutschvölkische Bund, which in turn became the Deutschvölkische Schutz und Trutzbund. In 1933, he joined the National Socialist Party. His political biography demonstrates the lack of continuity in extreme right-wing organizations. The impermanence of these parties is mirrored in the absence of continuity in support of *Mittelstand* organizations or against department stores.

In spite of all this, on an official level, animosity towards department stores in general and Jewish businesses in particular was not recorded as a major feature. There were many places in which the riots of the 1920s had antisemitic overtones, demonstrating that these underlying sentiments against Jews were increasingly breaking out in public.[31] Yet the picture is a complicated one as, while on the one hand, Hitler organized a putsch in Munich in 1922, on the other hand the assassination of foreign minister Walter Rathenau was publicly mourned. 'Kill off Walter Rathenau, The greedy goddamn Jewish Sow', had been chanted outside the Reichstag. Rathenau stood for everything radical right-wing groups hated: he was Jewish, a successful entrepreneur and a minister of the despised Republic. Denounced by the General von Ludendorff, of the First World War, and vilified by parties such as the NSDAP, he was murdered in June 1922. On the whole, however, the nation mourned the extremely capable diplomat and a state funeral, with all the trappings, was given him in Berlin.[32]

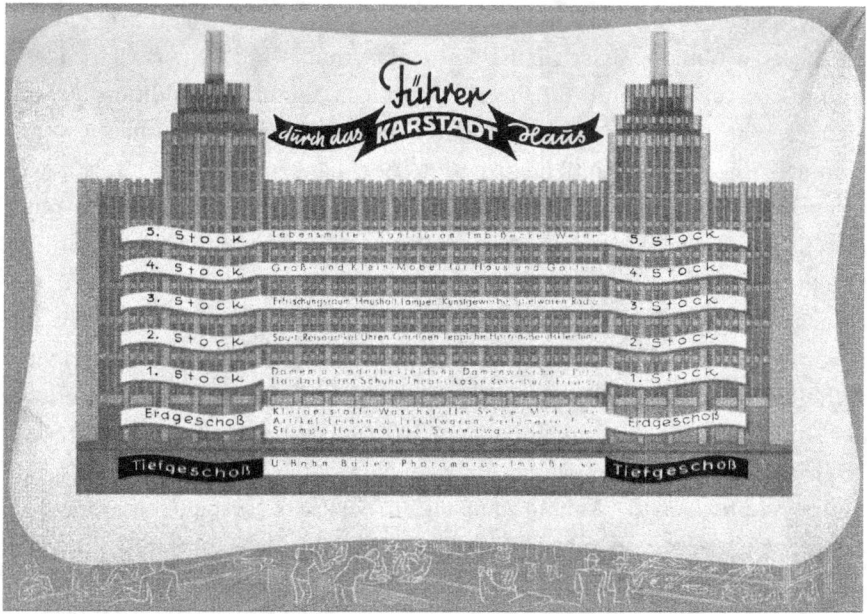

Figure 5.3 The gargantuan Karstadt store on the Hermannsplatz in Berlin had its own underground station and roof-top gardens. It was so vast; parts of the building had to be closed off shortly after it had been opened in 1929. © Author.

Expansion

Amidst all this chaos, department stores naturally struggled but, having mostly been established during an economic slump, found ways to carry on. Karstadt had merged with the Theodor Althoff AG, becoming the Rudolph Karstadt AG. The merger between the two companies in 1920 had become essential for several reasons. Most importantly, it resulted in savings in staffing and purchasing essential for both partners especially because of the economic depression. The united company could now rely on a single administration and purchasing department.[33] Capital for investment had become a desperate necessity as both companies had seen little or no innovation since before 1914, for different reasons. Althoff's rapid expansion before 1914 had come at a big price, and they had been forced to pay off all their loans before the First World War, which financially crippled the company. Karstadt, on the other hand, had invested in socks, blankets and just about anything that could be stored and might be useful if war broke out; this, however, now meant that the company had a large amount of unwanted stock.

The merger, which was more of an acquisition for Karstadt, brought the purchaser a dubious asset in the form of Althoff's industrious, if reckless, administrative staff and directors. The most significant addition to the management of Karstadt was Hermann Schöndorff, whose personality would dominate the company until he drove it to near-bankruptcy. Born into a family of horse traders, much like Oscar Tietz, Schöndorff was trained as a retail merchant and established a company making wooden bed frames, shop fittings and eventually railway carriages. He joined Althoff as an advisor in 1910, but quickly took on more responsibilities for the department store, ensuring, in the newly former Rudolph Karstadt AG, that both Rudolph Karstadt and Hermann Althoff left the board of directors.[34] This meant that the only significant German department store chain which had not been established by people of Jewish origin was now being run by one.

The addition of the Althoff company to Karstadt's brought them branches mainly in western and central Germany, including Essen. In 1885, Theodor Althoff had inherited his family's drapery store in the small town of Dülmen at the edge of the Ruhr. The company expanded and added a store in Dortmund covering 5,000 square metres and employing 500 staff in 1904. Althoff also had an elegant branch in Leipzig, a city that was the seat of a significant trade fair at which most department store proprietors, directors and managers would gather annually to inspect the latest manufacturing techniques and fashion trends. Naturally, this store, erected between 1912 and 1914, had to be especially well appointed if it was to be frequented by the employees of rival companies. The walls were covered in delicate inlay work in mahogany, pear wood, oak and rosewood. Three central halls brought natural light into the building and huge chandeliers lit the space at night. The name 'Warenhaus Althoff' remained after the merger, true to the established convention of trading under a locally known brand.

At first, Schöndorff, who had been awarded the honour and title of commercial councillor (*Kommerzienrat*) by the German Emperor for his services to the economy and charity, seemed to be on the road to success. He and his staff streamlined bookkeeping, rationalized inventory and ensured all branches ran according to the same principles of 'sheer military efficiency'. The 'horizontal integration' of manufacture and sales was furthered, along with the expansion of 'vertical integration' through associated branches (*Anschlussgeschäfte*). In the autumn of 1924, Karstadt floated on the stock exchange and was set, with American loans, on a course of expansion.[35] The company established its own haulage business and, most spectacularly, planned a new store in Berlin on the Hermannplatz.

Karstadt also introduced a so-called single price store (*Einheitspreisgeschäft*) called EPA to its portfolio. Woolworths (or Wohlwert), EHAPE and EPA stores were increasingly successful in Germany due to the simplicity of their concept. They exclusively sold the same low-cost, relatively good quality things that early department stores had concentrated on. This reflects a lack of disposable income at the time owing to which the general population appreciated the fact that everything in any given store cost exactly the same amount. One assumes that the idea behind these shops originated in America with Woolworths or with Marks & Spencer's Penny Bazaar in England; however contemporaries were not convinced that this was an Anglo-Saxon invention. Single price stores were a serious threat to established department stores. So as not to lose too much trade to these, department stores, including Karstadt, established their own single-price outlets; Leonhard Tietz founded a company to work alongside their other operations, while Knopf introduced a single price department (*Einheits Preis Abteilung*) into existing stores.

The entire German economy remained extremely fragile right up until the mid-1920s. Despite its instability, there were some advantages, depending on one's circumstances; for instance, hyperinflation meant that business loans could be repaid very quickly. For several department store companies, this meant that the properties they had purchased on credit to build their stores on were soon owned by them outright. Stores mainly reacted by rationalizing their operations even more than before, like Karstadt did with amalgamation or Schocken with stringent centralization. Proprietors of smaller companies had less capacity to make such large-scale savings. Yet, one chamber of commerce, presided over by Carl Werner, representing smaller retailers and craftsmen, had a radical solution to solving the problem: they believed a cleansing process would have to sweep the economy. The faster and more radically it could proceed, the better it would be for German business.[36] Companies that could not compete in such a market would have to perish for the benefit of those that were. Less drastic and more conservative voices, on the other hand, began calling for the protection of smaller businesses by the state. This could be financed by raising taxes on larger companies, such as department stores. On the initiative, of several groups of the *Mittelstand*, the Association of German Cities (Deutsche Städtetag) had already advised the German state governments to start taxing department stores on their capital as early as 1922, but this was not brought forward. The legislation may have as much as doubled taxation for some department stores, which were struggling no less than small businesses. Sally Knopf, in Freiburg, complained bitterly when the tax office failed to pay back his rebate on time, underscoring

Figure 5.4 Wertheim in Breslau was erected with the loans that had finally become available for large building projects in 1927. The horizontal window bands exuded the sophistication of the brief economic respite of the Weimar Republic. © Author.

that it was a disgrace if the state withheld funds from business when banks were being careful with investment.[37] New taxation was not introduced as the consequences were unforeseeable to the economy and social peace.[38] Department stores were much too important as they generated employment to risk their stability; unemployment was much too high as it is.

The golden twenties

To alleviate the situation, the Reichsbank introduced the *Rentenmark* in 1924 as an alternative to the ruined mark. First, the Dawes Plan, in the summer of 1924, and then the Young Plan, agreed in May 1930 retrospectively for September 1929, regulated the reparations Germany had to pay to the Allies at a manageable level.[39] By October 1925, an agreement was reached with the French occupying the Ruhr in the Treaty of Locarno. Earlier the same year, the president of the fledgling Republic, Friedrich Ebert died suddenly and was replaced by the reluctant Field Marshal Paul von Hindenburg – a more potent symbol of the old imperial order is hard to conjure up short of the Emperor himself. Gradually in this period turnover in retailing rose from circa 25 billion *Reichsmarks* in 1924 to 36 billion *Reichsmarks* in 1928.⁴⁰ Real change could be seen by 1927, and most entrepreneurs were hopeful of continued growth.⁴¹ Since the beginning of the First World War, consumer goods had not been easy to find. Department stores and *Mittelstand* companies had at times found it difficult to fill the shelves with the simplest things. In the early 1920s, Sally Knopf and Salman Schocken had complained about the difficulty of finding basic things such as velour, cotton, candles and soap.⁴² Around 1927, the markets eased up and goods were easier to come by.

Companies started making plans for the future: Hermann Tietz was set on expansion, and Schocken planned to do the same.⁴³ The relief that the economy was recovering was set in stone in Berlin by Karstadt. The new flagship store built, 1927–29, in Berlin-Kreuzberg, was of gargantuan proportions.⁴⁴ The shop had twenty-one escalators and twenty lifts that took customers from the store's own underground station to the roof terrace, which alone covered 4,000 square metres. It was so large that two entire floors remained unused until it was almost destroyed in 1945. A far cry from the parochial elegance of Knopf or the effortless modernism of Schocken, it was widely criticized for looking out of place architecturally and being an inappropriately grand statement in one of Berlin's poorer districts.

By 1925, the Wronker branch in Mannheim had been further enlarged to fifty-three departments and served a fifty-kilometre radius with home deliveries. In June 1927, Hermann Wronker became the majority shareholder of the Société Internationale des Grands Bazars S.A. This company include another store in Frankfurt, the Kaufhaus Hansa and Warenhaus Strauß in Nuremberg.⁴⁵ Hansa had originally been part of the Geschwister Knopf company under the Hermann Schmoller brand.⁴⁶ In 1929, the concern was renamed Hermann Wronker AG, turning it into a joint-stock exchange company.

In 1926, at the reopening of Frankfurt's most important bridge after restoration, a huge float, the size of a large canal boat, cruised down the main emblazoned with the word 'WRONKER' to mark the occasion. At the time of his sixtieth birthday, one year later, Hermann Wronker and his family were at their peak. Frankfurt and Mannheim were full of praise for Hermann Wronker as an entrepreneur, employer and philanthropist. His stores were not just among the most significant in these cities: the man had moulded economic lives of people, the Frankfurt *General-Anzeiger* stated. In Frankfurt, the 'business life of this city has, in great part, the character he gave it'.⁴⁷ 'With our best wishes for the man celebrating his birthday are united wide circles who revere in him one of the major proponents of the Frankfurt merchants' and indeed members of staff, representatives of the city council and delegations of trade and commerce were among those who personally attended the celebrations to mark the sixtieth birthday.[48] Letters and telegrams from all over Germany were read out on the occasion, as one paper put it, 'which bear witness to the general appreciation which the Wronker company enjoys'.[49] His staff even presented him with a bronze relief of himself.

The chorus of well-wishers was rounded off by the Frankfurt city council who considered it 'a great pleasure to see him at the pinnacle of his life's work, which could not afford prouder or happier reflection and anticipation'.[50] His good influence was felt beyond the bounds of his company and family within the city of Frankfurt itself. The city council recorded: 'At this juncture we must especially express that we appreciate your outstanding contribution to Frankfurt's economic life and your humanitarian efforts.'[51] The letter from Frankfurt city hall closed by wishing him sufficiently good health to enjoy the fruits of his labour.

Figure 5.5 Knopf's branch refurbishments and extensions throughout the 1920s were heralded as spiritual investments into the homeland. The lucrative construction contracts the department store gave were much welcomed by suppliers and craftsmen at a time little work was available. The refacing of the Knopf store in Freiburg, depicted here, was particularly considered a success by the local press. © Wolfgang Ziefle Collection.

Rooted into the landscape

Knopf's success was founded on localism, with the company and family feted for this very reason. When Knopf completely gutted and refaced the store in Freiburg in 1928, the local papers sang praises of their interiors: 'Freiburg's master craftsmen and suppliers were permitted to provide the best of their work'.[52] The exterior and interior, with its floors and panelling in highly polished Canadian birch, had 'the stamp of the well-bred and solid'. In Freiburg, as elsewhere, Knopf and their competitors used local craftsmen whenever they could. This naturally endeared them to the local guilds for giving large and lucrative commissions.

Max and his brother Sally Knopf had bought a property in Freiburg in 1898, expensively extending and improving it several times.[53] In 1927, Arthur Knopf, Sally's son, added a neighbouring house to the store. It was separated from the main building by a small alley running at a right angle to the high street. This alley connected the cathedral with the town hall and the civic bank (*Sparkasse*). It was this bank which complained when the architect suggested building a bridge across the alley to connect the two halves of the store. After a measured debate, the municipal arts commission demanded a full-size papier-mâché model be erected to gauge the effect. Permission was finally granted under complicated and detailed conditions, which included removing the art nouveau details from the older part of the building.[54] The renovated store was reopened to great applause on 10 November 1928. The Freiburg press was universal in its praise: 'For the advantage of the town's aspect', the store had 'a harmonious modern exterior' clad in the same sandstone as the cathedral. Retail space was sacrificed to achieve the desired effect, which was loss-bearing to the proprietor, as 'recently published accounts on the expensive square foot of land in Baden are in beautifully-scary competition to that of New York with this "dear corner of home land"'.[55] Articles praising the store were florid, almost poetic. Painting a tranquil picture in which the activity of the modern building was rounded off by the ancient and mighty cathedral, the bells of the cathedral's spire opposite 'mix their sonorous sounds into the homely bustle in the feverishly working house and the life on the street, encouraged by the evening hour'.[56] The great extent to which the company had gone in order to create such a store had been well worth it: 'one can justly say that the building client's business acumen has gone hand in hand with his good taste, to forge a link in Freiburg's future commercial life that gives a glorious and proudly heralded testimonial of the bustling activity of the Kaiserstrasse'.[57] Not even the sleek neon sign that had been ordered especially from Berlin could spoil Knopf's harmony with the city, its history and its economy. Working with local authorities paid off. Hermann Wronker and the Knopfs were considered benefactors to their cities each time they rebuilt or updated their buildings in the 1920s, as these provided visible signs in the cityscape of a more prosperous future and commitment to whatever town they had a branch in: 'When the company erected new buildings it did so in a manner that was architecturally valuable to the city's aspect, representative for the city and company, and functional in their interior and exterior design. In the execution of these intentions the company spared no expense.'[58] Karstadt, on the other contrary, had been permitted to develop the site for its enormous flagship in Berlin only on the condition that it lent funds to the municipality for building social housing.[59]

Arthur Knopf succeeded his father Sally, just as Margarete Levis took over from her father Max. The actual crown prince would surely have been Max's son Rudolf. Born in 1893, he went to the local grammar school (*Gymnasium*) and then to the universities in Berlin and Munich to study economics, before completing his PhD at the University of Heidelberg. When he died of influenza in 1924, it Max became greatly depressed. Only work kept him going, so his staff believed: 'With a superhuman willpower, he sought solace in his toil … in the perfection of his business, in the care of his employees.' Max allegedly worked until 21 October 1934, the day he died. Margarete completely took over the running of the family business with her husband Arthur Levis who, like his father-in-law, combined 'outstanding expertise with exemplary social understanding'. Just as Max Wronker became increasingly involved with his parents' business, so did Georg Tietz; Georg had since married Edith, who produced the heir, naturally named 'Hermann'. Oscar Tietz, the founder of Hermann Tietz, literally died in his boots, on hike in Switzerland in January 1923. Leonhard Tietz's eldest also made his mark on the family firm, expanding the business into Silesia.

On the contrary, Harry Jandorf – although he had been apprenticed to his father's associates at the Oberpollinger department store in Munich – did not follow in his father's footsteps. Adolf Jandorf's – initially unwilling – business partner, the Emden family, had sold all their stores to Karstadt, without consulting him. Max Emden retired to a palatial villa in Switzerland, where he dedicated himself to collecting art. This bitter taste of his own medicine, he had gone behind the Emden's back on more than one occasion in the past, caused Adolf Jandorf to sell his part of the firm to the Hermann Tietz company. The sons of Oscar Tietz played poker with Adolf Jandorf, and in a master stroke worthy of the best player he sold the store for a large and undisclosed cash sum, which he distributed

Figure 5.6 Erich Mendelsohn's iconic store for Schocken in Stuttgart. Having survived the bombings of the Second World War unharmed, it was pulled down to allow the road to be widened. © Author.

among his shareholding family. The fee for the solicitor who drew up the contract in 1926 was a staggering 150,000 *Reichsmark*, which one assumes reflects the sale price in some way.[60] Adolf had remarried after his first wife's untimely death and was the only one of the great department store entrepreneurs to enjoy the fruits of his labour in some small measure. He retired to a villa designed by his son and made entirely of timber on the Wannsee – a lake and district which was to become a byword for Hitler's disgustingly inhumane treatment of Jews. The logistics of the complete extermination of European Jews was decided in the vicinity at the so-called Wannsee Conference of senior Nazi officials.

Modernist architecture

At Schocken, the founder was sufficiently young to continue running the business. Salman found the company's commercial niche by embracing the new objectivity (*Neue Sachlichkeit*) and Bauhaus aesthetics. The company stood out from its rivals by elevating its stores to utilitarian temples – 'pure' retail spaces during the 1920s. His favoured architect would become Erich Mendelsohn, who had been part of Berlin's bohemian scene and had hardly any training or experience in the things Salman Schocken would want from him.[61] Mendelsohn would listen to music, sketching down broad strokes as it inspired the shapes of his building. The Nuremberg branch of Schocken was conceived during a performance of Bach's cello suite quartet.[62] This branch, Mendelsohn's first building for the family, was to be constructed keeping in mind the historic context of the city.[63] Mendelsohn replaced the vertical window bands, ubiquitous in department store architecture up until then, with bold horizontal stripes of glass and concrete. When Spedan Lewis had Peter Jones in London rebuilt, a team was dispatched to study the Schocken store in Chemnitz, which it still closely resembles, inside and out. As Salman's manager noted:

> We deliberately chose our buildings to go the way of modern design early, which was controversial at the time, not to the same extent today. The famous architect Erich Mendelsohn has, apart from our Nuremberg store, also built the Stuttgart store and, as crowning glory of his skills, supplied the designs for our biggest project in Chemnitz.[64]

Salman's passion for modernism was coupled with the company's need to stand out in the increasingly competitive market of retailing, indirectly turning his department stores into one of the most important patrons of modernist design in the Weimar Republic. Walter Gropius's Bauhaus pupils would design buildings, interiors and all items of publications from the typography to the complimentary slips of the company.[65] Salman believed his company attracted a better type of customer than others for two reasons: '1) Our small advertisements, 2) decoration. If we want to attract an elite clientele we must find a way that departs from the norm. We can be true to our system, but in a different way.'[66] By 'elite' he meant more discerning, not high class or moneyed. For instance, the extreme aesthete Schocken would insist on no decoration spoiling the store at Christmas; only fir trees were permitted as an adornment for the season.[67] By the 1930s, advertising at Schocken was done mainly through highly sophisticated handbills. The only embellishment to the plain type on these would be the 'S' logo, designed by the Mendelsohn studio. Further illustrations were supplied only if they were absolutely necessary to the understanding of the product. 'Ortos Health Shoes – keeps the feet young' features cross-sections of the shoe in a level of detail sufficient for an engineering project.

Schocken was the only department store that changed its public-facing operations in a significant way in the 1920s. Weathering the economic storm of inflation and depression, Salman Schocken and his staff had decided to give their stores an aura of exclusivity above that of his rivals. They dropped the type of advertising commonly used at the time – consisting mainly of price lists – as they did not want to 'pursue the tactic of selling at attractive prices items for which the price is generally known, and recouping with other objects', as Schocken's general manager wished it to be known.[68] Unlike most other stores, Schocken had always avoided making special offers but, by the late 1920s, amended its policy on this. Since hyperinflation, only popular and high-quality items were sold, as they posed a better investment, and the public had got accustomed to exchanging goods for cash, rather than saving. Salman Schocken would happily let his rivals try out innovative products, including them in his own stores' range once they had been optimized by the manufacturer and found to have a regular demand from the consumer.[69] This gave the impression of being a store selling sound and affordable wares of quality. 'The concept of quality is a mystical faith', Salman believed; only the quantity of work invested or the superiority of the raw materials could produce quality, and this was hard for the consumer to discern.[70] Maxims such as 'It is the task of the purchasing department to prevent products coming in which might be cheap, but do not correspond in their practical value to the money they cost' were printed and painted up in the stores as a means of advertising.[71] The quality control office of the Schocken AG was, however, not just a marketing ploy. It would rigorously check every item the purchasing department was considering acquiring.[72] Synonymous with the quality, rather than a bargain, was the legend 'own product' (*Eigenes Erzeugnis*) on the packet. Salman Schocken thought much of this classification, and insisted it be printed on every item that qualified.[73] Other companies would continue to use the more traditional forms of selection, advertising and retailing. Thanks to its perceived solidity, Schocken, however, was one of the very few department stores which remained independent from the banks after 1927.

By the 1920s, accounting techniques were sufficiently advanced to keep track of credit schemes, placing high-quality wares within reach of the working class. This was useful for stores at a time when purchasing power was low, but especially so for those that had to serve a large and less-affluent labouring demographic. As previously mentioned, some department stores took great relish in discounting products for those that had trouble affording them, others, especially Schocken, objected to the practice.

The importance of staff

Customers continued to be difficult to retain and satisfy. The poor economy and unstable situation meant they had less disposable income and were even more cautious. Well-trained staff were hence a key asset. The first tentative steps towards becoming department stores had been made within a family structure, but companies had only really expanded when customer-staff relations were developed as an important factor in maintaining and building consumer loyalty. Knopf training manuals in the 1920s offered myriad forms of guidance, reflecting the sort of expertise that was expected from an average assistant. Handbooks gave advice on how to display handkerchiefs, pointers on personal cleanliness and glossaries of textile retail jargon describing anything from laddered stockings (*Ameisengänge*) to imitation fur made of silk (*Zylinderplüsch*). These were not just part of the initial training, but were handed to all members of staff. A managerial memorandum enclosed with the pamphlet instructed the following to department heads: 'through repeated quizzing one is to verify if the expert knowledge discussed has been understood and kept in mind'.[74] Similarly strict control was kept on the circulation of the latest fashion magazines and staff members had to sign on a piece of paper pasted to the cover to show that they were up to date with the latest styles. At Schocken, a senior member of staff had to confirm that he or she had discussed the content of manuals with junior sales clerks.[75] Hence, training was time consuming and expensive, and although fashions changed from 1900 to 1930, well-polished staff was considered an investment in customer relations at any time. Knopf spent a great deal of its advertising space focusing on how well trained its staff were, announcing to the public that 'the service is as meticulous as ever'.[76]

Familiarity with the merchandise was essential to the new assistants' training, but understanding the psyche of the customer was key to the saleswoman's armoury. As the training manual put it: 'She must understand how to deal with this and that type of customer, and part of it is some study of human kind, which cannot be learned in a short time'.[77] Salman Schocken expected his staff to be immersed in a 'culture of service' in order to satisfy even 'the highest demands of our customers'.[78] Unlike in a personal space, such as in a small and familiar shop, the parties involved would not know each other in bigger stores; so new girls were trained to handle different types of consumers. Pamphlets, such as 'Sales Success', were hung from a string behind every counter at Knopf's stores in order to be ready at hand. The slim brochure, known to have been available in the 1920s, carried information on how to identify certain types of customer. A photograph of a typical customer would be followed by a caption, briefly outlining what the sales clerk had to expect from him or her. Ideally, if the system worked, a regular customer would feel at home and, as one shopper noted, looking back many years later, could 'find in the various departments a clerk that knew one's taste and served well. A personal chat was, if time permitted, also included.'[79] Eventually a proper relationship could be built, with mothers sending their daughters to certain members of staff with the advice: 'Go to Frau Seydlitz in the ladies' department, she will help and advise you gladly.'[80]

The close relationship between staff and employers ensured a detailed monitoring of salesmanship. For instance, at Schocken's Chemnitz store, when the management reviewed members of staff among themselves, each manager would be able to recognize personally by name all those working for them owing to their working relationship. Staff positions or their departments within the store are not mentioned in the verbatim protocol, assuming that everyone present knows exactly whom they are talking about. In 1931, the topic of discussion at a meeting was how senior members of staff ought to be more active in mentoring the newer employees. Copies of training manuals were supplied for staff to take home and read in their leisure hours. These manuals had specific spaces allotted in which the employee could note the date of the discussion of a particular topic with the appropriate member of staff. Staff were generally to be reminded that some customers required more attention, while others preferred to be left to their own devices.[81]

Understanding the wares on sale and the needs of the customer were two of the three pillars of good salesmanship. The third was to encourage interest in products the customer had not explicitly demanded. This was not just done by advertising, display and architecture, but by the appearance of the department and the assistant herself. Staff were told, in an undated pamphlet, that the 'appetite' of the customer for consumption would disappear 'if exquisite fashion items are presented by unclean, poorly maintained hands'.[82] The employees' clothes were to be simple, clean and unobtrusive: 'the most appropriate and refined clothing is black'.[83] Hair was to shine with cleanliness, not with grease, and to be modelled in a respectable style.[84] The orderliness of staff at Schmoller in Mannheim in the mid-1930s was well known that the 'beautifully dressed, reservedly elegant, well-styled staff caught the eye' of the customer to such an extent that it was remembered almost fifty years later.[85] Staff workplaces were also to be kept in the same pristine state as their personal appearance.[86] Every item had to be labelled with the purchasing and sales price. The decorations and arrangements had to be changed at least once weekly at which point 'special care is to be taken to account for changes in demand and the special popularity of certain articles', and the storeroom ordered accordingly.[87]

Staff were reminded 'that any advantage to the proprietor is to your own benefit and any disadvantage to him your own'.[88] For the Knopfs, family and business spheres were interwoven deeply, as reflected by the fact that Max Knopf was referred to lovingly as 'Papa Knopf' by his employees. In the 1920s and 1930s, the shop girls from Freiburg unanimously felt that it was not even the branch manager Mr Richter who represented the authority of the company, but rather Mrs Richter whose matriarchal strictness they feared in spite of her probably not even being a paid employee.[89] Various clubs and societies fostered the community spirit at Knopf. For instance, Friday was gymnastics evening at the Freiburg store in the 1930s, and each participant would receive supper at the expense of the company afterwards. As patrons of the local theatres and opera houses, the Knopfs had a large number of free tickets at their disposal which were distributed among employees. Department managers and their wives might go to the national opera in Mannheim, while the shop girls were more likely to be caught singing the hit 'All Men Are Criminals' ('Die Männer sind alle Verbrecher') in the store after a night at the revue.[90]

In contrast, at Schocken in the late 1920s, we find records of the poor working morale of the staff in most stores. The managerial board put this down to the great volume of negative criticism they were subjected to: 'We only criticize and give no praise. The staff misses this, which would usually be the way motivation would grow.' This had not always been so, and the absence of Simon Schocken's influence, after his death, as the genial and encouraging counterpart to Salman's cold and calculated manner caused difficulties.[91] Salman knew of his shortcomings: 'The main education meted out to the staff by my brother happened after the shop closed. The floorwalkers and sales clerks came to him to talk about this and that. He gave some pleasant words which were encouraging.'[92] The lack of the personal touch between staff and employee in modern companies was even described by his deputy Manasse as a 'curse'.[93] This problem was the cause of major concern. Instead, the Schocken system of staff-employer interaction was intensely codified after Simon's death. A handmade booklet was designed for managers and heads of departments: sheets of A6 paper were ruled in blue ink, and the name and occupation of every member of staff, their age, wage and date of joining the company were recorded in black. Names of heads of department were underlined twice, in black and red ink while that of their deputies was underlined once in black. Thus we know that a Mr Walter Kolb, forty-two years of age, was the head pastry cook and earning 70 *Reichsmarks*. The sheets with this information were placed into specially cut folders which fitted neatly into the managers' inside jacket pocket.[94]

Despite the fact that the Jews fought patriotically for their country during the First World War, they suffered defeat as did their countrymen. The first phase of the Weimar Republic was marked by war reparations, an economy at its knees, rioting in the streets and general political disorientation. Yet, in the same period 1918–23, the generation that saw active service stepped up to the mark as businesspeople, taking over their parents' firms and trying to make the best of the situation. We can trace a direct line from this new group of retailing executives to their ancestors in the Prussian provinces who went door to door selling linens. Over the generations, these families had seen gradual and positive change through some of the worst periods in German history, and they must have believed they would weather the economic and political storms of the new Republic too. Trade was not good, on the whole, but the public remained loyal to the Jewish-run stores, in spite of far-right groups continuing to blame them for the situation. A time of relative stability between 1924 and 1929, the second phase of the Weimar Republic, even gave reason for optimism, with easy money available to innovate, expand and improve businesses. In addition, overtly antisemitic voices remained disorganized and localized. For instance, in the election of 1928, the National Socialist Party's role was insignificant. The lasting improvement of the lives of Germans of Jewish origin and the growth of their businesses on the German high street seemed set to continue in tandem with the recovery of the economy. Unfortunately, the economic basis of the entire world was about to be shattered in the third – and final – period of the Weimar Republic.

6

Decline: 1929–32
'Voices of Envy'

The near-perpetual crisis of the Weimar Republic between 1929 and 1933 is crucial in understanding how the Nazis came to power and ultimately colours how we see the entire history of Jewish-owned department stores and Germany in general.[1] This chapter will show the drastic escalation of the situation in the Weimar Republic after the fragile house of cards that was the economy went tumbling down on Black Friday – a fateful day in October 1929. The Wall Street Crash destroyed what little recovery had been made in 1927–8. What few cash resources were left were finally wiped out, and investment ground to a halt. Mass sackings followed, and we will see how important this development was to the growth and crystallization of the critique of mass retailing in this chapter. Germany was devastated. Social unease, even unrest, and political consequences followed the economic downturn. Ever more people sought quick solutions to the complex problems that life had set before them. The ranks of the Nazi Party swelled.[2] As has been noted previously by historians, the National Socialists made more of the Jewishness of department stores than any group before.[3] Yet, it was not so much a dislike for Jews that was the cause of Nazi success, but more the dislike for other parties and 'the other' in general that made people turn to the National Socialist Party.[4] As other historians have shown, the Nazis promised to regulate the market to a much greater degree, which many people saw as key to improving their lives.[5] We will see how the situation on the streets became gradually more volatile again, mainly due to Nazi thugs. For instance, Wertheim's windows were smashed in Berlin, uncomfortably reminding contemporaries of the prolonged periods of rioting after the end of the First World War.[6] However, we must not forget, as one historian put it, that 'the Jewish question … rarely if ever surfaced in the remaining months of the Republic'.[7] This chapter will show that too and reveal – shockingly – how the financial gambles of 1927 would cost Jewish entrepreneurs their businesses even before the Nazis came to power.

„Was kann mer doch alles machen mit die Gojim! Ihren Christus haben ünsre Lait gehenkt am Kreuz und aus seinem Geburtstag machen wir ä Riesen-Geschäft . . . ."

Figure 6.1 'All the things we can do to the Goy! Our people hung him on the cross and on his birthday, we make a huge profit.' Although not widely read and sometimes obscene, *Der Stürmer*'s vicious caricatures are emblematic of Nazi rhetoric. © German Propaganda Archive, Calvin University.

The flight into retailing

There had been warning signs that things were not going well, but initially contemporaries found it hard to pinpoint what had gone wrong with the economy in 1928. Bad weather, spoiling the summer and autumn season, was blamed for low sales.[8] With the crash in autumn, customers had no disposable income left. Small retailers dreaded passing on growing overheads for fear of losing custom.[9] People were demanding an even wider range of products at even lower prices.[10] While Knopf in Karlsruhe invited around 1,500 people to their fashion show in March 1932, the narrow profit margins by which stores operated relied on a high turnover, and this was shrinking at speed.[11] Before the First World War, department stores had been relatively immune to depression – most had been founded during one – but the general drop in retailing turnover in Germany by 41 per cent between 1929 and 1933 was difficult to stomach even for the hardiest of veterans.[12] Department stores had a large number of fixed costs that did not change in good or bad economic situations.[13]

Meanwhile unemployment was growing. In 1927, approximately 1 million people were unemployed across Germany; by 1930, 3.5 million were out of work, rising to more than 6 million by 1932. In 1932, there was no area in Germany that had an unemployment rate of less than 19 per cent, with the industrial west, around Cologne, and east, in Silesia, hit with a rate of more than 34 per cent.[14] This meant 'sacked civil servants, merchants and workers without jobs move towards selling products to the consumer, by opening a store or by seeking their customers as door-to-door salesmen ... in almost every renovated or newly built apartment block a shop is being created'.[15] As not even a qualified doctor or lawyer could find work, let alone someone with only a high school certificate, more and more people tried running their own little businesses.[16] Shopkeeping seemed like a safe option, but soon there were simply too many people trying to subsist as retailers, accelerating an existing trend that was unhealthy for the economy. In Baden, the number of retailers and tradesmen that had grown in only a few decades, now ballooned out of proportion.[17]

In 1895, the city of Mannheim had the largest number of retailers and tradesmen than any locality in the state, with about 3,500; Karlsruhe followed with 2,400; then Heidelberg with 1,666 and Freiburg with 1,655.[18] Between 1895 and 1907, the number of retailing companies had increased by a third and the number of people they employed by 54 per cent. In 1925, when Field Marshall Paul von Hindenburg had just been made the German President, replacing the SPD politician Friedrich Ebert, the number of companies had gone up by a further 8.3 per cent and the people they employed grew by 28.6 per cent. In the same year, there were just over 8,000 companies in Mannheim, 5,000 in Karlsruhe, over 3,000 in Freiburg, just under 3,000 in Heidelberg and Pforzheim, 2,330 in Rastatt, with just over 1,000 in Konstanz, Bühl, Bruchsal, Offenburg and Lahr.[19] Of all the people employed in retailing and craft in Baden at the time, 84 per cent (571,651) of them worked in companies with fewer than four members of staff (including the owner or manager). Only 13 per cent worked in businesses with four to ten staff, while only 3.34 per cent people worked for a company with more than ten.[20]

Too many people were thus employed working in very small shops, like tobacconists and confectionery stores, that could be set up with little capital and little specialist knowledge or training. Yet, the increase in population did

Figure 6.2 'While the Angel of Christmas has its hand tied through the machinations of the World Bank Jews, the Department Store Jews, under the mask of the Christian's friend, sells his junk.' © German Propaganda Archive, Calvin University.

not require so many more suppliers of goods: in Mannheim between 1907 and 1925, the population increased by 44.2 per cent, while the number of retailers rose by 106 per cent and that of door-to-door salesmen by an astonishing 298.3 per cent.[21] In Berlin, the number of retailers almost doubled between the end of the First World War and 1923.[22] Even in the recovery years 1926–27, 75 per cent of retailers had a turnover of less than 20,000 *Reichsmarks*, meaning a minority of companies were achieving considerably higher rates than their

Figure 6.3 'Buy from the Jew, be a traitor to your people'. The names of the stores in these anti-department store propaganda caricatures are always anonymous or fictitious. The Jewish store round the corner was too familiar to attack directly. © German Propaganda Archive, Calvin University.

competitors.[23] The number of small companies employing few people and making little profit grew, making their existence unviable. Carl Werner, the president of the retail trading association in Freiburg, noted in his diary that 'the great banking troubles' had made things very difficult, causing the family to have to economize 'in the face of unprofitable business'[24] – and his company was large and well established. As early as 1926, the state publication for industry and commerce warned that the number of businesses that were small or badly run was unsustainable. Recovery in retailing could only be made permanent by a 'purge' from the economy of these tiny and ever-increasing unprofitable businesses.[25] Small shops were 'measly' and subject to the whim of their customers.[26]

Largely founded by people who had already lost employment once, these small businesses were destined to be unsuccessful. The *Frankfurter Zeitung*, looking back in 1935, noted that anyone who had failed in their own profession 'flees into retailing ... and contributes to endanger the basis of healthy competition'[27] – bolstering the ranks of a new class of people who were sacked from their previous employment and barely subsisted with shopkeeping. Due to the self-importance that various members of the *Mittelstand* attached to their new respective professions, they managed to project an image of themselves as champions of the home economy.[28] There were simply too many small shops trying to get a share of the same cake – a cake made even smaller by the Wall Street crash. The National Socialists used this to their own advantage. They believed department stores and cooperatives had conspired against their smaller rivals.[29] Single price stores were particularly suspected of stealing considerable amounts of business from *Mittelstand* businesses.[30]

Champions of the envious

When Georg Manasse addressed a newly admitted group of shopworkers in April 1932, he was echoing the thoughts of his boss Salman Schocken when he explained how it came about that department stores were increasingly being criticized publicly and why parliaments were called upon to restrict them:

> There are many people who through lack of diligence and through lack of sufficient education or through careless work but also as a result of the economic crisis are not successful ... and it is blatantly clear that these would speak of a company, which is healthy and has obviously expanded in the past years, with the voice of envy... It is always so, and that is part of human nature, that – when one is doing badly – one blames someone else.[31]

And the National Socialists blamed capitalism first and foremost. Although most of the population at the time were indifferent to Nazi policies, the existing political system never had a broad appeal. In 1928, an SPD organization recorded that the banner of the German Republic was no longer flown. In Freiburg, they noted thus: 'The flags of the old German Empire ... seem to have disappeared from the city's landscape, yet the new flag is not there in its place, but the state or municipal flag and varied fantasy flags which people have assembled out of embarrassment.'[32] Even the few wholehearted supporters of the Republic failed to show their conviction: Jewish and gentile businessmen would remain neutral by displaying the less controversial colours of the state or the city rather than those of the Republic.[33] The Republic was losing its republicans.[34]

The grand coalition government, uniting a broad centre spectrum headed by the social democrat Hermann Müller, collapsed on 27 March 1930. Heinrich Brüning, a reactionary of the Catholic Centre Party, was made chancellor and ruled largely by emergency decrees – Article 48 of the Weimar constitution that allowed for decisions to be made without the Reichstag. He did this largely with the consent of the SPD, who was itself under considerable pressure as working-class unemployed were increasingly supporting the Communist Party. This in turn, with the violent overthrow of the Russian Empire still fresh in people's memories, meant more conservative forces started gravitating towards radical right-wing parties, in particular the Nazis. Democracy was dying. The elections in September 1930 had made the NSDAP one of the most powerful political party in the Reichstag, backed by the German middle class, Protestant farmers and members of the working classes from those areas where the SPD was weak.[35] The SPD did however remain the strongest party in parliament, while the Reichstag – a cacophony at the best of times – became unmanageable under the rowdy interruptions of the large Nazi cohort.

The memory of Soviet councils ruling cities in November 1918 was still fresh and most businesses, including smallholders and Jewish retailers, were less concerned about which democrats were ruling them and more fearful of the possibility that communists might take over.[36] Even in historically relatively liberal states, antisemites had existed as a minority. As one historian put it: 'In countless speeches in beer houses and assembly halls throughout Baden, the antisemites argued that Jews were radically different than Germans, Catholic, or Protestant ... Crude but for that reason no less convincing, these appeals rested upon a binary language of work and trade: on the one side, Jewish department stores, unfair competition, commodity exchange swindles; middlemen of all sorts, on the other, small produce vendors, people who worked for every penny, craftsmen, tillers of the field.'[37] In addition, a myth which claimed Germany would have won the First World War if the Jews and the Social Democrats – and just about anyone one didn't like – had not given the German army a 'stab in the back' gained currency. Otto Schmidt who had been fearful of department stores bringing on proletarian rule was a Member of Parliament of the notoriously antisemitic constituency of Bretten. He represented the farmers' association (*Bund der Landwirte*). This sort of party, however, never had any significant support. Even at the height of their popularity in 1880–1920, in the 1893 and 1898 elections, parties with antisemitic tendencies won only 3 per cent of the votes.[38] When an antisemitic society formed in Donaueschingen in 1894, the local papers noted that they would refrain from commenting on its foundations as it might encourage something which 'certainly is not a blessing for humanity'.[39] Antisemitism and anti-capitalism, although existent, lacked a consensus and a broad base, making it an insufficient starting point from which to launch the National Socialists on a larger scale in Germany, particularly in more liberal areas.

The German people considered the threat of communism and open conflict breaking out on the streets as far more frightening than Jews as a people.[40] For some voters, the NSDAP provided a bulwark against communism, accepting antisemitism almost as a lesser evil to extreme left-wing politics. In 1923, the NSDAP had begun to gain some support in the environs of the industrial city of Mannheim, a traditional bulwark of the SPD. In contrast, in the countryside they took the place of small local or specialist antisemitic or right-wing parties. Making a concerted effort to gain votes in more rural areas such as Franconia, they gained 7 per cent of the seats in the state parliament of 1929.[41] There were, however, areas, such as the Catholic villages of the Black Forest, in which they gained only 0.6 to 3.4 per cent of the vote.[42] The membership of the Nazi Party itself grew rapidly, from 100,000 in the autumn of 1928 to 150,000 a year later.[43] So, they had managed to find some support in 1929 as a protest vote, but they needed to expand their appeal if they wanted to wield power. The *Mittelstand* was an ideal group to concentrate on as it was 'conservative and not radical. That makes a good impression – naturally also abroad when the party can show amongst its ranks many members of the *Mittelstand*', as one young boy noted his father saying.[44]

Agitators specializing in appealing to the *Mittelstand* voter were dispatched to the areas of Germany less inclined to vote for the NSDAP by 1930.[45] These National Socialists propagandists would prove masterful in blaming the crisis on the republican system and those who appeared to flourish by its support.[46] Here the Nazi rhetoric was less anti-communist and more anti-capitalist. Point 16 of the 1920 Nazi Party manifesto promised the creation of a healthy *Mittelstand* and the leasing of department stores to small businesses. In these early days of the party, they had but a tenuous grasp on how the economy worked. Department store owners were already aware of the party before it came to prominence. By 1931, the *Zeitschrift für Kauf- und Warenhäuser*, an official publication of the federation of department store owners, felt it necessary to dedicate an entire article to Nazism, an unusual defence for a magazine concerned usually with the minutia of accounting techniques, window displays and congratulatory notes to long-serving members of staff. In the article, they summarize the same arguments and stories that countless similar individuals and organizations had previously levelled against department stores, but which were now increasingly represented solely by the NSDAP. One such allegation against the department stores was they were no better than banks, companies listed on stock markets or consumer cooperatives,[47] and that they were out to dupe the masses out of their hard-earned money by selling products of poor quality. Something the department store magazine naturally denied. Their true role was, so the Jewish retailers believed, still in the supplying of good, mass-produced wares at reasonable prices thereby providing the population with the necessities of life at reasonable price during a period of intense economic depression.[48]

For the Nazis, department stores, banks, cooperatives and so on looked like they were successful because of their substantial presence on the high street, and most of these were seemingly run by Jews. However, the building projects that gave the impression of immense affluence had been financed at a time when credit was easy. In addition, more than 80 per cent of all Jewish-run retailing establishments in Germany were small or medium sized – so firmly placed within the boundaries of the *Mittelstand*.[49] Adept propagandists the Nazis established groups within their movement to appeal to social and political subgroupings, appealing to everyone from the steel worker to the diligent housewife. In an age before the internet or television and before the radio was widely used, the main medium of disseminating information was the press. The Germans were avid newspaper readers; nearly every political party had a local paper, with some being published daily in larger cities. Nazi press service published a newspaper in every German city. They featured propaganda specifically tailored for the area masquerading as serious local and international news.

As the city of Mannheim had more department stores than any other in the area, the local Nazi publication *Das Hakenkreuzbanner* crusaded particularly against the stores here. The other press who reported favourably on department stores did so only in return for bribes which took the form of lucrative advertising contracts, so they claimed. 'Whoever feeds off the Jew', the *Hakenkreuzbanner* warns the readers, 'will die from it.'[50] The Schmoller store, so the Nazi press claimed, had increased the working day by an hour and cut the pay of its staff simultaneously by 15 to 20 per cent: 'Unfortunately, today no member of staff dares to have the profit-Jew's hands inspected by the labour court.'[51] Instead, a commission of 'garlic and flat-footed Indians' had encouraged the distribution of chairs for staff to sit and rest upon; 'but woe betide the employee that dares make use of this welcome installation'.[52] How much, if any, of this was true is hard to say in retrospect. Certainly many stores had to make special arrangements for their workforce, or had to sack them altogether. It is clear, however, that the National Socialists were stirring up negative sentiment towards department stores on a level hitherto unheard of in the local press.

The year 1931, in which the above article was published, was summarized by one chamber of commerce as 'rock bottom'. Turnover fell by half, and even hitherto stable companies became victims of the 'economic catastrophe'.[53] *Der Führer*, another 'local' Nazi paper, took up the baton, demanding a taxation of department stores as only this would save the 'great majority of the people and the doomed *Mittelstand*'.[54] The National Socialists' anti-department store rhetoric placed a particular emphasis on the Jewish nature of this type of business which had been a rare occurrence previously.[55] They attempted in city councils to introduce measures against department stores that local authorities did not have the power to do. The National Socialists, however, managed to present the matter as if the established parties were unwilling, rather than unable, to consider the tax.[56] In Freiburg, the NSDAP even tried to force the mayor to present the problem before the umbrella organization of city councils.[57] In Karlsruhe, the Nazis managed in mid-May 1932 to exclude the department stores from the retail traders association.[58] Yet in Freiburg and Konstanz, the stores remained members, even having the presidents requesting that they be permitted to stay in the association. Their existence, so Carl Werner and his colleague said, did not have an adverse effect on trade. The National Socialists pounced on the statement, describing the men endorsing department stores as being 'hit with blindness', and acting like 'Little Red Riding Hood freely giving herself to be eaten by the Wolf'.[59] Salman Schocken lamented: 'We have never had such strong propaganda against us as now.'[60] Nazi rhetoric was 'like a revival meeting, and local shop owners, with big round eyes and open mouths, drank it all up ... It was only natural given a competitive environment that threatened to swallow them. Instead of adapting as he [Schocken] had advised them, these shopkeepers, especially the inexperienced ones with grievances, found in the Nazi views on race a convenient weapon to keep the modern "Jewish" commercial system at bay.'[61]

In Berlin, the NSDAP had a much stronger foothold than in the southwest. Georg Wertheim himself was physically attacked, and his shop windows smashed by SA brownshirts. To protect themselves, several large businesses in the capital established a society for their safety – effectively a private police. Under various guises, including the Combat Alliance for the preservation of the

German Mittelstand (Kampfbund zur Erhaltung des deutschen Mittelstandes), the NSDAP organized not just its thugs, but also quite respectable looking indexes of businesses in which it advised people to shop.[62] A good German, so the Nazis believed, could be a consumer, but only in a store not run by Jews.

Department store taxation

During almost the entire Weimar Republic, the issue of taxing department stores, branches or similar large retail businesses never got as far as the Baden Parliament. There are no calls of the *Mittelstand* for government protection from department stores in their records. That there were movements advocating such ideas at all is not discernible in parliamentary documents until 1932, when it is mentioned for the first time in the minutes of a plenary meeting. The parliamentary president's arms must have been stiff from ringing his bell calling the house to order: members were interrupting each other, behaving raucously and ostentatiously exiting the chamber when they didn't agree. Over the din, the prominent SPD politician Leopold Rückert was trying to make himself heard: 'Some business people complain about department stores' he bellowed; the National Socialists in particular were siding with them, 'which makes it quite interesting that you take money from the department stores'. He revealed that the National Socialists had approached Woolworths three times in the past year with a request for funding. Rückert pointed out the hypocrisy, adding: 'The language and tone of the National Socialists is not grown on native soil, it is an imitation, maybe a bad imitation, of fascism in Italy … It has been said by one of your men: "Politics is made of crooks." I never thought you knew yourselves so well.'[63] The chamber dissolved in laughter.

A month later, in May 1932, the question of department store tax was the subject of a parliamentary session in Baden for the first time since the First World War. A branch or chain store tax (*Filialsteuer*) was being considered on insurance companies, banks and department stores. It was brought forward by Friedrich Graf of the majority Catholic Centre Party (Zentrum).[64] The usual reasons that had been trotted out in 1900 for the tax were listed, including the destruction of local shops by department stores. The indifference of the public to these problems was, however, highlighted: 'It is almost senseless, for example, if on the one side some country folk make their purchases at chain stores and at the same time buy coconut fat, margarine and similar things, and then expect on the other side from the working class to buy butter, cheese, eggs etc. from the *Mittelstand*.'[65]

Both nationalist parties in parliament (which had nine seats) believed the proposed law did not go far enough. 'We are of the opinion ... that a department store tax must come and that the tax should be extended to the cooperative societies, ... either one wants to help the *Mittelstand* and really has the courage to do so or one doesn't.'[66] The communist Georg Lechleiter pointed out that the proposal would not help the *Mittelstand* at all, as they were neither the beneficiaries of the levy nor would branch stores be inhibited from operating. He was also concerned about the potential loss of jobs, not least in the manufacturing industry. Woolworths had bought German products worth 40 million *Marks* in the past year. Would they continue to do so if the tax was introduced, and 'what might the impact be on the German worker?'[67] The Communist Party hence decided to vote against the proposition as neither the *Mittelstand* nor the German worker would profit.

The SPD also considered the law useless for achieving what it set out to do. Graf believed that in a healthy economy choices were made by the consumer alone, which is why it seemed ridiculous to him that 'on the one hand we very often hear from those advocating the branch tax the call for a free market economy, the call for free market forces, but, on the other hand, as soon as any unpleasant competitor turns up they demand special taxes'.[68] The same would happen as before if the law was passed – department stores would pass on the increase to their manufacturers. Partisan politics were relatively unimportant for the average German shopping for necessity or pleasure, Graf emphasized. If one was able to see the political leanings of shoppers,

> one would find amongst them very many that made propaganda against department stores. Department stores are well visited by *Mittelstand* and the National Socialists from town and country. I say, it is a matter for the public, of the customers themselves. By one's own actions one might help the *Mittelstand* more than by taxation laws, which do not achieve what they set out to do.[69]

Historically, in time of economic distress, most established German politicians distanced themselves quite clearly from unreasonably taxing department stores. Nevertheless, the tax was passed in spite of misgivings from both sides. The idea was to support municipalities with the revenue, although actually the income (estimated at just 200,000 *Marks*) was to be used to support the 'value producing' unemployed.[70] This was hence not to be a way of supporting the *Mittelstand*. The law was not enforced immediately in 1932.[71] When the branch tax was agreed upon in principle, all parties endeavoured to ensure that the National Socialists could not claim it as their own achievement. The moderate parties agreed on this to prevent the Nazis gaining traction. A representative of the Communist Party even presented a copy of the Nazi's main newspaper, *Völkische Beobachter*, read aloud some of the anti-department store propaganda from it and then – amidst howling laughter from the other parties – produced a supplement from the pages of the newspaper of just such an establishment.[72] The finance minister Dr Wilhelm Mattes of the German People's Party(Deutsche Volkspartei) could not help closing the debate with a dig at the NSDAP by mentioning the millions of *Marks* of debt they had accumulated since sharing power in Thuringia and Brunswick.[73]

Unlike the department store introduced earlier in the century, this had the potential to majorly impact business as income was much lower than it was in 1900: While on the one hand, Georg Wertheim requested a deferment of payments, on the other, the board at Karstadt concluded that the company was in such a desolate state that the reintroduction of department store tax was the least of their worries.[74]

The banking crisis

On 11 May 1931, the Austrian Credit Bank (Österreichische Creditanstalt) had to admit that it had lost practically its entire capital. The Karstadt AG announced its greatest losses to date on the same day. Bank creditors in fear of their investment withdrew their money, causing a run on banks throughout Europe. By July, three major German banks, including the Dresdner Bank, announced their insolvency. All banks were closed on 14 and 15 July 1931 to prevent customers withdrawing their savings. By the end of the month, the cabinet under Chancellor Brünning had agreed on the establishment of the Akzept- und Garantiebank, an institution that gave state-backed credit to banks.[75] Where exactly the German state in turn was supposed to get the necessary backing was a mystery. The now practically state-owned Dresdner Bank was amalgamated with several other ailing banking institutions: 50 per cent of the Commerzbank was owned by the Reichsbank, with a further 14 per cent owned directly by the state, giving the state a share of 64 per cent of the business. The Deutsche Bank remained nominally independent, but had a third of its capital kept as guarantee by a state bank.[76] Most small banks collapsed altogether and larger ones were now controlled by the state, either directly by the treasury, via the Reichsbank or through an intermediate agency.

Figure 6.4 A promotional stamp from the Wronker company, the flagship store on Frankfurt's high street acting almost as a coronet to the 'W' emblazoned on the shield. © Author.

Figure 6.5 A display of sausages and cartoon pigs in the window of the same store in January 1932. By the end of that year, the company would no longer be owned by the Wronker family, poor financial management having forced Max Wronker into a purely managerial position. The name was changed to HANSA in 1934 to sever all connections to the family of Jewish origin. © Author.

Collapses of Karstadt and Wronker

Karstadt's new stores, new factories, hotels and haulage company had all been fuelled by the easy credit available before the New York Stock Exchange and Banking Crash. The company was on the edge of financial ruin, and yet still Schöndorff drove the expansion further and his critics off the board. He even purchased the department stores of Lindemann & Co. AG.[77] The fiftieth anniversary of the founding of the first Karstadt store and Rudolph Karstadt's seventy-fifth birthday were not marked in 1931 – so desolate was the financial situation. The flagship store on the Hermannplatz in Berlin now looked like the work of a megalomaniac. The banks, which had gradually become the majority shareholders, took control, evicting Schöndorff. The new board in 1931, chosen by the consortium of banks and creditors, consisted entirely of members of non-Jewish origin. They handed back a branch of Lindemann & Co., sold assets, closed stores, liquidated associated companies and sold much of the property.[78]

Although Wronker proclaimed itself 'a masterpiece of mercantile organization' in 1931, the company was not in good financial shape.[79] In 1929, the turnover had been 31.14 million *Marks*, but by 1930, this had dropped to 27 million.[80] In the 1930–1 financial year alone, the company lost 2 million *Marks*.[81] By 1931, the firm had debts in excess of 7 million *Marks*: the firm was bankrupt. 'The cause of this breakdown is, according to a periodical for clothes retailers, down to the economic crisis, and in particular due to the declining purchasing power and losses caused in the stock room', a Mannheim paper noted.[82] The Dresdner Bank and the Mannheimer Hypothekenbank, the main creditors, put the Wronker company up for sale. Dr Bacharach, a director of the Dresdner Bank, took over as chairman of the board and offered to waive the personal debt Hermann Wronker had accumulated if he handed over the company entirely to the creditors.[83] A price of 7 million *Marks* was considered a ludicrous sum for the shipwrecked department store and selling the company as a whole was impossible as little of it was profitable.[84]

Salman Schocken was subsequently approached by Bacharach as a potential investor. Schocken agreed to look at the accounts to see what might interest him. He was soon disenchanted with the prospect, dismissing much of the content of the books presented to him as 'fantasy'.[85] The company had 'a faulty design' at its core he concluded.[86] It was clear that Hermann Wronker had managed to siphon off money from the company into his own pocket. Salman Schocken commented in private that he got 'the impression the business is worse than it looks' and blamed this on the unhealthy influence of Hermann Wronker's wife Ida.[87] In September 1932, the creditors were assembled a last time, and by the end of that year the Wronker family had departed from their business, leaving only Max Wronker as a salaried manager of a Frankfurt branch.[88]

Well-established and familiar retailing empires fell victim to the economic crisis, among them were two of the best known, Karstadt and Wronker. While their names – for now – remained the same, at the core they were already different companies run by banks as investors, not families and long-term shareholders.

Wronker and Karstadt were not the only department stores to suffer under the financial collapse. The brief economic respite in the mid-1920s had caused some companies to overstretch themselves. According to Georg Wertheim, up to the end of the 1920s, 'banks almost pursued one with offers of credit'.[89] Wertheim's turnover continued to rise each year between 11 per cent and 27 per cent between 1924 and 1933.[90] This, however, did not reflect a rise in profits. In 1932, the company made a loss of 43 per cent. Wertheim could only salvage its position by jettisoning its foreign branches and had to accept most unfavourable conditions in August 1932 from the Akzept- und Garantiebank.[91]

The Hermann Tietz company was no better off. They had purchased the entire business of Adolf Jandorf, most of whose stores needed considerable renovation. The KaDeWe, also part of the package, had spent hundreds of millions on adding two extra levels to it. In addition to which they still had 8 million *Reichsmark* to pay Jandorf's son Harry. Hermann Tietz had been on the verge of collapse before. In 1900, their main source of credit, the Pommernbank, had gone bankrupt.[92] In the book on his family's firm, Georg Tietz turns the alarming altercations between himself and the director of the Deutsche Bank before the First World War into a tale of paternal affection, later claiming the head of the bank had simply wanted to teach him a valuable life lesson, whereas in fact the company was on the brink of collapse.[93]

When Knopf, with easy credit, completely gutted and refaced the store in Freiburg in 1928, the local papers sang praises of their interiors and

Knopf continued improving their building stock, in spite of economic problems. Expanding the branch in Pforzheim in 1931, the company was praised in the highest tones by the local paper: 'That it has, just at the present time of the collapse, the general depression and the giant unemployment [embarked on this project] is an act of a strong business mind, an expression of the soundness of the company and at the same time a charitable act. Many craftsmen and workers found rewarding employment in the conversion and approximately 70 staff members will have to be gradually employed.'[94] On the same occasion, another journalist described Max Knopf as a 'solid old business man' who trusted in 'his lucky star and *German work ethic*'.[95] Similar articles, voicing the gratitude of the local people for the work and employment department stores gave can be found in newspapers whenever a new building project was completed by a department store. Work was hard to come by, and anyone who provided it welcomed.

The same year a small party was held in the grand carpet department of the main Knopf store in Karlsruhe to mark the fiftieth anniversary of the company's founding. Present were family, employees, colleagues and representatives of the chamber of commerce and the authorities.[96] Those of the company who had lost their lives during the war were remembered during the celebration, after which Max Knopf received congratulatory speeches, not only from his managers, the staff representatives, the sister company in Freiburg and the department store association, but also from the chamber of commerce. The president of the chamber made a speech in which he reported 'from his own experience of the past fifty years and from his personal relationship with the founder of the store'.[97] Max Knopf was presented with the highest honour of the chamber of commerce, just before the president of the State Centre for Retailing (Landeszentrale des badischen Einzelhandels) spoke of 'the many services of Mr Knopf in the work of his organization'.[98] Less than two years before the National Socialists took power, and in the midst of a horrible financial crisis, the representatives of the *Mittelstand* celebrated the Jew from Poznan.

Continued success at Schocken

As the German treasury had influence over most banks by the end of 1932, the majority of large department stores were de facto owned by the Reich.[99] The only exception was Schocken. They had quite drastically changed their operation system in the 1920s: fewer and higher quality products were sold in return for a greater mark-up. After the First World War, the firm had expanded greatly. From 1926 onwards, Schocken moved from concentrating on Saxonian towns and villages to locations throughout southern and central Germany.[100] New stores were opened in Nuremberg, Stuttgart and Chemnitz. The designs by Erich Mendelsohn used for these stores set standards for modern architecture. Overnight the Schocken branch at Nuremberg became the most profitable department store in Germany.[101] By 1933, the company had thirty branches of which Salman was incredibly proud: 'There are four companies that are bigger, much bigger. But maybe we are – without being conceited – the best equipped, and we are also the company that has expanded most strongly in recent years.'[102]

Salman had been running the company by himself for a few years, together with his loyal director Georg Manasse, when Wronker became bankrupt. In the end, Salman chose to salvage just one Wronker branch in the town of Pforzheim, renowned for its quality and small-scale manufacture of precision instruments. Taking over the Pforzheim store was not ideal for Schocken: 'Before I cause myself a nuisance with an old business, with inventories, personnel, which must be dismissed if not appropriate, I have opened a new store that is our speciality.'[103] Although reluctant at first to purchase the store, Salman's meticulous research gave him sufficient confidence that there was a market for his company in Pforzheim.

In the late 1920s and early 1930s, Pforzheim had approximately 80,000 inhabitants employed mainly in high-end manufacturing. It was not unlike Zwickau or Regensburg and mirrored the type of demographic Salman Schocken had successfully dealt with in the past. 'To anyone who doesn't know Pforzheim and sees it for the first time it gives an impression of particular wealth. This may be an illusion, but it could also be a reflection of the actual conditions …, the industry [is] an industry of small entrepreneurs. From this comes a certain wealth across the board.'[104] There was clearly a clientele for Schocken's superior goods. As Knopf 'is inferior in taste and as a whole the nature of the business is below our genre' and 'there are virtually no speciality stores', there was clearly a gap in the market Schocken could fill. Although the building was not to Salman's liking – he had got too used to the sleek lines of Mendelsohn – the Wronker branch at Pforzheim was purchased.[105] It is remarkable that Schocken made a success of the old Wronker store in Pforzheim, which reopened in late September 1931 in the midst of the financial crisis. It speaks of Salman's optimism that the firm managed to make the store a success. Continued improvement since its foundation had made Schocken incredibly competitive in spite of the dour outlook on the economy.

The *Pforzheim Rundschau* could excitedly report of the masses jostling into the store – so great was the crush that the doors had to be closed to prevent accidents. 'The external appearance of brightness, clarity and straightforwardness characterizes also the inner nature of the company. Brief words on the pillars etc. indicate the inventory from afar, the same goes for the clean price tags which make asking almost superfluous.'[106]

By the end 1932, department stores, most of which had been established over fifty years ago, were household names, almost part of the family for staff (of which there were tens of thousands) and customers (of which they had millions). Though their actual percentage of retail was negligible, at their height in the late 1920s, department stores accounted for just 5 per cent of national sales,[107] they were regarded as large and visible examples of successful business. One could even say their sustained existence was almost patriotic, continuing a tradition of backing Germany as a nation and an economy. Since the Empire's foundation and through the First World War and the tumultuous years of the founding of the first republic, they had provided necessary and beautiful items to every strata of German society and granted lucrative contracts to German industry. Unfortunately, that vision was a hollow one. Department stores had become 'too big to fail'. De facto the businesses were largely owned by banks, who in turn were supported by the state. Thus on the eve of the Nazi's victory over the German democratic system, many Jewish names emblazoned across the department stores in German cities were no more than historic evidence of former ownership.[108] The Reichstag elections of July and November 1932 saw the NSDAP emerge as the party with the most seats in the national parliament. The parties who had supported the Weimar Republic were now a minority. In order to prevent any left-wing coalition forming, the conservative politician Heinrich von Papen, taking over as chancellor from Heinrich Brüning, formed a weak government tolerated by President Hindenburg and the National Socialists. The chancellorship was within Hitler's grasp. By January 1933, he was in power and the symbiotic bond between retailers of Jewish origin and the German population was questioned seriously and violently for the first time.

7
Fall: 1933–9
'Two Million Hitler Portraits'

From the 1880s to the late 1920s, Jewish department stores in Germany were viewed by trade and retail authorities as rivals and colleagues, by the government as economically legitimate, by local administrators as accommodating businesses, by staff as good employers, by the press as welcome investors and by customers as efficient and pleasant shopping venues. The month Hitler took power, the German Federation of Department Stores was able to publish a quietly optimistic piece regarding the future: 'There are still families which have, for generations, purchased their wares from the same department store', and key to that success was the personal relationship between customer and store, and the trust in the quality of their products.[1] Fiery anti-capitalist, antisemitic and supposedly pro-*Mittelstand* rhetoric was ineffectual for almost fifty years.

The National Socialists, who would establish this hate as a core part of their model of German society, had no traditional support for their policies in the population, were unsuccessful at the ballot box in 1928, were belittled by established parties and yet grasped the reins of power firmly by March 1933. Only a few years earlier in 1927, Carl Werner, a prominent and some-time chair of the chamber of commerce and of retail in Freiburg, had been to Italy and was horrified at the fascist regime there. The beauty of the landscape alone allowed him to get over 'the nationally less pleasing' sides of Italy.[2] However, in the years since, like so many of his fellow shopkeepers, Werner had listened to Hitler on the radio, had even read *Mein Kampf* and, although he admitted the NSDAP's methods took some getting used to, agreed in principle with the 'constructive ideas' that promised to bring stability to Germany.[3] Eventually owned by practically everyone, it was a rare occurrence to have actually read Hitler's tirade of a book, and so Werner was making quite sure he made a well-informed choice at the ballot box. This chapter will show how the belief in 'constructive ideas' for a better future alarmingly and swiftly escalated into violence and murder, bringing

Figure 7.1 'Mutual cheating ... intended to transform the world ... into one big department store, in the lobbies of which the busts of the most cunning profiteers ... were to be stored for eternity.' Adolf Hitler, in *Mein Kampf*, on Jewish run-department stores. Adolf Hitler in a widely available reproduction of a portrait by Heinrich Knirr. © German Propaganda Archive, Calvin University.

centuries of Jewish life in Germany to a hideous end. It will become apparent just how haphazard and sometime ineffective the discrimination of people with Jewish origins was, making the mass-killing of a large section of this part of the German population, under the eyes of the rest of society, even more shocking.

On 30 January 1933, Georg Wertheim noted in his diary: 'Hitler called by Hindenburg to govern'.[4] Apart from the day he spent with the Emperor, back in the days of the old regime, Georg could keep the thoughts he confided to his diary very brief at quite momentous occasions. One might assume that, although moved, he was sticking to this cool style. However, antisemites like Hitler had been around for a long time, not in quite such prominent positions, but nevertheless a factor to be considered in life ever since Georg and any other Jewish-born person could remember. In Italy, indeed, many Jews had been members of Mussolini's Fascist Party since its foundation in 1919, some becoming government ministers. By the time the first antisemitic legislation was passed in 1938, a third of all Italian-Jewish adults were party members.[5] The Nazis introduced censorship a few days after Hitler was made chancellor. Within just weeks, in the wake of the burning of the Reichstag on 27 February 1933, basic rights were suspended. Arrests could be made without charge. At the national elections on 5 March, the NSDAP lost some of their constituencies. To bolster their majority, the communist members of the Reichstag were simply excluded. Tolerated by the Catholic Centre Party, Hitler's government could now rule without consent of parliament.

The Nazis' success at the ballot box, now heavily funded by big business, and the partially engineered Reichstag configuration in March 1933 did not, however, reflect the distribution of power in the states or municipalities across Germany. Yet the parties that may have prevented them taking over failed to unite in opposition. On the left, the communists and the SPD bickered, while the centre-right had a myriad of issues, with Protestants against Catholics and libertarians against conservatives. The German states (who controlled the police force for instance) and powerful local authorities (who were responsible for a great deal of schooling) were still in the hands of a variety of political parties. For the country the Nazis wished to create, such a diversity of authority was unacceptable. Days after the election, members of the Nazi Storm Detachment (Sturmabteilung), commonly referred to as brownshirts, forcibly entered government and municipal buildings all over Germany to hoist the swastika flag.[6] Prussia, the largest and most influential state, was already governed by a leading Nazi, Herman Göring, so there was no problem there. In Freiburg, the brownshirts marched on the town hall, hanging out the Nazi Party flag against the protestations of the mayor. In Karlsruhe, officials took the flag down again, only to have it rehoisted by brownshirts amidst 'Heil Hitler' calls from the crowd below. In Mannheim, as noted by a young lady in her diary, the swastika was seen banner flying from the palace and town hall.[7]

To the symbolic act of the victorious conqueror, the National Socialists added intimidation, confusion and mayhem with an aim of discrediting established authority. In Freiburg, a mixture of defamation and physical abuse ousted the mayor, Dr Bender, causing him to leave office in spite of wide support from the population, the resident archbishop and university vice chancellor.[8] The man who succeeded him was the editor of *Der Alemanne*, the same paper that had created a smear campaign against Bender. Nazi sympathizers massed on the streets of Karlsruhe chanting and molesting passers-by. The police were unable – and some unwilling – to keep control.[9] Similar incidents occurred all over the country, with the Nazis creating havoc. People in authority, if not members of the NSDAP, were asked to hand over their posts in order to guarantee public peace – a peace the Nazis themselves had disrupted. If they refused, they were dragged from their offices.[10] State prime ministers were replaced with loyal party members. Robert Wagner, the senior Nazi for Baden, who had the Centre Party head of government thrown onto the streets, announced the future 'spiritual regeneration' of state and economy: 'We are unwilling to have our work disturbed by the Centre Party, their press or their long obsolete government.'[11] The just wrath of the German people had brought them to power, he claimed, yet a great deal of brutality and persuasion was necessary to cement it.[12] The National Socialist Party alone was to direct every aspect of German life in future. The complete reorganizing of politics, administration, industry and education reaching far into the private sphere and home was dubbed 'coordination'. By mid-March, the swastika banner had officially replaced the republican flag.[13] The German states, the bedrock of the federation for almost a millennium, lost their independence in March and April 1933, becoming nothing more than administrative units. Parliaments became rubber stamps. Jewish delegates were taken into, what the National Socialists called, protective custody during May 1933.[14] The civil service – never entirely happy with the loss of its imperial and unquestioned status – was brought to heel more or less willingly.[15] With political institutions firmly in their grip, the Nazis gradually gained control of courts, unions, professional organizations and nearly every part of public life, including their own version of Protestantism. During the entire process, Jews were eliminated from public life first and foremost, followed by all things that were considered Jewish, including communism and socialism, liberalism and pacifism, and artistic and sexual freedom. Similarly, capitalism, where it did not fit into the Nazi's plan for a war economy, was branded 'Jewish'. The official handling of department stores was now subject to the inconsistent whims of the national NSDAP agencies and civil servants.

Consolidating power

During March 1933, the brownshirts had organized protests against Jewish stores in some German towns. In Brunswick, the events were so violent they were later dubbed the 'Storm on the Department Stores'. In Karlsruhe, in contrast, the police acted swiftly, bringing the main perpetrators to account. The Nazi leadership officially denounced the protests.[16] On 1 April, however, the first nationally organized so-called boycotts were staged. Jewish shops and department stores – even those with merely Jewish sounding names – were besieged by SA men, daubing windows with antisemitic slogans, haranguing those who tried to enter shops and photographing those that did. The campaign had previously been announced in the press, including lists of the stores to be targeted. The German Association of Department Stores had warned its members of the potential assault on their businesses and advised them to stay closed wherever possible.[17] In Berlin, some had heeded the advice; in the provinces, few did.[18] On the day in question, as the brownshirts marched down the high street, the branch manager of Knopf in Freiburg instructed the burly men from the carpet department to pull down and fasten the shutters, and the staff was ordered to stand well away from the windows. Once the SA men had departed, the shutters went up and business continued as normal.[19] In Karlsruhe, customers found a way around the boycott:

> In the Knopf store there was a very cosy cafe where the ladies enjoyed meeting each other in the afternoon. On the afternoon of 1 April, my mother went with some girlfriends, as agreed, to the entrance of the store, where SA men blocked their access. However, the women knew what to do. There was a staff entrance on the Zähnringerstrasse and through entering here they still got into the cafe.[20]

Georg Wertheim's stores, in spite of the fact that he had converted, were not spared entirely. He tried to contact Hitler and Göring through his banker Emil Georg von Stauss. Stauss only got as far as an adjutant of Hitler, who in turn contacted the Ministry of the Interior explaining that, in spite of being Jewish-owned or having Jewish staff, department stores were in debt to the state via government-controlled banks.²¹ Stauss later regretted not having exerted his influence to protect other stores, but it is hard to say how effective he was. Wertheim was not spared by the brownshirts, even if he was not forced to close as a result of their actions. According to the propagandist Julius Streich, when it came to department stores, 'religion does not enter into it. Jewish businessmen and dissidents who have been baptised Catholics or Protestants are Jews.'²²

The public displays in the streets were not well received by the German population. It was the SA that was identified as the alien element in the calm bustle of the main road in Freiburg.²³ By pre-empting the assault on their shops or closing briefly, the storeowners managed to appear as the active agent on the high street, meaning the brownshirts were robbed of their stage. Almost all photographs of the day from various cities show a half a dozen brownshirts posing in front of shuttered Jewish shops – gaped at by the local ragamuffins, with people with bags and baskets standing further back waiting to continue their shopping. The unsuccessful boycotts forced the Nazi press to exaggerate the success of the day's events.²⁴ The Council Jews of Baden (Badischer Oberrat der Israeliten), of which various department store managers were members, declared in the press the next day their willingness to help with the rebuilding of Germany and their deep connection to their 'Badische Heimat'.²⁵ Privately, Germans noted in their diary that they thought the events of the day had been 'horrible processions'. One lady, who had been harangued by an SA officer for shopping at Knopf, came home 'completely distraught and cursed the regime'.²⁶ In many places, people demonstratively broke through the lines to enter Jewish shops.²⁷ A popular pro-department store song in Mannheim at the time went as follows:

> For only fifty Pfennigs one can, from Schmoller and Company,
> Kit out a pretty young lady, from head to the knee:
> For ten Pfennigs the petticoat, for twenty the shoe,
> For thirty the dress – and a scarf too!
>
> Refrain: Listen up! That is a business. That still brings a profit.
> Not everyone can do that: You must understand it!²⁸

People would distinguish between their affable Jewish neighbour and the evil Jewish capitalist or communist.²⁹ For over fifty years, department stores had been a good neighbour and provider of essential and lovely things, too long to fall into the category of 'evil'. The National Socialists, now in power, were confronted with two problems. First, the German population was not prepared to tolerate open violence on the street, especially not from the ruling party.[30] One of the reasons the Nazis had been elected was because they had promised public order. Second, department stores were a significant economic force. The stores were too important as employers and creditors to be closed.[31] In the Nazi's 'battle for work', they could not afford to have as one of their first policies any measure that would put tens of thousands of people out of work and ruin the supply chains of major German manufacturing businesses. As department stores were now largely owned by banks, and those in turn propped up by state guarantee, department stores had been practically nationalized anyway. The Nazis needed to come up with some other way of dealing with them.

Official documentary evidence on retailing is lacking, and proof of how Jewish influence was ousted from business is even scarcer; perpetrators were not keen to leave a paper trail. Georg Tietz's history of his family's businesses, published in 1965, ends in 1923, drawing a veil over the imprudent investments in Jandorf. In addition, the Nazi leadership did not provide a unified front against department stores. While, on the one hand, Hitler is reported to have reprimanded Finance Minister Alfred Hugenberg for proposing to act severely against department stores, on the other, his successor as minister, Kurt Schmitt, apparently needed to convince Hitler to do the opposite.[32] This has led to confusion in popular German history over the process. In postwar Germany, there has been a tendency towards reporting the years after 1933 in a clear-cut manner, as the years of the brutal calculating Nazi profiteer and the subjugated passive Jewish entrepreneur. Symptomatic of this is the tendency of historians to sum up the entire process under the neat heading of 'Aryanization', a word seldom used by the Nazi hierarchy. For a while, the regime evens struggled to define what a Jewish business was, relying on trial and error to find out, which was their usual modus of operation.[33] Unlike with the laws for the restoration of the German civil servant of April 1933, there is no single moment at which all Jews were simultaneously expelled from business. This means there was no coherent way Jewish owners were expelled, reflecting the Nazis' conflicting policies and actions.[34] The large wholesale plunder was completely disorganized. 'Pillaging' may be a more suitable term.

Due to department store's economic importance, the National Socialists embarked on a haphazard and often clandestine path, promising their followers a more concerted effort against stores once the economy had stabilized.[35] The National Socialists were not organized in the approach, while the Jewish businessmen were more ingenious in dealing with challenges. Although some Nazi hotheads continued to physically assault shoppers at Schocken and photograph those at Knopf and Tietz, they did so without support from the party leadership.[36] Lists were published itemizing the sorts of thing that hitherto had been done on an ad-hoc basis against Jewish businesses, expressly forbidding the use of any of them.[37] In December 1933, the NSDAP forbade the disruption of the Christmas shopping season. Salman Schocken, however, complained that the party was clearly not able or willing to stop their local ruffians.[38] At first glance, 1934–7 could be considered a respite for Jews from Nazi harassment; however, Jewish businessmen were slowly ousted from their firms in a variety of ways which were almost imperceptible to the public and thus much more devious.[39]

Department stores continued their operations as best they could after the boycotts of 1 April 1933. A month later, on Labour Day, Georg Wertheim had the red and white swastika banner hoisted above his flagship store for the first time.[40] It seems just about anything was done to appease; anything to keep the business going. Advertisements become more frequent, and by December Knopf's central hall in Karlsruhe was turned into a winter wonderland, complete with reindeer and Saint Nicholas. As recorded by one customer:

> It glittered and sparkled everywhere and a delicate fragrance came from the decorated fir trees. Christmas sounds filled the space. My mother headed for the giant railway landscape, crafted with great love of detail. The beautiful landscape of mountains, lakes, villages, animals and small dolls took up my whole attention. It was such an exhilarating experience for me and I forgot time and space.[41]

To the consumer, things had gotten back to 'normal'. Yet, in the background, the Nazis passed laws restricting department store activities gradually in their puppet parliaments.[42] The list of punitive measures is long.

In March 1933, stores were prohibited from running events that were not associated with their trading. The same month they were prevented from expanding their stores or opening further branches 'in the interest of public peace and security as well as the protection of the *Mittelstand*'.[43] In some states, civil servants were forbidden to shop at department stores in as early as 1 March 1933. A national law prohibiting civil servants from frequenting department stores was not however passed until 1938.[44] Losing this relatively financially secure demographic was an enormous blow. In more than one department store, members of staff turned informant. In one case, a head of personnel was 'not interested in the revenue of his employer, but spent his entire working time busily noting down the names of those civil servants that continued to buy in Jewish department stores'.[45]

The Department Store Federation Committee was forcibly evicted and replaced with non-Jewish members early in 1933 – these were men who previously had no noticeable role in the organization, but towed the party line. On 25 March 1933, Dr Walther Spieker was announced as Salman Schocken's successor as president of the Department Store Federation.[46] Spieker had been the president of the Federation of Medium and Large German Retailers (Reichsverbandes der Mittel- und Grossbetriebe des Deutschen Einzelhandels). He became a department store owner only after he acquired the Landauer business based in Stuttgart.

Permission to raise a department store tax was given on 15 July 1933, but only Anhalt and Hamburg chose to do so.[47] In the same month, department stores were also banned from selling perishable goods which meant the loss of food halls and delicatessen departments. The struggle to prevent the closure of food halls and refreshment rooms was highly emotional elsewhere, as agriculture and suppliers had grown dependent on orders from department stores.[48] They were a key factor in the economy. In addition, apprentices from department stores were gradually more penalized by guild examination boards, and marriage loans issued from 1933 by the state could not be redeemed in large stores.[49]

Rapidly these measures proved to be more effective than publicly denouncing Jews. In October 1933, Schocken, so proud of its financial independence, felt it necessary to begin economizing; the first way to make savings within the company was to reduce the number of staff.[50] With the changed political landscape, Schocken felt it necessary also to adapt the tone of correspondence with their suppliers. In future, letters turning down unsolicited or unreasonably high manufacturers' offers were to be phrased more carefully.[51] They had, after all, weathered several severe economic downturns and a world war. Plenty of people continued to shop at Jewish stores, and the savvy entrepreneurs ensured this remained as pleasant as possible. In order to protect his customers from the thugs, Salman Schocken decided to stop using the company's iconic logo on their wrapping thereby anonymizing purchases.[52] Most stores had learned to deal with an emotionally tense German population in the previous decade. While in the 1920s, aggression had not been levelled at shops in particular, during the Weimar Republic one became used to brawling, demonstrations and even riots spilling into the stores: 'Today these march, tomorrow those, and one can say only bad things of the other. There is hardly a country where the political passions descend upon each other with such vehemence as Germany.'[53] Even if this new type of violence was aimed directly towards the stores, it could be dealt with by giving the Nazis as little chance to act public as possible; shutters could simply – like in April 1933 – be pulled down.

Cashing in on Jewish businesses

The combination of many small official measures and the public acceptance of the sort of skin-deep antisemitism that had always existed in part of German society meant it slowly became apparent that stores could not weather this storm as they had done in the past, in spite of their best efforts. It was estimated in 1934 that concerted efforts against Jewish-owned shops and businesses had lost them 135 million *Reichsmark* in sales.[54] The Nuremberg Laws, passed in November 1935, stated Jews together with 'Gypsies, Niggers and Bastards' were a danger to German blood. These laws did not affect department stores directly; yet they set down officially the policy and thoughts the Nazis had pursued from the very beginning. Each store was subjected to a different process by which Jewish influence was ousted. No single group was instrumental in ejecting Jewish owners. Wherever we look, it is a combination of national and local authorities, now firmly under Nazi control, employees and, above all, banks.

The Nazis had initially assumed that Karstadt was a Jewish business, in spite of its non-Jewish ownership and name. All other department stores had been founded by Jews and many of Karstadt's associated stores were too, which was sufficient for the NASDAP's brownshirts to organize a rogue boycott against it. Karstadt quickly tried to improve its standing with the new ruling party by sacking its Jewish staff and stopping all special events. Employees that were forced to leave had to go to court to receive any kind of compensation. Hermann Schöndorff, sacked in 1933 from his post at Karstadt, had left Germany as early as April 1933 to live in Switzerland, where he died in 1935. His villa in Berlin, built by the same architect who had designed the gigantic store on the Hermannplatz, is now the Israeli Embassy. His brother Albert, with whom he had established his original bed-making business, was not so lucky and was murdered in Auschwitz in 1942.

The Hermann Tietz company, now headed by Oscar's son Georg, had overstretched itself considerably with the purchase of the Jandorf stores and the KaDeWe, their flagship store, in the 1920s. Even though, after the so-called boycotts, the Dresdner Bank, among others, threatened to cancel their credit, the Ministry of the Economy warned that a folding of Hermann Tietz would make 14,000 people unemployed and cost German agriculture 130 million *Reichsmark* in lost income. Harming the sister company Leonhard Tietz would similarly put 20,000 people out of work.[55] At the time, the children and relatives of Oscar Tietz held approximately 24 million *Reichsmark* worth of shares in the Hermann Tietz business. Wilhelm Keppler, an early follower of Hitler and one of his main links to industry, valued them at only 8 million, forcing the price to plummet, eventually meaning the family had to sell for just 800,000 *Reichsmark* – this was legalized robbery, via the stock exchange. Hermann Tietz became 'Hertie', a brand which still inspires confidence in the German consumer today, or 'Kaufhaus Union'. In 1934, 53 per cent of Leonhard Tietz was still owned by family of the founder. The value of the shares of the company had, however, plummeted, between 1930 and 1933. During 1933 and 1934, members of management who were of Jewish origin left and the was business renamed Westdeutsche Kaufhof AG.[56]

Those stores that had run into financial difficulty in the late 1920s were already de facto owned by the German state. Here, the process was relatively straightforward. At the end of 1932, before the Nazis came to power, the Wronker family had lost control of their company entirely to the bank due to financial difficulties. Max Wronker had stayed on as a manager of one of the branches into 1933, but was sacked in 1934 along with all staff of professed Jewish faith. The company changed its name to the more Germanic sounding Hansa AG. In terms of ownership, when it came to the Tietz department store businesses and Karstadt – a company that need not be renamed as it was of non-Jewish origin – an economic process that had begun even before the Nazis came to power was completed.[57] The fate of the Wronker company demonstrates what may have befallen it even if the National Socialists had not come to power – that is the replacement of the upper echelons of the company with people who suited the banks that owned them. The difference after 1933 was that this now had a political element with strong antisemitic motivation, involving new managers running the company, the renaming of the business and the wholesale sacking of all people of Jewish origin.

Staff turn on their employers

Other department stores managed to maintain their business for longer. From the summer of 1933, Arthur Knopf's staff in Freiburg began seeing less of him. His customary morning greeting remained, though he would never be seen without his hat and coat, either arriving or leaving the store in haste. The retreating of Jewish entrepreneurs into their businesses was by no means unusual at the time.⁵⁸ Instead, Fritz Richter, the branch manager and general deputy, became the public face of the company. So much so that by the time people were entering the company in 1937, Arthur Knopf had entirely disappeared from view.⁵⁹ In 1934, Arthur Knopf signed up no fewer than sixteen new assistants, fulfilling the implied condition for his further existence by acting as an employer. He was also displaying a degree of optimism in the future of his ancestral company. The new girls were happy to be in apprenticeship, receive a good wage and work for a respectable company that had an exemplary ethos towards its staff and a still excellent reputation among its customers.⁶⁰ By their own admission, the girls knew little of the involvement of the company with the Nazi Party and its unions; at that time some of these girls were not even beyond their mid-teens. After the Second World War, Arthur Knopf's lawyers would assert that his client had been put under pressure by the shop steward and head of personnel during this time.⁶¹ Unfortunately no records exist of how the works committee forced his hand. Apart from giving the manager the title of 'company leader', the newly issued company regulations in 1934 at Knopf in Freiburg were almost identical to those published ten years previously.⁶² At least on paper, the relationship between management and staff had not changed. However, the National Socialist Workers' Union (Nationalsozialistische Betriebszellenorganisation, NSBO) issued pamphlets on how to put pressure on Jewish employees.

Before the stores changed hands, the NSBO at Hermann Tietz and Wertheim in Berlin were being told by Nazi headquarters to negotiate with their companies for two months' pay in advance and the sacking of Jewish employees.⁶³ Even here, there is no evidence showing how the proprietors reacted to the demands of the NSBO.⁶⁴ At the Nuremberg branch of Schocken, the NSBO was particularly active and exceptionally violent in character. The manager was beaten up by members of staff, but the incident covered up and the perpetrators were subsequently protected from sacking by the NSBO.⁶⁵ However, it is hard to ascertain these facts in retrospect.

Some members of the Knopf store in Karlsruhe made the management's life extremely difficult, spending their entire working day finding ways to obstruct the working business of the store:

> Advertising manager Rinner, a long-time employee of the company in an important position, developed into a representative of the Nazis, who was not only employee of the company but also spy of the party. The latter he took very seriously and saw to it that the manager [Martin Klopstock] was daily, if not hourly, exposed to chicanery.⁶⁶

Martin Klopstock, whose sister Eva had married Max Knopf, was the managing director of the company's flagship store. The consistent bullying from the National Socialist members of staff caused him considerable physical pain in the chest, which was diagnosed as angina pectoris. After a particularly unpleasant run-in with Nazi agitators in front of the store, Klopstock collapsed on the street. According to his family, the chest pain had probably been a symptom of the stress that caused a restriction of blood to the tissue of the heart muscle. His widow records his dying words on 24 December 1935 as follows: 'The Nazis have managed to break me as a good German and the company too.'[67]

With the legal restrictions on department stores and the internal pressures put upon those managing them, trade began slipping. The accounts from this time no longer exist, but between 1931 and 1934, the overtime averaged in the Knopf haberdashery workshops was ten days per worker per annum, the highest the store had in its history. In 1936 and 1937, it fell to four and a half.[68] Although this shows that the stores were still frequented and staff kept busy, the company lost 300,000 *Reichsmarks* in 1937 through a combination of falling sales and high taxation.[69] Jewish department stores had various levies forced upon them, including the so-called Adolf-Hitler-Donation of the German Economy (Adolf-Hitler-Spende der deutschen Wirtschaft).[70] Although the Nuremberg Laws of 1935 did not affect Jews in business directly, the financial situation of the companies was becoming ever more precarious. The correspondence between Knopf's lawyers and creditors was vast.[71] Arthur Knopf's branches had been able to service their debts since the rebuilding of the flagship store in 1927 from their profits. A fall in these resulted in an increasing cash flow problem.[72] The clearing houses Knopf had been dealing with had their Jewish staff removed, and others were reluctant to help. Eventually the combination of official hostility, internal pressures and, above all, the desperate financial state of the company forced Arthur Knopf to sell his business to his manager Fritz Richter. On 18 March 1937, after six hours of negotiation, the core of his business, the flagship store in Freiburg and two branches of Knopf were sold for just over 800,000 *Reichsmarks* plus 700,000 *Reichsmarks* for the furnishings, fixtures and equipment.[73] To the outside world, this may have looked like a completely legitimate sale.[74] How exactly Arthur Knopf was brought to the point of sale and why the price was fixed is impossible to determine now. It is likely that the sum was not the result of negotiations between Knopf and Richter, but was set by the highest-ranking official of the Ministry of Finance in Freiburg, Johann Stöckinger. Knopf's former manager and his lawyer Dr Roth were also accused of conspiring against their employer. The relationship between Richter and Knopf was complex. They had been life-long colleagues, possibly friends, until the forced sale of the business; they even returned to a partnership with each other after the Second World War. It is more likely that the civil service and the Sparkasse (civic bank) put pressure on them. Stöckinger was known for holding sales consultations 'before the Jewish entrepreneur was aware of this' and quite simply didn't care if the company liked the prospective buyer or not.[75] Richter was probably put under pressure to sell a large portion of the land to the Sparkasse subsequently.

Margarete Levis, who had taken over the Geschwister Knopf branch in Karlsruhe when her father Max died in 1934, had to sell her portion of the Knopf company to different individuals. The flagship store was formally taken over on 24 September 1938 by Friedrich Hölscher and two associates from Berlin.[76] The Rastatt store was sold to a manager that same month, while the other stores followed until Geschwister Knopf finally ceased to exist as a company in May 1939.[77] The properties were still nominally owned by Margarete and her husband, but were requisitioned gradually by the state in lieu of the Jewish wealth tax (*Judenvermögensabgabe*) and once they had left Germany to cover the so-called flight tax (*Reichsfluchtsteuer*).[78] Independent valuation had set the price for the three major Knopf properties at 4,884,900 *Reichsmark*s, the state paid just 2,180,000 *Reichsmark*s,[79] a sum that Margarete Levis would never receive.

Final sale

The owners of companies that were more financially sound before 1933 managed to retain some control for longer, as did businesses with links abroad that were considered important for bringing foreign currency into the country.[80] Salman Schocken, to avoid the fate of other Jewish businesses as much as possible, sold two-thirds of his shares of the Schocken AG to a British business contact, Sir Andrew McFadyean, while a significant minority of the shares and the property remained in Salman's hands.[81] The board of directors was completely replaced with non-Jews, and, by 1936, the turnover of the company became slightly more stable as a result. Some newspapers even dared to run advertisements for the company.[82] Salman's ruse only worked as a temporary measure and in anticipation of his hand being forced, he arranged for two Dutch banks to sell all his and Sir Andrew's shares to a consortium headed by the Deutsche Bank and the Reichskredit-Gesellschaft.[83] The sale went through for only 5 per cent of the estimated value of the company. The largest individual stockholder of the renamed Merkur AG was the deposed Emperor Wilhelm II, living in Dutch exile, who had visited Wertheim with his entourage in 1910.[84]

The financial and economic crisis of the past years had taken its toll on the Wertheim business too, and the family's income was now controlled by a consortium of banks, which owned the department stores and all associated companies. In April 1934, Georg Wertheim gifted his entire fortune to his Protestant-born wife Ursula and simultaneously wrote his last will that stipulated that his wife and children should inherit it. Thus, he had given away his estate twice over – possibly as a means of securing it in the family as best he could, given the political circumstances. The will further stipulated that his children, Albrecht and (the younger) Ursula, should receive their portion only after they turned forty-one years old. Wertheim, possibly because it had been allowed to retain its original name for longer or because it was still run by people appointed by the founder-retailer and not a bank, actually managed to increase its sales gradually by 1936.[85] There are reports in 1937 of customers standing in queues outside stores with Jewish names.[86] In 1938, Ursula Wertheim junior went on a trip to America, where she met her future husband, and England, where she met Harry Gordon Selfridge. In the same year, she and her brother enjoyed aristocratic country pursuits and even managed to settle most debts.[87] This monetary relief was granted to them not just by relatively good sales, but also when a large portion of their land was purchased for building Hitler's bombastic chancellery. The year 1938 was one in which the elder Wertheims went through divorce or were forced to sell the shares Ursula senior owned. Nazi leadership had given the couple the ultimatum that Ursula would have to sell her part of the company.

On 1 January 1939 – the same day Albrecht Wertheim was enlisted in spite of being a 'half-caste' – all Jews were forbidden not just from owning a retail business, but also from running it. By this point, many companies had already changed hands, but for Wertheim and Schocken. The legal fiction of their ownership no longer offered protection. Many members of the Wertheim family had to all but surrender their shares. Martha Wertheim gave hers to her estranged adoptive daughter, who was thus became the second most influential shareholder, while Fritz Sternberg, a nephew of Georg Wertheim, was forced to sell his considerably under value. Emil Georg von Stauss, who had been so helpful to the company with his contacts to leading Nazis, also helped himself to a portion.[88] The 'Abraham Wertheim AG' was renamed 'AWAG' (Allgemeine Warenhaus Gesellschaft AG). By the end of that year, Georg Wertheim passed away. By 1940, the AWAG was considered sufficiently respectable by the haphazardly inconsistent National Socialist leadership to be asked to take over the Schocken/Merkur company; the proposition was not, however, followed through.

Under new management

The change of ownership was advertised in the press by all the department stores, who were eager to encourage customers back. Characteristically loyal to his former employer, Fritz Richter's advertisement simply depicted the flagship store and the legend 'this company from 1 April 1938: *Kaufhaus Fritz Richter KG*'.[89] Other new owners were more detailed as to how the changes would affect the company. In the case of Schmoller and Knopf, the illustrations of the stores – as easily recognizable icons of the firms – were central to the 'Aryanization' advertisement, but the former names were emblazoned alongside, crossed out and informative texts reproduced as to how the companies had changed with the takeover. A break with the past and continuity had to be simultaneously

Figure 7.2 Albert Brosmann, front, in the accountancy office at Knopf in Freiburg. He would marry one of the ladies from the shop floor and went on to take over some small department stores in the Swabian Alps after the Jewish owners had been forced to leave. Bizarrely, his former Jewish employer Arthur Knopf congratulated him on his business acumen. © Wolfgang Ziefle Collection.

implied. Hansa, formerly Wronker, had for some time called itself a 'German shopping house', avoiding the taint of the word *Warenhaus*, now declaring itself a 'Christian company'. The entire process of 'Aryanization' had little to do with the antisemitism of those involved.[90] Profiteering was merely clothed in antisemitic language to give it legitimacy, which does not mean that one could not be both prejudiced and profit-oriented.

Some cases of 'Aryanization' seem bizarre due to their peripheral connection with Jewish families during the process. In April 1936, Albert Brossmann, a loyal member of staff at Knopf in Freiburg, was presented with a hand-illuminated certificate of thanks from the management of the company in recognition of his twenty-five years of service to the firm. He had worked his way up in the managerial department and met Helene Ziefle, known as Helenchen, a girl who worked on the hosiery counter. They fell in love, married and continued working for the store. Shortly after his twenty-fifth jubilee with Knopf, Albert became aware of the possibility of purchasing a recently Aryanized haberdashery and clothes shop – a small department store – in Esslingen in Württemberg. The bizarre state of affairs before the final ejection and expulsion of the former Jewish owners of department stores becomes apparent: furnished with manuals, blank receipts and pattern books supplied by his former Jewish employer, Albert and Helenchen headed to the Swabian Alps to become 'Aryanizers'. The now Jew-free Kaufhaus Albert Brossmann even received a congratulatory telegram from Arthur Knopf on the opening day![91]

Slow decline in the *Volksgemeinschaft*

The departure of Jewish owners, managers or shareholders from the stores did little to improve sales. They remained as good or as bad as they had been. The National Socialist Party programme had been an instrument to gain votes rather than a considered economic policy, and this became a problem not just for businesses, but for the whole nation, as soon as they had gained power.[92] Wertheim, after passing into non-Jewish hands, had no significant rise in turnover.[93] In many cases, non-Jews had, after all, been fronting the company for some time, and the change in name seemed more like a logical consequence than a radical break.[94] Carl Werner, who with the amalgamation of *Mittelstand* trading organization into the NSHago (Nationalsozialistischer Kampfbund für den gewerblichen Mittelstand) had lost his position as president of the retail traders, noted that competition had stiffened: 'Since 1 April '37 the Knopf department store has gone into Aryan hands, and with that has become a more significant competitor again, which again offers products which the Jewish store apparently was not allowed to.'[95] Although, with the Knopf family gone, the stationery departments started offering 'two million' Hitler portraits in various shapes and sizes,[96] department stores continued to have almost the same restrictions placed upon them as before. This was compounded as all retailing continued to suffer from the lack of disposable income.[97] Members of the NSDAP would be allowed to shop there again, bringing much needed business, but the refreshment rooms remained closed, the food halls shuttered and all forms of business not connected directly with that of a department store were prohibited. Civil servants were forbidden to shop at department stores until 1940. The infringements were placed on the business because it was a department store, not just because it was once Jewish, revealing the complex interweaving of antisemitism and the agenda of *Mittelstand*-protectionism.

In addition, the German economy was being turned into a command-led system in which stores were no longer free to choose what items they wanted to sell. Wools and cottons were being adulterated with man-made fibres, and real silk was being replaced with artificial.[98] Carl Werner, whose entire diary was hitherto free of antisemitism, believed it was 'international Jewry' that was preventing the goods being sold to Germany – rather than the conversion to a war economy. Depots of department stores were filled with products no self-respecting company would have considered selling previously. The retailers that remained due to their ownership being virtuous in the eyes of the authorities were degraded to nothing more than distributors of goods. Department stores could, in theory, advertise again, but lacked the staff and products to deliver what these advertisements might promise.[99] National Socialist cronies continued to collude. The authorities in Freiburg, in the shape of Mayor Kerber and a civil servant called Stöckinger, continued to force their will on the Knopf department store even after it had changed hands, refusing to end locally imposed sales prohibitions. The council even intervened on behalf of the Sparkasse bank, who had been jealous of part of the property of the store ever since Knopf purchased it in the 1920s. They forced the new owner Fritz Richter to sell it. Many people were out to profiteer and turn cronyism and bullying to their own advantage regardless of religious or political affiliations. The victims were Jewish, which made them antisemitic in spite of what many may have claimed afterwards.

Figure 7.3 A bust of Hitler and swastika banners take centre stage at Labour Day celebrations on 1 May. With the departure of the Knopf family from the helm in Freiburg, Fritz Richter (seated centre) took over the company under his own name. © Author.

Figure 7.4 The female staff at the Richter department store showing off their 'Strength Through Joy' gymslips. © Author.

The employee in the *Volksgemeinschaft*

Internally, the structure of companies changed gradually to reflect the new order, especially the relationship between employers and staff. Employees, sacked for being of Jewish origin, were not always replaced successfully. The loss of a well-trained and loyal workforce was far more of a problem for department stores as a business than the departure of Jewish management.[100] The new rule book, still introduced under Jewish ownership, at Knopf in 1934 had been written in collaboration with the Nazi employees' union, and undermined the core of the Knopf's staff relations. The first changes entailed referring to the manager as *Betriebsführer* (company leader) and mentioning the business as part of the *Volksgemeinschaft* (people's community, a mystic unity of the German people). The entire familial structure, on which the company was founded, was challenged. New assistants were not just to be good sales personnel, knowledgeable in the goods they sold and well versed in handling customers, but to be a 'useful member of the Volksgemeinschaft'.[101] Further still, 'only continual striving and an honest self-appraisal' will enable the employee to 'take up the battle of life with a chance of success'.[102] Those that paid their full dues to the Nazi state and were members of a coordinated organization were to be paid fully during their time of absence which was spent attending party functions.[103]

The patriarchal element was replaced by allegiance to the *Volksgemeinschaft*:

> Those who run the company will, 'by their best endeavours ensure the welfare of their followers ... so shall their followers be always aware of their loyal commitment to the company and the company's leader, that only trusting, companionable and sincerely cooperative work, will serve to promote the common goal.[104]

The alterations made to the staff rule book in 1937 were more drastic, however. With the remaining workforce conforming to the Nazis' Aryan concept, the stores could now fully integrate into the *Volksgemeinschaft*.[105] The staff rules of 1937 for the new Fritz Richter KG made the company's coordination into the Third Reich evident.

The company was now firmly planted into the *Volksgemeinschaft*. Indeed it was seen as a seed for it: 'Only when the community at large thrives, can the cell flourish and grow... All work and influence in the company and for its economic purposes must therefore always be at the same time service to the national community.'[106] As before, the close and almost confidential relationship between employer and employees was emphasized, yet now these dynamics were seen less as a way of increasing the reputation of the company and more as a means of fostering the *Volksgemeinschaft*. Coordination at the workplace was accomplished by insisting that every employee be a member of the German Workers' Front (Deutsche Arbeitsfront). Junior members of staff had to be members of the Hitler Youth or the Federation of German Girls (Bund Deutscher Mädel). In line with the Nazi policy to drive up the birth rate, married persons with a new-born received 50 *Marks*; this could include unmarried women with children, who, like their male counterparts, received up to 26 *Marks* until the child was sixteen.[107] Holiday pay was now reserved only for those who earned 350 *Marks* or above, and the company would be 'especially considerate, if possible, of those taking holidays to participate in Strength through Joy trips'.[108] The 'Kraft durch Freude' travel opportunities were offered to those who made themselves particularly helpful to the new regime. At a time where foreign travel was practically unheard of for the vast majority of the population, a trip to another part of Germany for politically approved holidays was an enormous treat.

The coordination was made clear not only in the text, but in the presentation of the rule book. The *Kraft durch Freude* (strength through joy) swastika and cogwheel adorned the first page rather than the company's logo. The main annual celebrations of the store were moved from Christmas to 1 May – the day Wertheim first flew the swastika banner in 1933. Ceremonies honouring deserving staff and the retired were framed by the decorations of the new regime. Hitler's bust and swastika banners artistically assembled formed the backdrop to function rooms. The swastika would also feature on the store's gymnastics team *Kraft durch Freude* leotards.

The final days

On the day after Arthur Knopf's departure from the company in 1937, Fritz Richter announced that Mr Knopf was 'retiring to his Swiss business'.[109] The Knopf family rearranged its routine, fleeing into domesticity. Every morning Arthur Knopf would have his chauffeur Herr Gilbert pick him up from his villa in Freiburg and drive him to Basel, from where he ran the Swiss part of his business. He, his wife and child continued to live in their house in the best part of town. On Sundays, they would take the car up into the Black Forest for afternoon tea at the Hotel Adler, where the department store had supplied the uniforms for the waiting staff. The family celebrated Christmas as usual, and the chauffeur's daughter was presented customarily with a new frock. In 1937–8, the same year he was forced to sell the company, Arthur Knopf's life remained bizarrely normal. He even embarked on renovating his mother's house.

However, on the night of 9 November 1938, on the day generally known as *Kristallnacht*, this half-life was brought abruptly to an end. While their own men were searching the cellar, the SA set fire to the synagogue in Freiburg. As the building burned, lighting the sky, Arthur, whose father had been a founding member of the Jewish community in Freiburg, was rounded up together with hundreds of others that night and interned in Dachau. In Berlin, of the 50,000 Jewish businesses that had existed before 1933, only 3,637 survived on the eve of *Kristallnacht*.[110] The ratio of depletion was probably the same in Freiburg. About half the Jews in Freiburg could eventually flee, a quarter was sent to the internment camp at Gurs and the rest were murdered elsewhere.[111] Arthur Knopf was set free again late in December on the condition that he leaves the country. Taking his wife and child with him, they moved to Basel permanently. His cousin Margarete and her husband Arthur Lewis had no foreign business interests to fall back on. They were forced to pack up their belongings and flee to Lisbon in 1940. The possessions they had arranged to be sent on never arrived. Taking a parcel steamer, they eventually ended up in New York in 1941, where they managed to keep their heads above water as home workers.[112] Most of the Knopf family survived, with the exception of an aunt who was killed for being mentally deficient and thus, in the eyes of the Nazi regime, not worthy of life. Hermann Tietz's great-nephew Georg and his wife also managed to flee successfully to the United States. Other members of the family fled via Holland to Palestine, where they ran a small guest house in Tel Aviv.

Salman Schocken's work for the Zionist movement had guaranteed his involvement with the foundation of the state of Israel. To allow their children an uninterrupted education, the Schockens had already moved there permanently in the mid-1930s, where Mendelsohn would build them an iconic modernist home to settle into.[113] Here the Schockens led a life almost indistinguishable to their German one: in the baking heat they would entertain guests at dinners at which suits had to be worn. In the middle of the desert, they cultivated a rose garden.

The Wronkers, however, were not lucky enough to escape with their lives. The systematic destruction of Jews was decided at the Wannsee Conference on 20 January 1942. While their son Max successfully fled to the United States, Hermann and Ida Wronker had moved to France in the hope of being safe closer to home. They were imprisoned in 1942 and murdered the same year in Auschwitz.

Twenty members of the Wertheim family escaped, while five were imprisoned in concentration camps of which four were murdered. Fritz Wertheim, Georg Wertheim's nephew was, in spite of being the son of a department store entrepreneur, a qualified cook, as skill which made him useful enough in Theresienstadt to be spared the gas chamber. Ursula Wertheim, Georg's wife, married Arthur Lindgens, a long-time friend of the family who not only had been instrumental in the improvement of their estate at Sassleben, but was now also the front of the new AWAG department store business.[114] Albrecht Wertheim, Ursula's son, never returned to the business after he left the Wehrmacht. The brand 'Wertheim', unlike those of the other stores, was considered sufficiently popular after the Second World War to be resurrected – after all, it did mean 'home of value'.

Department stores continued to fare badly during the war. Even when not run by Jews, constraints on large retailers remained regardless of the owner's origin. The new managers lacked the experience to dexterously handle the restrictions of a war economy as their Jewish predecessors had. In the First World War, Germany had profited from Jewish retailers' ability to adapt to situations and their contacts. The Nazis had destroyed this; thus a key element in the successful feeding and clothing of a civilian population during a conflict – retailing – had been severely damaged by those wanting a war.

Early in 1933, before the Nazis seized power, it would have been impossible to imagine how dramatic the lives of all Germans would change over the course of that year. The swift and tragic escalation of the situation for citizens of Jewish origin was unforeseen and took a complex course. Immediately upon gaining power, the Nazis made Jewish existence intensely difficult. Although most German department store founders had a common origin, they and their children had very different fates. It is frustratingly hard to instil order into the chaos of Nazi rule retrospectively, especially when it comes to understanding human relationships and interactions. Within six years, lives were shattered, property plundered and many killed.

Conclusion

The Wertheims, the Tietz families, Margarete Levis, Arthur Knopf, Max Wronker and Salman Schocken all returned to West Germany when peace was declared after the Second World War in the hope of regaining some portion of their respective companies. Although the Wronker department stores had not been owned by the family since 1932, Max Wronker attempted to get compensation for the loss of his family's business. His granddaughter remains

> confused about this question ... I know that my grandfather Max started claims for restitution for the family's business assets immediately after the war. He worked on this for the rest of his life, and this cost him not only money but an enormous amount of stress and discouragement ... I think that if there was no family interest in the business, what was Max trying to do by trying to take action against the German government?[1]

Emotional trauma was not deemed worthy of compensation during the early attempts at restitution directly after the war, if this is what Max was looking for. Martin Klopstock's heart attack as a result of stress was not considered an effect of the Nazi rule.[2] Financial loss was something that – if systematically worked out – could be claimed for, but personal tragedy, which was profound for the people who lost their family businesses, was not something that could be measured.[3] Margarete's husband, Arthur, as a former state prosecutor, took it upon himself to represent his wife's interest. The couple had been instructed to leave the company's archive with the bank Feuchter & Co. when they fled, a firm that was taken over by the Dresden Bank after the war. To Arthur Levis's amazement, he was told that the fireproof safe in which the documents had been placed had been burnt out during an air attack. All files regarding 'Aryanization' had been lost and conveniently remained so. The documents of the banks, government departments and chambers of commerce involved are usually reported to have been destroyed by enemy action.[4] The value of the Knopf company and the compensation for Margarete and her husband Arthur

Levis had to be reconstructed from memory. Something similar was done for Arthur Knopf. Although on paper his and Fritz Richter's lawyers battled out terms and conditions, the two men went into partnership again after the Second World War.

In the Merkur company, formerly the Schocken AG, the modus of operation had changed little with the departure of Salman from its helm. In 1946, there were some members of the Merkur management that looked forward to the return of their former boss. Although a large chunk of the company was lost in the Soviet sector, Salman received 51 per cent of the shares of the West German portion of the department store in 1949.[5] Pleasingly, for Salman, on his return the structure and most of the staff of the company were as he had left them.[6] The principles of management, customer service and employment practice had not changed under the new name.[7] His son took over the day-to-day running for a while, during which Salman found the time to open a new branch of Schocken in Heilbronn in 1951. The following year Salman sold his store to a former apprentice of Leonhard Tietz, Helmut Horten. Horten had purchased the department store Gebrüder Alsberg in 1936, a firm he had previously worked for.[8] The Helmut Horten AG would be the fourth largest department store company in the Federal Republic of Germany after the war, universally recognizable by the so-called Horten-tiles.

After the Second World War, department stores became an expression of the West German economic miracle of the 1950s. Their success was not founded on the loosened ties with their former Jewish owners, as has been suggested,[9] but on their continued appeal to customers and the great wealth individual Germans enjoyed. Until the 1990s, they were robust businesses that dominated the German high street, gradually amalgamating over the decades to become larger companies. For instance Hertie, formerly Hermann Tietz, was taken over by Kaufhof.[10] Yet, gradually, by the end of the twentieth century, a decline set in. Currently it is assumed to be due to the convenience of online shopping.

Most former Wronker stores would eventually become part of a different company or cease to exist altogether. By 2014, only one former Knopf department store remained operational as such. Hölscher would eventually give up and sell the former Knopf store to the Karstadt AG. This old flagship store of the company, gutted but with completely intact façade, still dominates the main road in Karlsruhe as a reminder of the Jews from Birnbaum and a testimony to the power of the consumer. The Knopf branches in Freiburg and Lörrach became Kaufhaus für Alle after the Fritz Richter AG became jointly owned by Arthur Knopf. The company folded due to poor management after Richter's and

Knopf's departures. Other Knopf branches continued just into the twenty-first century as Kaufhaus Schneider or Kaufhaus Krauss, but were in small-town locations that were no longer viable and hence closed down. In the last days of Arthur Knopf's life, a favourite outing for his past employees was to take their children on a day trip to visit their former boss. In Basel, Arthur would allow the children to sit in the front of the chauffeured Benz and treat them to cake, while the grown-ups talked about old times. The trip down there involved a train journey along the same line that Arthur's grandfather had founded his first stores.

All the stores located in the Soviet sector, which later became the German Democratic Republic (GDR), became so-called publicly owned enterprises (*Volkseigene Betriebe*, VEB). In cities and larger towns, they were all re-branded as *Centrum* department stores and in smaller places called *Konsument*. Branches of Karstadt, Tietz and Schocken mainly befell that fate. The products they offered were overwhelmingly made within the GDR and reflected what one could manufacture with the raw material and labour that the closed economy had to offer. After 1990, many were no longer viable. The Mendelsohn's Schocken in Chemnitz now serves as the Natural History Museum of the State of Saxony, while Hermann Tietz across the road is a shopping mall. The Kaufhaus zum Strauß in Görlitz was owned by Karstadt when it was taken over by the state. This extremely rare example of a completely preserved art noveau department store was the inspiration for the research into this book when it was still open in 2008. It closed in 2009, but used as the set for the film *Grand Budapest Hotel*. Modelled on the Wertheim on the Leipziger Strasse, it serves as a reminder of the Emperor's favoured department store, which itself was bombed and then pulled down. Its foundations lay beneath the death strip between east and west Berlin for the rest of the century.

*

The history of Germans of Jewish origin has been seen mainly in the light of the Holocaust since the end of the Second World War. Postwar attempts at reparation, at first with monetary compensation and later in the twentieth century increasingly with memorials, continue to this day. The same difficulty the historian is faced with tracing what happened to businesses associated with Jews after 1933 are those faced by lawyers and courts. Business records in general are not kept for long periods of time, and those that had benefitted from the forced exit of Jewish entrepreneurs were not keen to have documentary evidence of their machinations. The lack of records is usually excused by claiming they were destroyed by enemy action. In some cases, this may well be true, but it does remain astonishing that there does not seem to be a bank, chamber of commerce or governmental institution that has proper documentation relating to the sale of department stores after 1933. One suspects the perpetrators ensured there was as little evidence as possible.

This has partially been the reason why professional historians – and amateurs, mostly journalists – reach for simplistic explanations. Anti-Jewish and anti-capitalist pamphlets, books and articles have survived, as have the late-nineteenth- and early-twentieth-century works of fiction portraying department stores as the harbingers of evil. The records of the businesses they targeted have not. Neither have the millions of shopping lists, coupon books, treasured Christmas and birthday presents, tins of meat, bars of soap, enamel washbasins and tons of cake consumed in refreshment rooms in department stores across Germany. This is because shopping was an everyday occurrence – mostly mundane – but in the best of cases spiced with a little joy or excitement over a bargain or an opulent display of crisp white linen. Department stores and the Jewish-sounding names above their doors were part of German life – a part taken for granted by the customer except for the purpose of acquiring necessary goods and little luxuries. Most shoppers will not have read Zola's fictionalized attack on department stores, would have been unconcerned about shoplifters, shopgirl's wages or the apparent death of independent retailers of the high street: they wanted the *Mark* in their pocket to go as far as it could. The shoppers were, in that sense, no different from English, American or French people. The German ruling and political class recognized this, even celebrated it. From the Emperor to the social democrat, the department stores were seen as a necessary element of German society, even something to be feted.

Jewish entrepreneurs understood themselves as good Germans and presented themselves as such. That does not mean necessarily that they were accepted as such. However, despite societal challenges, perhaps even because of them, department store owners constructed their identities as integrated Germans through their efforts as businesspeople. This would allow people who engaged in non-rabid, private antisemitism or had qualms about the business model to shop at Jewish-owned stores and enjoy the products, services and experiences. Instances of antisemitism were academic, physical, public, private, casual, institutionalized, economic and deeply rooted, but little generalization can be made about time, place or type. In the history of Jewish run-department stores, we can see this existed, but that it was fairly simple to overlook in the light of the retailers' successes.[11] The ancestors of those Jews who enjoyed this success had eked out a more or less meagre existence in the Prussian provinces, and when the German Empire was formed, liberating the economy and the Jewish people to a great extent, they saw a business opportunity. Everything they did made commercial sense, and was geared towards the customer as a major active agent. The bonds of kinship that tied them together were a reliable system of guaranteeing credit. The concentration on certain geographic areas – at first – made logistic sense and reflected Germany's provinciality, rooting them, in spite of their Jewish origin, deep within the German cityscape and a common sense of belonging. The establishing of branches increased orders. Going straight to the manufacturer reduced the purchase price. Introducing affordable luxuries encouraged well-to-do people to shop with them. Erecting purpose-built stores gave local craftsmen lucrative business contracts. Ensuring the architecture was a statement of restrained grandeur elevated the shopping to an experience and the store to a welcome feature on the high street. The customer service enforced Germany's rigid class structure and allowed every member of society to feel comfortable while shopping. Women were employed because their wages were lower than those of men. Training staff, giving them career opportunities, holidays and perks meant they were fresh-faced, eager and qualified to serve customers – a perfect advertisement for the business.

Gradually these families of Jewish origin became financially comfortable and recognizably middle class. They did so at a time when many Germans were reaping the rewards of the country's industrial boom. People moved to the cities, and the most successful settled in affluent and leafy districts lined by villas – regardless of their religion. They became active in philanthropy, both for faith-specific and general causes, not because they were trying to overcome a prejudice in particular, but to be seen as wealthy and generous was, again, good business no matter who you were. The businessmen – for although women were heavily involved with the running of the firms, it was still the patriarch's name that graced the polished plaque by the main door – received accolades from their staff. Their *Mittelstand* rivals celebrated them as shrewd commercial minds and good employers. The German monarchs even tried to ennoble them or at the very least give them medals for their work.

Quite naturally, there were people who disliked the stores, their owners and what they thought they stood for, especially those engaged in other forms of retail and those who perceived department stores as 'un-German'. Jealousy most likely motivated the former, and social and racial prejudice the latter. Sometimes this was cloaked in language that suggested the *Mittelstand*, the backbone of the German economy, was at threat. Deeper down was an antisemitic streak in disguise. As the documentary material for these groups still exists and is available in most German university libraries, this is often the framework in which the story of Jewish retailers is told. We have, however, seen that there is also another side to Jewish existence in Germany. Although antisemitism existed, it is rarely directly associated with department stores until after the First World War, even then only sparingly until the Nazis became a force to be reckoned with. The anti-department store agitators were not a homogenous group. Until the National Socialists came to prominence, they had no consistency in their agency. They were lone wolves or organizations that were often small and local. They formed, argued and disbanded in various guises being no real threat to retailers at all. However, parallelly, the continued growth and expansion of department stores – with and without their Jewish names – reflects their acceptance by the population. The existence of a department store in every provincial town is proof of the Germans' love for shopping and the success of Jewish life in Germany.

As we have seen, antisemitism and those who grumbled about the commercialization of German society were an ambient noise of the lives of the people who ran department stores, but did not seem like something to worry about. The main concern of those running department stores was the success of the business. The peddler ancestors had, like themselves, gone through many political storms and economic upheavals. If anything, since 1871 their businesses and lives had improved drastically. The First World War, in which German Jews threw themselves into the war effort just as patriotically as any other Germans, was a blow to pride, business and doubtless to their soul, having lost their own 'homeland' in Prussia to the Poles. The lack of basic necessities, almost from the first months of the war, made retailing a dire prospect. With defeat came the frustration, inflation, hunger and rioting. Violence on the streets and a lack of disposable income was more or less the norm during the years of the Weimar Republic. Department stores adapted as best they could, merging with rivals, introducing new business models, floating on the stock exchange and when a little credit was available around 1927 investing heavily – like any shrewd entrepreneur would.

The National Socialists had evolved from a vilified bunch of ruffians to a dangerous force in German society. Through target-specific propaganda, promising whoever they were talking to whatever they wanted and a mixture of legal and brutally enforced political manoeuvring, they managed to unite the previously scattered groups on the right-wing – and sometimes left-wing – fringe. Antisemites, monarchists, opponents of capitalism, champions of a mythical form of a Teutonic past and a general assortment of thugs joined their ranks. Increasingly, so did the *Mittelstand*, civil servants and employees who had lost their livelihoods and any sense of security. Department stores, which had been a beacon of Germany's commercial success, lauded in the press and by the authorities, suppliers of good quality sanitary products and elaborate hats, were now twisted into being exactly that which was wrong with the nation. Anti-Jewish hate, mistaken views on the way staff were treated, rumours of dumping prices, allegedly dangerous products and a good deal of chapbook tales were conflated to present department stores as the harbingers of evil in a way that they had never been seen before. The Nazis pledged to tax them out of existence, close them, nationalize them or make them hand over the retailing space.

When they finally got into power, they found that the Germans were more attached to this form of retailing than they had thought. SA brownshirts daubing the windows of shops with Jewish-sounding names, photographing customers and generally making a spectacle were disliked and often even ignored. Not least, one suspects, as the Nazis had come to power with the promise to stop the almost perpetual aggravation Germans had to witness in public places during the Weimar years. The new men in power may have been astonished when they realized that department stores were already de facto owned by the state. The loans available in 1927 and 1928 were now underwritten by state-owned or state-controlled banks. Doing away with large stores would mean a huge loss for banks, a big drop in employment and a huge and visible gap on the high street. Nazis needed the banks on side to move to a war economy and had come to power pledging work for the German people. Moreover, the Germans – even those who had antisemitic views – were devoted to the stores that had served them for more than fifty years and sometimes over generations. Through a series of back-room manoeuvres by unscrupulous officials, profiteers and store employees, the Jewish directors and staff were evicted. The main tool was financial; the banks would simply no longer deal with anyone who did not fit into Germany's new order; this cloaked antisemitism in a legitimate transaction. For the customer, however, on the face of it, very little changed. In many cases, the new non-Jewish names of the companies very closely reflected the old brand. Continuity was not unimportant, even if the new management lacked the experience to run the businesses successfully. Most consumers were as indifferent to the nominally Christian ownership of the store as they were to the Jewish – they continued to want good quality products at a reasonable price, regardless of who was selling it. The war preparations of the National Socialists, however, soon put paid to that. Not until the 1950s and Germany's economic miracle would customers be able to enjoy the delights of department stores on a level similar to those experienced in the 1910s.

The postwar treatment of people of Germans of Jewish origin is shocking. Questions of restitution rage on until today and may, sadly, never be fully resolved due to a lack of evidence to support material claims and the inability to measure emotional distress. Can one – or should one – quantify the rape of Jewish life in Germany? We have to try, but admit that we will always fail. Time marches on and the wrongs committed recede further into the past, but the tragedy continues: in the fight for restitution, Germans of Jewish origin are still seen as the 'other'. The memorialization of German Jews emphasizes their Jewishness, not their Germanness and with that, they are being excluded from German society for a second time. Commemoration of Jews in Germany should be that of an integral and multifaceted part of society which included those of strong Jewish belief and identity and those for whom their religion was a matter of ancestry. Department stores in Germany were founded by Germans who happened to have been born into families whose faith was Jewish. Some of these Germans went on to convert to Christianity or embrace their Jewish religion more seriously; however, in their commercial lives, their Jewishness was often of secondary importance to themselves and – they may have hoped – to others. These were successful and innovative commercial individuals who helped build Germany and enabled it to flourish in a uniquely German way, balancing the international phenomenon of department stores with provincial and traditional ideals. Their absence after the Second World War must be seen as an impoverishment of Germany and a bitter loss for their non-Jewish countrymen.

Historians have often examined the deep roots of antisemitism in Europe, from the Middle Ages to the nineteenth century, to explain what happened under the Nazis. This book shows that attitudes and beliefs were not as broad or ingrained as we believe. Within this, we find a cautionary tale for our own time. It is not necessary for intense, widespread and prolonged prejudice to exist within a society for a group to be the target of horrific persecution. Kauder muses that 'in the end … it was the "irrational", the unannounced and the unforeseen, that would make all the difference' to the history of Jews in Germany.[12] More profoundly, there may be a principle here for a better understanding of history: Given the wrong circumstances, a highly assimilated group can find itself excluded, even murderously hunted down, without a great deal of warning, by the very same people who seemingly accepted them before.

Notes

Introduction

1 Stadtarchiv Freiburg (StAF) F202/32, 7030.
2 Deutsches Tagebucharchiv (DTA) 19495/II 1–2, Diary of Hedwig Rahmer, 1 April 1933 (Mannheim, 1933), p. 48.
3 DTA 13,2, Diary of E. C. Halder (Karlsruhe, 1933), 1 April 1933, p. 17.
4 Simone Ladwig-Winters and Erica Fischer, *Die Wertheims: Geschichte einer Familie* (Berlin, 2007), p. 50.
5 See http://www.documentarchiv.de/wr/1920/nsdap-programm.html.
6 Adolf Hitler, *Mein Kampf* (Munich, 1942), pp. 31, 270 and 291.
7 Ibid., p. 170.
8 Michael B. Miller, *The Bon Marché, Bourgeois Culture and the Department Store, 1869–1920* (London, 1981), p. 20.
9 Tim Dale, *Harrods, the Store and the Legend* (London, 1986); Peter Cox, *Spedan's Partnership: The Story of John Lewis and Waitrose* (Cambridge, 2010).
10 Helmut Frei, *Tempel der Kauflust* (Leipzig, 1997), p. 43, quoted in Alarich Rooch, *Zwischen Museum und Warenhaus. Ästhetisierungsprozesse und sozialkommunikative Raumaneignung des Bürgertums* (Bremen, 2000), p. 136.
11 Aux Ligueurs, *La Revendication*, 20 September 1888.
12 Miller, *The Bon Marché*, pp. 190–7, 205–8 and 213–15 and Georg Tietz, *Hermann Tietz – Geschichte einer Familie und ihrer Warenhäuser* (Stuttgart, 1965). On small shopkeepers, see: Robert Gellately, *The Politics of Economic Despair: Shopkeepers and German Politics 1890–1914* (London, 1974), pp. 40–8. For middle-class fears and anxiety surrounding the department store, see: Tim Coles, 'Department Stores as Retail Innovation in Germany: A Historical-Geographical Perspective on the Period 1870–1914', in Geoffrey Crossick and Serge Jaumain (eds), *Cathedrals of Consumption: The European Department Store, 1850–1939* (Aldershot, 1999), pp. 72–96, 79; Jennifer Jenkins, *Provincial Modernity, Local Culture and Liberal Politics in Fin-de-Siècle Hamburg* (London, 2003), pp. 272–80; Jürgen Kocka, *Industrial Culture and Bourgeois Society: Business, Labor and Bureaucracy in Modern Germany* (New York, 1999), pp. 209–31; Wolfgang J. Mommsen, *Imperial Germany 1867–1917: Culture and Society in an Authoritarian State* (New York, 1995), pp. 183–7.
13 Erica Rappaport, *Shopping for Pleasure: Women in the Making of London's West End* (Princeton, 2000), p. 143; Miller, *The Bon Marché*, p. 190.

14 Paul Lerner, 'Circulation and Representation: Jews, Department Stores and Cosmopolitan Consumption in Germany, Circa 1880s–1930s', *European Review of History*, Vol. 17, No. 3 (June 2010), pp. 395–413, 397; Paul Lerner, *The Consuming Temple: Jews, Department Stores, and the Consumer Revolution in Germany, 1880–1940* (Ithaca, 2015).
15 Philip W. Walker, *Zola* (London, 1985), p. 157.
16 I am indebted to Prof. Robert D. Lethbridge of the Faculty of Modern and Medieval Languages at the University of Cambridge for this information. Émile Zola, *Au Bonheur des Dames* (Paris, serialized, 1883).
17 Detlef Briesen, *Warenhaus, Massenkonsum und Sozialmoral – Zur Geschichte der Konsumkritik im 20. Jahrhundert* (Frankfurt, 2001), p. 12.
18 Lerner, *The Consuming Temple*, p. 15.
19 Ibid., p. 17.
20 Thomas Lenz, 'Veblen im Warenhaus: Theorien der reaktionären Modernisierung als Erklärungsansatz für die Warenhaus-Debatte im deutschen Kaiserreich', in Godela Weiss-Sussex and Ulrike Zitzelsperger (eds), *Das Berliner Warenhaus: Gesichte und Diskurse* (The Berlin Department Store: History and Discourse) (Frankfurt, 2013), pp. 53–62, 54–5.
21 Briesen, *Warenhaus, Massenkonsum und Sozialmoral*, p. 332.
22 Lerner, 'Circulation and Representation', p. 398.
23 Hal Hansen, 'Rethinking the Role of Artisans in Modern German Development', *Central European History*, Vol. 42, No. 1 (March 2009), pp. 33–64, 34.
24 DTA 592, Diary of Heinz Wittmann (Mannheim, 1933), p. 38.
25 Rembert Unterstell, *Mittelstand in der Weimarer Republik. Die soziale Entwicklung und politische Orientierung von Handwerk, Kleinhandel und Hausbesit 19–1933* (Frankfurt, 1989); Adelheid von Saldern, *Mittelstand im Dritten Reich: Handwerk – Einzelhändler – Bauern* (Frankfurt, 1979); and Heinrich A. Winkler, *Mittelstand, Demokratie und Nationalsozialismus: Die politische Entwicklung von Handwerk und Kleinhandel in der Weimarer Republik* (Cologne, 1972), p. 52.
26 Uwe Spiekermann, *Warenhaussteuer in Deutschland, Mittelstandsbewegung, Kapitalismus und Rechtstaat im späten Kaiserreich* (Frankfurt, 1994), p. 9.
27 Paul Lerner, 'An All Consuming History? Recent Works on Consumer Culture in Modern Germany', *Central European History*, Vol. 42, No. 3 (September 2009), pp. 509–43, 519.
28 Martin Lange, *Antisemitic Elements in the Critique of Capitalism in German Culture 1850–1933* (Bern, 2007), p. 265.
29 Werner E. Mosse, 'Jewish Entrepreneurship in Germany 1820–1935', in Werner E. Mosse and Hans Pohl (eds), *Jüdische Unternehmer in Deutschland im 19. und 20. Jahrhundert* (Stuttgart,1992), pp. 54–66, 65.

30 Gellately, *The Politics of Economic Despair*, p. 8. The German is not translated in the original. It refers to a class system based on ancient social groups, each with its own role in the functioning of society.
31 Spiekermann, *Warenhaussteuer in Deutschland*, p. 10.
32 Lerner, 'Circulation and Representation', p. 396.
33 Werner E. Mosse, *The German-Jewish Economic Elite 1820–1935: A Socio-Cultural Profile* (Oxford, 1989), p. 223.
34 Lerner, 'An All Consuming History?', p. 513.
35 Steven E. Aschheim, ' "The Jew Within": The Myth of "Judaization" in Germany', in Jehuda Reinharz and Walter Schatzberg, *The Jewish Response to German Culture* (London, 1985), pp. 212–41, 212–13 and 238; Mosse, *The German-Jewish Economic Elite*, p. 298.
36 *Stadtzeitung Karlsruhe*, 25 April 2014.
37 Peter Lambert, 'Paving the "Peculiar Path": German Nationalism and Historiography since Ranke', in Geoffrey Cubitt (ed.), *Imagining Nations* (Manchester, 1998), pp. 92–109, 94.
38 Georg Bollenbeck, 'German Kultur, the Bildungsbürgertum, and Its Susceptibility to National Socialism', *German Quarterly*, Vol. 73, No. 1 (January 2000), pp. 67–83, 79; see also: Anthony Kauder, *German Politics and the Jews: Düsseldorf and Nuremberg, 1910–1933* (Oxford, 1996), p. 56.
39 See, for instance: Hagen Schulze, 'Is There a German History?', *The 1987 Annual Lecture of the German Historical Institute* (London, 1987), pp. 9–20; Georg Iggers, 'Nationalism and Historiography, 1789–1996: The German Example in Historical Perspective', in Stefan Berger, Mark Donovan and Kevin Passmore (eds), *Writing National Histories: Western Europe since 1800* (London, 1999), pp. 5–29, 15 or Lambert, 'Paving the "Peculiar Path" ', pp. 92–106.
40 Jürgen Kocka, 'The European Pattern and the German Case', in Jürgen Kocka and Alan Mitchell (eds), *Bourgeois Society in Nineteenth-Century Europe* (Providence, 1993), pp. 3–39, 6–7; Thomas Childers, 'The Social Language of Politics in Germany: The Sociology of Political Discourse in the Weimar Republic', *American Historical Review*, Vol. 95, No. 2 (April 1990), pp. 331–58, 331.
41 Christopher Kopper, 'Wirtschaftliche Selbstbehauptung im sozialen Ghetto. Jüdische Wirtschaftsbürger im Dritten Reich', in Dieter Ziegler (ed.), *Grossbürger und Unternehmer: Die deutsche Wirtschaftselite im 20. Jahrhundert* (Göttingen, 2000), pp. 204–14, 205.
42 Leo Colze, *Berliner Warenhäuser* (Berlin, 1908), p. 11.
43 Coles, 'Department Stores as Retail Innovation in Germany', pp. 75 and 81.
44 Briesen, *Warenhaus, Massenkonsum und Sozialmoral*, p. 14.
45 David Blackbourn, *Populists and Patricians, Essays in Modern German History* (London, 1987), p. 87.

46 Hermann Lebovics, 'Reviewed Work: Mittelstand, Demokratie und Nationalsozialismus: Die politische Entwicklung von Handwerk und Kleinhandel in der Weimarer Republik by Heinrich August Winkler', *Journal of Modern History*, Vol. 45, No. 3 (September 1973), pp. 539–40, 539.

47 Spiekermann, *Warenhaussteuer in Deutschland*, p. 10.

48 Oded Heilbronner, *Catholicism, Political Culture, and the Countryside: A Social History of the Nazi Party in South Germany* (Michigan, 1997), p. 233.

49 Hansen, 'Rethinking the Role of Artisans', pp. 62–4.

50 Anthony McElligott, *Rethinking the Weimar Republic, Authority and Authoritarianism, 1916-1937* (London, 2014), p. 70.

51 Briesen, *Warenhaus, Massenkonsum und Sozialmoral*, p. 14.

52 Ibid., p. 44

53 Amos Elon, *The Pity of It All: A Portrait of Jews in Germany 1743-1933* (London, 2004).

54 Robert Gellately, *Backing Hitler. Consent and Coercion in Nazi Germany* (Oxford, 2001), p. 24; Till van Rahden, *Juden und andere Breslauer. Die Beziehung zwischen Juden, Portestanten und Katholiken in einer deutschen Grossstadt 1860-1925* (Göttingen, 2000), p. 17.

55 Lerner, 'Circulation and Representation', p. 410.

56 Peter Pulzer, *Jews and the German State* (Oxford, 1992), p. 271; Kauder, *German Politics and the Jews*, p. 182.

57 Rahden, *Juden und andere Breslauer*, p. 28.

58 Till von Rahden, 'Jews and the Ambivalences of Civil Society in Germany, 1800-1933: Assessment and Reassessment', *Journal of Modern History*, Vol. 77, No. 4 (December 2005), pp. 1024–47, 1030.

59 Richard J. Evans, *The Third Reich in Power* (London, 2006), p. 2.

60 Rahden, 'Jews and the Ambivalences of Civil Society in Germany', p. 1031.

61 Ladwig-Winters and Fischer, *Die Wertheims* and Konrad Fuchs, *Ein Konzern aus Sachsen, Kaufhaus Schocken als Spiegelbild deutscher Wirtschaft und Politik, 1901-1953* (Stuttgart, 1990).

62 Armen Avakin and Franz A. Paulus, *Die Familie Sternberg* (Bad Kissingen, 2003); Tietz, *Hermann Tietz*; Nils Busch-Petersen, *Oscar Tietz* (Berlin, 2004); Nils Busch-Petersen, *Adolf Jandorf, vom Volkswarenhaus zum KaDeWe* (Berlin, 2008); Rudolf Lenz, *Karstadt, Ein deutscher Warenhauskonzern 1920-1950* (Stuttgart, 1995).

63 Anthony David, *The Patron: A Life of Salman Schocken* (New York, 2003).

64 Spiekermann, 'Der Mittelstand stirbt!', in Weiss-Sussex and Zitzelsperger, *Das Berliner Warenhaus*, pp. 33–52, 51.

65 David Cook and David Walters (eds), *Retail Marketing, Theory and Practice* (Hemel Hempstead, 1991), p. 4.

66 Friedrich Heubach, 'Produkte als Bedeutungsträger. Die heraldische Funktion von Waren. Psychologische Bemerkungen über den kommunikativen und imaginativen Gebrauchswert industrieller Produkte', in Reinhard Eisendle and Elfie Miklautz (eds), *Produktkulturen. Dynamik und Bedeutungswandel des Konsums* (Frankfurt/Main, 1992), pp. 177–98, 178; Mommsen, *Imperial Germany*, p. 184.
67 Cook and Walters, *Retail Marketing*, p. 331.
68 Jenkins, *Provincial Modernity*, pp. 148 and 265.
69 Celia Applegate, *A Nation of Provincials, the German Idea of Heimat* (Berkley, 1990), p. 150.
70 Detlef Briesen, 'Die Debatte um das Warenhaus: Vom Deutschen Kaiserreich bis zur Bundesrepublik Deutschland', in Weiss-Sussex and Zitzelsperger, *Das Berliner Warenhaus*, pp. 17–32,18.
71 Crossick and Serge Jaumain, *Cathedrals of Consumption*, p. 75; cf. August Sartorius von Waltershausen, *Deutsche Wirtschaftsgeschichte, 1815–1914* (Jena, 1923), p. 537.
72 Marks & Spencer, Bainbridge's, Jenners, Robert Sayle and Fenwick's are all early provincial foundations.
73 Michael John, 'Jews as Consumers and Providers in Provincial Towns: The Example of Linz and Salzburg, 1900–1938', in Gideon Reuveni and Nils Roemer (eds), *Longing, Belonging, and Making of Jewish Consumer Culture* (Leiden, 2002), pp. 139–62, 145.
74 Frank Trentmann, 'Beyond Consumerism: New Historical Perspectives on Consumption', *Journal of Contemporary History*, Vol. 39, No. 3 (July 2004), p. 375; Rappaport, *Shopping for Pleasure*, but especially pp. 5, 5–11; Mary Douglas, 'In Defence of Shopping', in Eisendle and Mikautz, *Produktkulturen*, pp. 95–116, 107; Laura Ugolini, *Men and Menswear, Sartorial Consumption in Britain 1880–1939* (Aldershot, 2007); Michael Bell and Simon Gunn, *Middle Classes, Their Rise and Sprawl* (London, 2002), pp. 42 and 54.
75 Tina Dingel, *Shopping for Masculinity: Constructing the Male Consumer in Germany, 1920s to 1950s* (Limerick, 2008).
76 Werner J. Mommsen, *Bürgerliche Kultur und politische Ordnung. Künstler, Schriftsteller und Intellektuelle in der deutschen Geschichte 1830–1933* (Frankfurt, 2000), p. 182.
77 Lerner, 'An All Consuming History?', p. 520.
78 Carole E. Adams, *Women Clerks in Wilhelmine Germany, Issues of Class and Gender* (Cambridge, 1988).
79 Miller, *The Bon Marché*, pp. 190–2; Susan P. Benson, *Counter Cultures* (Chicago, 1986), p. 126.
80 The K is pronounced explosively, like in 'Cook'.
81 Aschheim, 'The Jew Within', p. 317.
82 Mosse, *The German-Jewish Economic Elite*, p. 5.

83 Marion Kaplan, 'Friendship in the Margins: Jewish Social Relations in Imperial Germany', *Central European History*, Vol. 34, No. 4 (2001), pp. 471–501, 472.

1 Foundation: 1834–90 – 'Travelling Sons of David'

1. Attributed to Georg Tietz.
2. *Zeitschrift für Waren- und Kaufhäuser*, January 1933.
3. R. Clouston, *Letters from Germany and Belgium by an Autumn Tourist* (London, 1839), p. 173.
4. Ibid., p. 177.
5. Jerome K. Jerome, *Three Men on the Bummel, Three Men in a Boat and Three Men on the Bummel* (Oxford, 1998), p. 323..
6. Richard J. Evans, *The Coming of the Third Reich* (London, 2004), p. 15.
7. Werner Sombart, 'Das Warenhaus ein Gebilde des hochkapitalistischen Zeitalters', in Deutsche Waren- and Kaufhausverband, *Probleme des Warenhauses* (Berlin, 1928), p. 77.
8. Marie Baum, *Drei Klassen von Lohnarbeiterinnen in Industrie und Handel der Stadt Karlsruhe* (Karlsruhe, 1906), p. 144.
9. Ibid., p. 143.
10. Rudolf Knopf, *Die Wirkung der Kartelle der Textil- und Bekleidungsindustrie auf die Abnehmer* (Karlsruhe, 1915), p. 55.
11. Richard J. Evans, *The Pursuit of Power, Europe 1815–1914* (London, 2017), p. 327.
12. Aschheim, 'The Jew Within', p. 212.
13. Ladwig-Winters and Fischer, *Die Wertheims*, p. 15.
14. Ibid., p. 20.
15. Ibid., p. 35.
16. Tietz, *Hermann Tietz*, p. 15.
17. Ibid., p. 12.
18. Clouston, *Letters from Germany*, p. 154.
19. NilsBusch-Petersen, *Leonhard Tietz* (Berlin, 2014), p. 24.
20. Ibid., p. 26.
21. Ibid., pp. 18 and 22.
22. Hermann Tietz was Chaskel Tietz's brother.
23. Clouston, *Letters from Germany*, p. 110.
24. Ibid., p. 122.
25. Tietz, *Hermann Tietz*, p. 30.
26. Anecdotal evidence has it that he was also involved in the conservation of historic buildings in Frankfurt and was instrumental in the establishing of the Internationale Luft- und Raumfahrtausstellung in Berlin.

27 *Volkszeitung*, Frankfurt, 4 August 1927.
28 *Neue Mannheimer Zeitung*, 5 August 1927.
29 *Volkszeitung*, Frankfurt, 4 August 1927.
30 Archiv Südwestdeutsche Druck- & Verlagsgesellschaft GmbH (ASDV), undated and unattributed newspaper article, possibly from 4 April 1931.
31 ASDV, undated and unattributed type-written sheets, probably by Martin Klopstock.
32 ASDV, undated and unattributed newspaper article, possibly from 4 April 1931.
33 However, official records state that Bruchsal was opened as early as 1889 and Rastatt in 1890. Badisches Statistisches Landesamt (ed.), *Handel und Verkehr in Baden im Jahre 1925* (Kalrsruhe, 1927), p. 145.
34 Jürgen Schwarz, *Architektur und Kommerz: Studien zur deutschen Kauf- und Warenhausarchitektur vor dem Ersten Weltkrieg am Beispiel der Frankfurter Zeil* (Frankfurt, 1995), p. 229.
35 Generallandesarchiv Karlsruhe (GLAK), 480 7223.
36 Schleese Family Collection (SFC), *Tafel-Lied zur vermählungsfeier seiner lieben Schwester Hedwig mit Herrn Jacob Steilberger am 18. Dezember 1872. Gewidment von Albert Knopf.*
37 See Table 1.1 where some relationships between the retailing dynasties are given a graphic representation.
38 Elon, *The Pity of It All*, p. 208.
39 Ibid., p. 227.
40 I am indebted to Dr Emma Harris, Director of Studies at the Woolf Institute, Cambridge, for this insight into her own family's history.
41 Badisches Statistisches Landesamt, *Handel und Verkehr in Baden im Jahre 1925*, p. 146. Staatsarchiv Freiburg (StAF), Landesarchiv Baden-Württemberg, A 25/1 300/2.
42 ASDV, undated and unattributed typewritten sheets, probably by Martin Klopstock.
43 ASDV, Martin Klopstock, *Max Knopf als Persönlichkeit* (Karlsruhe, April 1931).
44 Ibid.
45 Ibid.
46 Clouston, *Letters from Germany*, p. 7.
47 Leo Baeck Institute (LBI), ME 335, Jandorf, Harry, *Erinnerungen an meinen Vater Adolf Jandorf*.
48 LBI, AR3144, Adolf Jandorf Collection.
49 Clouston, *Letters from Germany*, p. 10.
50 Ibid., p. 15.
51 Richard Thassilo, 'Graf von Schlieben', *Deutsche Allgemeine Zeitung*, 22 January 1932.
52 Ibid.

53 LBI, ME 335.
54 Lenz, *Karstadt*, p. 51.
55 David, *The Patron*, p. 2.
56 Clouston, *Letters from Germany*, p. 38.
57 Ibid., p. 39.
58 Ibid., p. 48.
59 David, *The Patron*, p. 51.
60 Stadtarchiv Chemnitz (StAC) 33309/39, Georg Manasse, *Einkauf, Verkauf und Organisation im Schocken-Konzern*, 6 June 1926.
61 Fuchs, *Ein Konzern aus Sachsen*, p. 35; see also: Schocken Library Jerusalem (SLJ) 111/191, p. 4.
62 StAC 33309/36, Karl Püschner to Georg Manasse, dated 15 June 1935, but should be 1934.
63 StAC 31451/449, examples from 24 August 1931 and 26 March 1934.
64 David, *The Patron*, p. 161.
65 Jeremy B. Jeffreys, *Retail Trading in Britain, 1850–1950: A Study of Trends in Retailing with Special Reference to the Development of Co-operative, Multiple Shop and Department Store Methods of Trading* (Cambridge, 1954), p. 18.
66 Stadtarchiv Freiburg (StadtAF) K1/139 3b, Carl Werner, 24 December 1918.
67 StadtAF K1/139/2m, p. 9.
68 Ibid., p. 10.
69 Ibid., handwritten notes which formed the basis of *100 Jahre C. Werner-Blust*, p. 9.
70 Badisches Statistisches Landesamt, *Handel und Verkehr in Baden im Jahre 1925*, p. 97.
71 There were even attempts made to introduce the term *Vollwarenhaus*, meaning a department store that also sold food. Käthe Lux, *Studien über die Entwicklung der Warenhäuser in Deutschland* (Jena, 1910), p. 175.
72 'In Mannheim wie auch in allen anderen Städten, findet man bei vielen kleineren Geschäften sehr oft die Bezeichnung "Kaufhaus". Das hat mit der Grösse der einzelnen Betriebe absolut nichts weiter zu tun.' Hans Meißinger, *Die Entwicklung des Detailhandels in Mannheim* (Heidelberg, 1931), p. 40.
73 Deutsche Waren- and Kaufhausverband (ed.), *Probleme des Warenhauses*, p. 39.
74 Meißinger, *Die Entwicklung des Detailhandels*, p. 40.
75 'Unter Kaufhaus … ist im allgemeinen Sprachgebrauch ein Textilfachgeschäft zu verstehen, in dem eine Reihe von verschiedenen Artikeln in verschiedenen Abteilungen zusammen feilgeboten werden, das also nicht den Charakter eines Spezialgeschäftes hat.' Meißinger, *Die Entwicklung des Detailhandels*, p. 40.
76 Lenz, *Karstadt*, pp. 22–5; who doesn't come to a conclusion and decides it isn't important after all.
77 'eine Sammlung von Sortimentsgeschäften aller Branchen unter einem Dach und unter einheitlicher Leitung'. Meißinger, *Die Entwicklung des Detailhandels*, p. 12.

78 Martin Müller, *Der Interessenskampf zwischen grosskapitalistischen und mittelständischen Einzelhandel* (Freiburg, 1933), p. 111.
79 Jeffreys, *Retail Trading in Britain*, p. 60.
80 Tim Coles, 'Department Stores as a Retail Innovation in Germany', in Crossick and Jaumain, *Cathedrals of Consumption*, p. 85.
81 Joseph Bach, *Die Organisation des gemeinsamen Einkaufs im Warenhaus und Einzelhandel* (Munich, 1933), pp. 15–17.
82 Michael Prinz, *Brot und Dividende, Konsumvereine in Deutschland und England vor 1914* (Göttingen, 1996), p. 80.
83 David Peal, 'Self-Help and the State: Rural Cooperatives in Imperial Germany', *Central European History*, Vol. 21, No. 3 (September 1988), pp. 244–66, 245.
84 Prinz, *Brot und Dividende*, p. 237.
85 Badisches Statistische Landesamt, *Handel und Verkehr in Baden im Jahre 1925*, p. 59.
86 Ibid., p. 60.
87 'Wodurch ein besonders günstiger Boden für die Entwicklung des Konsumvereinswesens gegeben war.' Meißinger, *Die Entwicklung des Detailhandels*, p. 25.
88 Badisches Statistische Landesamt, *Handel und Verkehr in Baden im Jahre 1925*, p. 60.
89 Peal, 'Self-Help and the State', p. 248
90 Lux, *Entwicklung der Warenhäuser*, p. 44.
91 Dingel, *Shopping for Masculinity*, p. 116.
92 Lux, *Entwicklung der Warenhäuser*, p. 46.
93 Knopf, *Die Wirkung der Kartelle*, p. 3.
94 Lux, *Entwicklung der Warenhäuser*, p. 73.
95 GLAK 56 13. The General-Intendanz of the royal household declared the postcard 'unwürdig' and asked for it to be removed from circulation by the police. Ten thousand of them had been produced at a cost of 210 *Marks* within a day and sold in the store. Hundred packs were sold at 4 *Marks* to door-to-door salesmen. They were taken out of circulation 27 October 1907.
96 Knopf, *Die Wirkung der Kartelle*, p. 18.
97 Lux, *Entwicklung der Warenhäuser*, p. 151.
98 Ibid.
99 Map 1 shows only the stores and branches discussed in this book, but illustrates the extent to which branch-based mass retailing had spread across Germany in just around ten years.
100 Paul Lerner, 'An All-Consuming History? Recent Works on Consumer Culture in Modern Germany', *Central European History*, Vol. 42, No. 3 (2009), pp. 509–43, 513.

101 Coles, 'Department Stores as a Retail Innovation in Germany', p. 72.
102 Cf. Lerner, *The Consuming Temple*, p. 11.
103 Applegate, *A Nation of Provincials*, p. 11.
104 Mosse, 'Jewish Entrepreneurship in Germany 1820–1935', p. 279.

2 Expansion: 1890–1900 – 'Each Sale – A Piece of Renown'

1 Miller, *The Bon Marché*, pp. 190–3.
2 Spiekermann, *Warenhaussteuer in Deutschland*, p. 10.
3 Briesen, *Warenhaus, Massenkonsum und Sozialmoral*, p. 14.
4 Max Cohen-Reuß, 'Die sozialen Probleme des Warenhauses und ihre Weiterentwicklung', in *Probleme des Warenhauses* (Berlin, 1928), p. 116.
5 Lux, *Studien über die Entwicklung der Warenhäuser*, p. 160.
6 *General-Anzeiger*, 1 December 1900.
7 Woolworth is usually credited with bringing this sales technique to Germany, but it seems it was already being used in the first years of the twentieth century. Wronker was advertising a 95-*Pfennig* week in September 1905 in the *General-Anzeiger*.
8 Lux, *Studien über die Entwicklung der Warenhäuser*, p. 184.
9 Mrs E. Pastecki, Mannheim, 17 February 2011.
10 Lux, *Warenhäuser in Deutschland*, p.142. The company name Maggi is synonymous with a savoury seasoning made of vegetable protein. Initially intended as a cheap and nourishing replacement for beef extract, the brown liquid became a near-universal condiment in the German-speaking word by 1900. See: Annatina Seifert, *Der Nahrungsmittelkonzern Maggi: Auswirkungen des Ersten Weltkriegs auf ein schweizerisches Unternehmen*, Dissertation Universität Zürich (Zürich, 2006).
11 Mrs I. Plfiegensdörfer, Bad Schönborn, 15 February 2011.
12 F. Richter, *Die tüchtige Verkäuferin, Aus der Praxis für die Praxis* (Freiburg, before 1925), p. 13.
13 Ibid., p. 15.
14 Ibid., p. 13.
15 Tietz, *Hermann Tietz*, p. 85.
16 Richter, *Die tüchtige Verkäuferin*, p. 13.
17 Mrs I. Plfiegensdörfer, Bad Schönborn, 15 February 2011.
18 Richter, *Die tüchtige Verkäuferin*, p. 12.
19 Otto Kitzinger, 'Warenhaus und Spezialgeschäft', in Deutsche Waren- and Kaufhausverband, *Probleme des Warenhauses*, p. 109.
20 Dingel, *Shopping for Masculinity*, p. 107.
21 Kitzinger, 'Warenhaus und Spezialgeschäft', p. 109.
22 Cf. Ugolini, *Men and Menswear*, p. 176.

23 Ibid., pp. 4–5.
24 Dingel, *Shopping for Masculinity*, p. 111.
25 *Verkaufserfolg durch Menschenkenntnis* was published by L. Schottlaender & Co. (no author or date), probably 1920s, p. 11.
26 Richter, *Die tüchtige Verkäuferin*, p. 15.
27 Tietz, *Hermann Tietz*, p. 89.
28 Mrs I. Plfiegensdörfer, Bad Schönborn, 15 February 2011.
29 The Christ-child brings presents to German children on Christmas eve.
30 Cf. Lerner, *The Consuming Temple*, p. 4, who claims the opposite.
31 Lux, *Warenhäuser in Deutschland*, p. 170.
32 StAC 33309/39, Georg Manasse.
33 Richter, *Die tüchtige Verkäuferin*, p. 12.
34 Mrs V. Senft, Mannheim, 21 March 2011.
35 StAC 33309/39, Georg Manasse.
36 Ibid., p. 12.
37 Tietz, *Hermann Tietz*, p. 89.
38 StAC 33309/39, Georg Manasse, 19 April 1933.
39 Julius Hirsch, 'Die Bedeutung des Warenhauses in der Volskwirtschaft', in Deutsche Waren- and Kaufhausverband, *Probleme des Warenhauses*, p. 60.
40 Tietz, *Hermann Tietz*, p. 45.
41 Fuchs, *Ein Konzern aus Sachsen*, p. 22.
42 *General-Anzeiger Mannheim*, 15 May 1906.
43 Ibid.
44 Ibid.
45 Reichstagsprotokoll, 20 November 1903.
46 Blackbourn, *Populists and Patricians* and Gellately, *The Politics of Economic Despair*. See also: Unterstell, *Mittelstand in der Weimarer Republik*; Winkler, *Mittelstand, Demokratie und Nationalsozialismus* and Saldern, *Mittelstand im Dritten Reich*.
47 Reichstagsprotokoll, 15 January 1913.
48 Reichstagsprotokoll, 20 November 1903.
49 Spiekermann, *Warenhaussteuer in Deutschland*, pp. 122–31.
50 *Verhandlungen der Stände-Versammlung des Großherzogtums Baden vom Landtag 1903/04 III. Beilagenheft* (Karlsruhe, 1904).
51 David Blackbourn, *Class, Religion, and Local Politics in Wilhelmine Germany: The Centre Party in Württemberg Before 1914* (Connecticut, 1980), pp. 144–5.
52 Evans, *The Pursuit of Power*, p. 330; *Verhandlungen der Stände-Versammlung des Großherzogtums Baden vom Landtag 1899/1900 II. Protokoll* (Karlsruhe, 1900). Kammer, 22 June 1900; *Verhandlungen der Stände-Versammlung des Großherzogtums Baden vom Landtag 1901/02 Protokoll* (Karlsruhe, 1902).

53 *Verhandlungen der Stände-Versammlung des Großherzogtums Baden vom Landtag 1903/04 III.*
54 GLAK 231 5016, Union of independent merchants and tradesmen of Baden, 12 June 1902.
55 *Verhandlungen der Stände-Versammlung des Großherzogtums Baden vom Landtag 1903/04 III.*
56 Ibid.
57 GLAK 231 5016 and also paraphrased in: *Verhandlungen der Stände-Versammlung des Großherzogtums Baden vom Landtag 1903/04 III.*
58 *Verhandlungen der Stände-Versammlung des Großherzogtums Baden vom Landtag 1903/04 III.*
59 GLAK 231 5016.
60 *Verhandlungen der Stände-Versammlung des Großherzogtums Baden vom Landtag 1901/02 IV.*
61 *Verhandlungen der Stände-Versammlung des Großherzogtums Baden vom Landtag 1903/04 III.*
62 Ibid., p. 168.
63 *Verhandlungen der Stände-Versammlung des Großherzogtums Baden vom Landtag 1903/04 III.*
64 Ibid., p. 150.
65 *Verhandlungen der Stände-Versammlung des Großherzogtums Baden vom Landtag 1903/04 III.*
66 Tietz, *Hermann Tietz*, p. 105.
67 Ibid., p. 65.
68 Ibid., p. 46; Spiekermann, 'Der Mittelstand stirbt!', in Weiss-Sussex and Zitzelsperger, *Das Berliner Warenhaus*, p. 47.
69 Reichstagsprotokoll, 20 November 1903.
70 Briesen, *Warenhaus, Massenkonsum und Sozialmoral*, p. 14.
71 Cf. Miller, *The Bon Marché*, p. 205.
72 Briesen, *Warenhaus, Massenkonsum und Sozialmoral*, p. 101.
73 Cf. Miller, *The Bon Marché*, p. 183 and Lerner, *The Consuming Temple*, p. 4.
74 Rappaport, *Shopping for Pleasure*, p. 5.
75 Ibid., pp. 10–11.
76 Miller, *The Bon Marché*, p. 190.
77 Spiekermann, *Warenhaussteuer in Deutschland*, p. 10.

3 Labour: 1890–1930 – 'Qualified Young Ladies'

1 Miller, *The Bon Marché*, p. 190.
2 Briesen, *Warenhaus, Massenkonsum und Sozialmoral*, p. 16.

3 Lerner, 'Circulation and Representation', pp. 395–413, 405.
4 Miller, *The Bon Marché*, p. 192.
5 S. P. Benson, *Counter Cultures, Saleswomen, Managers and Customers in American Department Stores 1890–1940* (Chicago, 1986), p. 125.
6 Ibid., p. 128.
7 Baum, *Drei Klassen von Lohnarbeiterinnen*, p. 122.
8 GLAK 480 7223.
9 StAC 33309/39, Georg Manasse, 5 April 1932.
10 There is no evidence as to the faith of the employees. Employees from the 1920s and 1930s report that the religious make-up reflected that of the town, with either a large proportion of Catholics or German Protestants, with a few Jewish employees. Upper management especially was however dominated by men with surnames that might well have been Jewish.
11 Adams, *Women Clerks in Wilhelmine Germany*, p. 11.
12 Sombart, 'Das Warenhaus ein Gebilde des hochkapitalistischen Zeitalters', p. 87.
13 Adams, *Women Clerks in Wilhelmine Germany*, p. 12.
14 *Berufszählung. Die berufliche und soziale Gliederung des deutschen Volkes*, Band 408 (Berlin, 1931), p. 703.
15 Published by Karstadt Karlsruhe on the occasion of the extension of the store: *Der Fächer* (Karlsruhe, 1990), p. 3.
16 Miller, *The Bon Marché*, p. 171.
17 Adams, *Women Clerks in Wilhelmine Germany*, pp. 36–8.
18 Hirsch, 'Die Bedeutung des Warenhauses in der Volskwirtschaft', p. 68.
19 Deutsche Waren- and Kaufhausverband, *Probleme des Warenhauses*, p. 36; Lux, *Studien über die Entwicklung der Warenhäuser*, p. 24.
20 Stadtarchiv Pforzheim (StadtAPf) Rj Schoc 14262 2. Ex., p. 30.
21 Richter, *Die tüchtige Verkäuferin, Aus der Praxis für die Praxis*, p. 3.
22 Baum, *Drei Klassen von Lohnarbeiterinnen*, p. 149.
23 Ibid., p. 135.
24 Baum, *Drei Klassen von Lohnarbeiterinnen*, p. 145.
25 Ibid., pp. 142 and 150; see also: Adams, *Women Clerks in Wilhelmine Germany*, p. 9.
26 Lux, *Studien über die Entwicklung der Warenhäuser*, p. 24.
27 Baum, *Drei Klassen von Lohnarbeiterinnen*, p. 150.
28 GLAK 480 7223 and StAC 31451/387.
29 StAC 31451, Schocken-Konzern & Nachfolger 387.
30 Ibid.
31 Schleese Collection, *Tafellied von Sigfried Raphael*, 13 May 1906. A line-up of Knopf's sales staff during a fashion show: Illustration 23.
32 Benson, *Counter Cultures*, p. 126.

33 Baum, *Drei Klassen von Lohnarbeiterinnen*, pp. 140–1.
34 Adams, *Women Clerks in Wilhelmine Germany*, p. 108.
35 StAC 31451/387.
36 Max Cohen-Reuss, 'Die sozialen Probleme des Warenhauses und ihre Weiterentwicklung', in Deutsche Waren- and Kaufhausverband, *Probleme des Warenhauses*, p. 117; Lux, *Studien über die Entwicklung der Warenhäuser*, p. 37. As confirmed by Frau Hinzle on 9 March 2010.
37 Julius Hirsch, *Das Warenhaus im Westdeutschland: Seine Organisation und Wirkung* (Leipzig, 1909), p. 10.
38 Knopf, *Die Wirkung der Kartelle*, p. 17.
39 Baum, *Drei Klassen von Lohnarbeiterinnen*, p. 123.
40 Firma Knopf, *Betriebsordnung der Betriebsgemeinschaft* (22 May 1925), p. 10 and Firma Knopf, *Betriebsordnung der Betriebsgemeinschaft* (30 June 1934), p. 12.
41 Baum, *Drei Klassen von Lohnarbeiterinnen*, p. 123.
42 Ibid., pp. 123–4.
43 Adams, *Women Clerks in Wilhelmine Germany*, p. 57.
44 Lilly Braun, *Die Frauenfrage* (Bremen, 2010), reprint from 1901, p. 483.
45 Paul Göhre 'Das Warenhaus', *Die Gesellschaft* (1907), p. 78.
46 Firma Knopf, *Betriebsordnung der Betriebsgemeinschaft* (30 June 1934), p. 6.
47 Hirsch, *Das Warenhaus in Westdeutschland*, p. 12.
48 Baum, *Drei Klassen von Lohnarbeiterinnen*, p. 150.
49 Hirsch, 'Die Bedeutung des Warenhauses in der Volkswirtschaft', p. 63.
50 Baum, *Drei Klassen von Lohnarbeiterinnen*, p. 164 and for comparison with factory workers, see p. 53.
51 Ibid., p. 168.
52 Lynn Abrams, *Workers' Culture in Imperial Germany, Leisure and Recreation in the Rhineland and Westphalia* (London, 1992), p. 27.
53 StAC 33309/39, Georg Manasse, 5 April 1932.
54 StAC 31451/387.
55 StAC 33309/39, Georg Manasse, 15 June 1931.
56 StAC 31451/387, Arbeitsordnung der Firma S. Wronker & Co., 25 July 1921, p. 6.
57 Lux, *Studien über die Entwicklung der Warenhäuser*, p. 28.
58 Firma Knopf, Firma Knopf, *Betriebsordnung der Betriebsgemeinschaft* (30 June 1934), p. 2.
59 StAC 33309/39, Georg Manasse, 19 April 1933.
60 StAC 33309/39, Georg Manasse, 5 April 1932.
61 Badisches Statistische Landesamt, *Handel und Verkehr in Baden im Jahre 1925*, p. 146.
62 Firma Knopf, Firma Knopf, *Betriebsordnung der Betriebsgemeinschaft* (30 June 1934), pp. 9–10.

63 Lux, *Studien über die Entwicklung der Warenhäuser*, p. 26.
64 Adams, *Women Clerks in Wilhelmine Germany*, p. 16.
65 Baum, *Drei Klassen von Lohnarbeiterinnen*, p. 128.
66 Lux, *Studien über die Entwicklung der Warenhäuser*, p. 40.
67 StAC 31451/387, Arbeitsordnung Wronker (1921), p. 2.
68 Ibid., p. 2.
69 Ibid., p. 3.
70 Stadtarchiv Karlsruhe (StadtAK) 1Bauakte Kaiserstraße BOA 3240; for the Strassburg store, see: Josef Durm, *Handbuch der Architektur* (Stuttgart, 1902) p. 88, and for the one at Mannheim, see: Leopold Stober, *Mannheim und seine Bauten* (Mannheim, 1906), p. 244.
71 Lux, *Studien über die Entwicklung der Warenhäuser*, p. 33.
72 Staatsarchiv Basel-Stadt (StAB) DI-REG 5a 4-20-5 (1) 45, Arbeitsordnung 1920.
73 Lux, *Studien über die Entwicklung der Warenhäuser*, p. 35.
74 StAB DI-REG 5a 4-20-5 (1) 45, Arbeitsordnung 1920.
75 Richter, *Die tüchtige Verkäuferin*, p. 16.
76 StAC 31451/387, Arbeitsordnung Wronker (1921), p. 7.
77 Ibid., p. 4.
78 Tietz, *Hermann Tietz*, p. 89.
79 Ibid.
80 *Verhandlungen der Stände-Versammlung des Großherzogtums Baden vom Landtag 1903/04 III*, p. 166.
81 Fuchs, *Ein Konzern aus Sachsen*, p. 123.
82 Schleese Collection, *Tafellied von Siegfried Raphael*, 13 May 1906. See Illustration 24.
83 Newspaper clipping, unattributed, dated '1916', probably 13 March 1916, Stadtarchiv Frankfurt (StadtAFra), Zeitungsarchiv Wronker, S3 R2075.
84 Martin Klopstock, 'Max Knopf als Persönlichkeit', *Zeitschrift für Waren- und Kaufhäuser*, Vol. 29, No. 14 (Berlin, 1931), p. 1.
85 StAC 31451/387.
86 StAC 33309/39, Georg Manasse, 1 May 1934.
87 Fuchs, *Ein Konzern aus Sachsen*, p. 118.

4 Apogee: 1900–14 – 'The Kaiser Is Impressed'

1 Leo Colze, *Berliner Warenhauser* (Leipzig, 1908), p. 9.
2 Warren G.Breckman, 'Disciplining Consumption: The Debate about Luxury in Wilhelmine Germany, 1890–1914', *Journal of Social History*, Vol. 24, No. 3 (Spring 1991), pp. 485–505, 499.

3 Alarich Rooch, *Zwischen Museum und Warenhaus: Ästhetisierungsprozesse und sozial-kommunikative Raumaneignung des Bürgertums* (Bremen, 2000), p. 21.
4 Lerner, 'Circulation and Representation', p. 410.
5 Rahden, 'Jews and the Ambivalences of Civil Society in Germany', p. 1030.
6 Kaplan, 'Friendship in the Margins', p. 500.
7 StAC 33309/39, Georg Manasse, 19 April 1933; and Meißinger, *Entwicklung des Detailhandels*, p. 13.
8 Meißinger, *Entwicklung des Detailhandels*, p. 38.
9 Ibid., p. 13.
10 Knopf, *Die Wirkung der Kartelle*, p. 17.
11 Meißinger, *Entwicklung des Detailhandels*, p. 38.
12 *General-Anzeiger Pforzheim*, 27 March 1915.
13 Oskar Trost, 'Abschied vom alten Marktplatz', *Lebendige Vergangenheit*, Heft 11 (February 1962), p. 20.
14 Stadtarchiv Pforzheim (StadtAPf), B64 Westliche Karl-Friedrichstraße.
15 *Pforzheimer Anzeiger*, 27 March 1915.
16 StadtAPf, B64 Westliche Karl-Friedrichstraße.
17 *General-Anzeiger*, Pforzheim, 9 December 1911.
18 *General-Anzeiger*, Pforzheim, 5 December 1911.
19 *General-Anzeiger*, Pforzheim, 9 December 1911.
20 *Pforzheimer Kurier*, 28 February 1913.
21 Ibid.
22 *Pforzheimer Freie Presse*, 21 November 1931.
23 *Pforzheimer Rundschau*, 21 November 1931.
24 Kreis's career successfully spanned the Kaiserreich, the Weimar Republic and the Third Reich, right into the Federal Republic, building the Hygienemuseum in Dresden alongside numerous other noteworthy institutions.
25 Nanni Harbordt, *Bernhard Sehring – Das Warenhaus Tietz an der Leipziger Strasse* (Ravensburg, 2010), p. 2.
26 Reichstagsprotokoll, 24 April 1908.
27 The store still exists, the exterior largely unaltered to this day, as a branch of the Karstadt AG.
28 *Zeitschrift für Waren- und Kaufhäuser*, 14 (1931), pp. 1–5, 2.
29 *Badische Presse*, 24 April 1914.
30 Ibid.
31 'Ein Bau allergrössten Stiles und ersten Ranges', *Badische Presse*, 24 April 1914.
32 Eberhard Grunsky, 'Das ehemalige Warenhaus Knopf (heute Karstadt) in Karlsruhe', *Denkmalpflege in Baden-Württemberg* (April–June 1979), pp. 57–64.
33 Mrs I. Plfiegensdörfer, Bad Schönborn, 15 February 2011.
34 Lux, *Warenhäuser in Deutschland*, p. 80.

35 Ibid., p. 171.
36 StAC 33309/39, Georg Manasse, *Einkauf, Verkauf und Organisation im Schocken-Konzern*, 6 June 1926.
37 LBI, Hermann Tietz Collection, AR 1943, 1, 1.
38 Gustav Stresemann in1900 quoted in *Monumente*, October 2009.
39 Busch-Petersen, *Leonhard Tietz*, p. 32.
40 Quoted in Lerner, *The Consuming Temple*, p. 174, where he proves himself wrong about the acceptance of Jewish department stores in the provinces.
41 Schwarz, *Architektur und Kommerz*, p. 223.
42 Lux, *Warenhäuser in Deutschland*, p. 171.
43 Mrs I. Plfiegensdörfer, Bad Schönborn, 15 February 2011.
44 *General-Anzeiger*, 13 June 1912.
45 Rappaport, *Shopping for Pleasure*, p. 143.
46 *Badische Presse*, 24 April 1914.
47 Cf. Lerner, *The Consuming Temple*, p. 94.
48 *Zeitschrift für Waren- und Kaufhäuser*, 31 May 1925
49 Ladwig-Winters and Fischer, *Die Wertheims*, p. 50.
50 The whole event was covered in the press. For example: *Berliner Tageblatt*, 24 January 1910 or *Berliner Volkszeitung*, 24 January 1910.
51 *Staatsbürgerzeitung*, 16 December 1912, quoted in Ladwig-Winters and Fischer, *Die Wertheims*, p. 174.
52 Reichstagsprotokoll, 15 January 1913.
53 Amos Elon, *The Pity of It All*, p. 223.
54 Compare, for instance, with the ridiculous figure of Diederich Hessling in Heinrich Mann's *Der Untertan*.
55 Elon, *The Pity of It All*, p. 284.
56 Ladwig-Winters and Fischer, *Die Wertheims*, p. 171.
57 Reichstagsprotokoll, 15 January 1913.
58 Elon, *The Pity of It All*, p. 225.
59 Ladwig-Winters and Fischer, *Die Wertheims*, p. 142.
60 Ibid., p. 57.
61 Ibid., p. 172.
62 StAC 31451/386.
63 David, *The Patron*, p. 191.
64 Fuchs, *Ein Konzern aus Sachsen*, p. 251.
65 David, *The Patron*, p. 174.
66 Ibid., p. 171.
67 Well known for financially supporting progressive publications on economy and society in Baden.

68 Levis Family Collection (LFC), collection of papers including certificates of thanks and letters of recognition by the royal household.
69 Heinz Schmitt, *Juden in Karlsruhe* (Karlsruhe, 1988), p. 165. This book is very poorly researched, and the claims made within it are hard to check up on as the sources are not always cited.
70 SFC, engagement announcement, wedding programme and menu.
71 GLAK 480 7379, Nr. 1.
72 Ibid.
73 LBI, Lili Wronker Collection, AR25255, 956.
74 StadtAFra S3 R2075, newspaper clipping, unattributed, dated '1916', probably 11 March 1916.
75 Italics in original, *General-Anzeiger*, Frankfurt, 3 August 1927.
76 Göhre, 'Das Warenhaus', p. 90.
77 Tietz, *Hermann Tietz*, p. 104.
78 LBI, Adolf Jandorf Collection, AR3144.
79 Ibid.
80 Ladwig-Winters and Fischer, *Die Wertheims*, p. 64.
81 Tietz, *Hermann Tietz*, p. 65.
82 Ibid., p. 94.
83 GLAK 231 5738.
84 *Verhandlungen der Stände-Versammlung des Großherzogtums Baden vom Landtag 1911/12 Protokoll* (Karlsruhe, 1910), p. 198.
85 Walter Rüegg and Otto Neuloh (eds), *Zur soziologischen Theorie und Analyse des 19. Jahrhunderts* (Göttingen, 1971), pp. 145–62.
86 GLAK 231 5126.
87 GLAK 231 5056.
88 Ibid.
89 *Verhandlungen der Stände-Versammlung des Großherzogtums Baden vom Landtag 1909/10 Protokoll*, p. 285.
90 Karlheinz Reich, *Die Liberalen Parteien in Deutschland 1918–1933* (Osnabrück, 1979), p. 13.
91 Italics added. *Verhandlungen der Ersten Kammer*, 25 June 1910, p. 683.
92 Ibid., p. 683.
93 *Beilage zum Protokoll der Sitzung der Zweiten Kammer*, 28 April 1912, p. 23.
94 Ibid.
95 Peter Stuerzebecher, 'Warenhauser', Leopold Stober, *Mannheim und seine Bauten* (Mannheim, 1906), p. 5.
96 Breckman, 'Disciplining Consumption', pp. 485–505, p. 490.
97 Elon, *The Pity of It All*, p. 223.

98 Oded Heilbronner, 'From Antisemitic Peripheries to Antisemitic Centres: The Place of Antisemitism in Modern German History', *Journal of Contemporary History*, Vol. 35, No. 4 (October, 2000), pp. 559–76, 565.

99 The pinnacle of this perceived superiority of the German Jew may be seen in the formation of a youth movement in which Jewish boys and men went hiking in the woods to commune with their German heritage. Glenn R. Sharfman, 'Between Identities: The German Jewish Youth Movement Blau-Weiss, 1912–1926', in Michael Berkowitz, Susan L. Tananbaum and Sam W. Bloom (eds), *Forging Modern Jewish Identities, Public Faces and Private Struggles* (London, 2003), pp. 198–209.

5 Survival: 1914–29 – 'Dear Corner of Homeland'

1 Heinz Kramer, *Warenhausprobleme der jüngsten Zeit* (Würzburg, 1931), p. 90.
2 Cf. Lerner, *The Consuming Temple*, p. 8.
3 Kauder, *German Politics and the Jews*, p. 89.
4 Heilbronner, 'From Antisemitic Peripheries to Antisemitic Centres', p. 568.
5 Tim Grady, *A Deadly Legacy: Jews and the Great War* (New Haven, 2017), p. 7.
6 Ladwig-Winters and Fischer, *Die Wertheims*, p. 202.
7 Knopf, *Die Wirkung der Kartelle*, p. 4.
8 Ibid., pp. 21 and 78.
9 Busch-Petersen, *Adolf Jandorf*, p. 67.
10 Grady, *A Deadly Legacy*, p. 119.
11 R. Vogel, *Ein Stück von uns: Deutsche Juden in deutschen Armeen, 1813–1976* (Mainz, 1977), p. 149; Elon, *The Pity of It All*, p. 338.
12 LBI, ME 335.
13 Elon, *The Pity of It All*, p. 344.
14 Italics added, StadtAF K1/139/3b, 24 December 1918.
15 Ibid.
16 Evans, *The Coming of the Third Reich*, p. 83.
17 Busch-Petersen, *Jandorf*, p. 7.
18 Tietz, *Hermann Tietz*, p. 212.
19 StadtAK 8/PBS X 1139.
20 Stadtarchiv Mannheim (StadtMa), Anker Kaufstätte.
21 *Badische Presse*, 2 February 1922.
22 *Zeitschrift für Waren- und Kaufhäuser*, 4 January 1920.
23 *Zeitschrift für Waren- und Kaufhäuser*, 26 February 1922.
24 I am indebted to Dr Christoph Popp of the municipal archive in Mannheim for this information.
25 *General-Anzeiger Mannheim*, 16 October 1928.

26 Ibid.
27 Evans, *The Coming of the Third Reich*, p. 173.
28 Hitler, *Mein Kampf*, p. 172.
29 Ibid., p. 291.
30 Heilbronner, 'From Antisemitic Peripheries to Antisemitic Centres', p. 568.
31 Ernst O. Bräunche and Ulrich Nieß, *Geschichte im Plakat 1914–1933, Katalog zur Ausstellung der Stadtarchive Karlsruhe und Mannheim* (Karlsruhe, 2004), p. 37.
32 Heinko Haumann and Hans Schadek, *Geschichte der Stadt Freiburg* (Stuttgart, 1996), Volume III, p. 282; *Volkswacht*, 1 September 1921; StadtAF C4/VI/15/5; Johnpeter H. Grill, *The Nazi Movement in Baden 1920–1945* (Chapel Hill, 1983), p. 22.
33 Lenz, *Karstadt*, p. 86.
34 Ibid., pp. 75–9.
35 Lenz, *Karstadt*, p. 92.
36 *Oberbadisches Industrie- und Handelsblatt*, 1 January 1926.
37 StAF F196/1 3628/2 [171].
38 StadtAF KXIV/17/14, correspondence dated 30 May 1922, 15 November 1922 and 15 May 1923.
39 McElligott, *Rethinking the Weimar Republic*, p. 52.
40 Unterstell, *Mittelstand in der Weimarer Republik*, p. 25.
41 Fuchs, *Ein Konzern aus Sachsen*, p. 129.
42 StAF F 196/1 3628/2 and Fuchs, *Ein Konzern aus Sachsen*, pp. 53–7.
43 David, *The Patron*, p. 192.
44 Lenz, *Karstadt*, p. 103.
45 *General-Anzeiger*, Frankfurt, 3 August 1927.
46 Schwarz, *Architektur und Kommerz*, p. 223.
47 *General-Anzeiger*, Frankfurt, 3 August 1927.
48 Ibid.
49 StadtAFra S3 R2075, newspaper clipping, unattributed, dated '1916', probably 13 March 1916.
50 StadtAFra MA S2739 2, Magistrat Frankfurt am Main, 5 August 1927.
51 Ibid.
52 *Breisgauer Zeitung*, 9 November 1928, this paper even included a list of the craftsmen involved.
53 StaatAF A25/1 300/ 1 and 2.
54 StadtAF K-C4 I/26/6.
55 The term *teuer* means both expensive and loved, so 'dear' seems the best translation. *Oberreinischer Beobachter*, 10 November 1928.
56 *Oberrheinischer Beobachter*, 10 November 1928.
57 Ibid. Also, cf. Lerner, *The Consuming Temple*, p. 8.

58 Klopstock, 'Max Knopf als Persönlichkeit', p. 2.
59 Anthony McElligott, *Contested City. Municipal Politics and the Rise of Nazism in Altona, 1917–1931* (Ann Arbor, 1998), p. 135.
60 LBI, ME 335. Germans would have earned 30–50 *Reichsmark* a week at the time.
61 David, *The Patron*, p. 148.
62 Ibid., p. 150.
63 Ibid., p. 149.
64 StAC 31451/387, Georg Manasse, Press Conference, 22 September 1931.
65 David, *The Patron*, p.165.
66 StAC 31451/449.
67 Ibid.
68 StAC 33309/39, Georg Manasse, *Einkauf, Verkauf und Organisation im Schocken-Konzern*, 6 June 1926.
69 Fuchs, *Ein Konzern aus Sachsen*, pp. 111–13.
70 StAC 31451/449, 13 June 1931.
71 StAC 33309/39, Georg Manasse, 19 April 1933.
72 Fuchs, *Ein Konzern aus Sachsen*, p. 128.
73 StAC 31451/449, 20 June 1932.
74 This example from a memorandum in the Ziefle Collection.
75 StAC 31451/449, 28 October 1931.
76 Ziefle Collection, Zeitungsauschnitte, cutting dated 13 December 1933.
77 Ziefle Collection, Fritz Richter, *Die tüchtige Verkäuferin*.
78 StAC 31451/449, 28 October 1931.
79 Mrs I. Plfiegensdörfer, Bad Schönborn, 15 February 2011.
80 Ibid.
81 StAC 31451/449, 28 October 1931.
82 Richter, *Die tüchtige Verkäuferin*, p. 6.
83 Firma Knopf, *Betriebsordnung der Betriebsgemeinschaft* (22 May 1925), p. 10; Firma Knopf, *Betriebsordnung der Betriebsgemeinschaft* (30 June 1934), p. 12.
84 Richter, *Die tüchtige Verkäuferin*, p. 5.
85 Mrs I. Plfiegensdörfer, Bad Schönborn, 15 February 2011.
86 Firma Knopf, *Betriebsordnung der Betriebsgemeinschaft* (22 May 1925), p. 10; Firma Knopf, *Betriebsordnung der Betriebsgemeinschaft* (30 June 1934), p. 12.
87 Richter, *Die tüchtige Verkäuferin*, p. 7.
88 Ibid., p. 4.
89 Mrs A. Stillhahn, Freiburg, 30 January 2010; Mrs A. Hinzel, Freiburg, 9 March 2010; Mrs G. Nestelberger, Freiburg, 9 March 2010.
90 Mrs K. Hipp, Freiburg, 1 and 2 February 2010.
91 StAC 31451/449, 28 October 1931.
92 Ibid., Salman Schocken, 28 October 1931.

93 Ibid., Georg Manasse, 28 October 1931.
94 Several of these can be found at: StAC 31451/607, Schocken-Konzern & Nachfolger.

6 Decline: 1929–32 – 'Voices of Envy'

1 Henning Grunwald, 'Die "Vertrauenskrise der Justitz" in der Weimarer Republik: Justizkritik als Krisendiagnostik', in Henning Grunwald and Manfred Pfister (eds), *Krisis! Krisenszenarien, Diagnosen, Diskursstrategien* (Munich, 2007), pp. 177–99, 177.
2 Evans, *Coming of the Third Reich*, p. 211.
3 Wolfgang Mönninghoff, *Enteignung der Juden: Wunder der Wirtschaft, Erbe der Deutschen* (Hamburg, 2001), p. 70.
4 Kauder, *German Politics and the Jews*, p. 167.
5 Briesen, *Warenhaus, Massenkonsum und Sozialmoral*, p. 66.
6 Ladwig-Winters and Fischer, *Die Wertheims*, p. 103.
7 Kauder, *German Politics and the Jews*, p. 176.
8 StadtAF, *Handelskammer Kreis Freiburg Jahresbericht 1928*.
9 *Oberbadische Handels- und Wirtschaftszeitung*, 1 January 1929.
10 Ibid.
11 *Zeitschrift für Kauf- und Warenhäuser*, 5 March 1932.
12 Hrant Pasdermadjian, *The Department Store. Ist Origins, Evolution and Economics* (London, 1954), p. 45.
13 Ibid., p. 56.
14 Evans, *Coming of the Third Reich*, p. 256.
15 Meißinger, *Die Entwicklung des Detailhandels*, p. 11.
16 StAC 33309/39, Georg Manasse.
17 Badisches Statistische Landesamt, *Handel und Verkehr in Baden im Jahre 1925*, p. 8.
18 Ibid., p. 9.
19 Ibid., p. 10.
20 Ibid., p. 19.
21 Meißinger, *Die Entwicklung des Detailhandels*, p. 29.
22 Saldern, *Mittelstand im Dritten Reich*, p. 23.
23 Unterstell, *Mittelstand in der Weimarer Republik*, p. 25.
24 Deutsches Tagebuch Archiv, Emmendingen (DTA) 1798, 7, Werner, Carl, p. 76.
25 *Oberbadisches Industrie- und Handelsblatt*, 1 January 1926.
26 Cohen-Reuss, 'Die sozialen Probleme des Warenhauses und ihre Weiterentwicklung', p. 114.
27 *Frankfurter Zeitung*, 12 May 1935.
28 *Handelskammer Kreis Freiburg Jahresbericht* 1928.

29 Kramer, *Warenhausprobleme jüngster Zeit*, p. 97.
30 *Volkswacht*, 10 April 1929.
31 StAC 33309/39, Georg Manasse, 5 April 1932.
32 StadtAF C4/XIII/24/5.
33 DTA 1798, 7, Diary of Carl Werner, p. 68.
34 Grunwald, 'Die "Vertrauenskrise der Justitz"', p. 179.
35 Evans, *The Third Reich in Power*, p. 9.
36 Julius Sternberg, owner of the department store MK Sternberg in Spandau, Berlin, had also voiced similar concerns. Avakin and Paulus, *Die Familie Sternberg*, p. 46. Heilbronner emphasizes the great fear that the farmers, another branch of the diverse *Mittelstand* family, had of communism. Heilbronner, *Catholicism, Political Culture, and the Countryside*, p. 236.
37 See, for example, the speech of Viktor Welcker (the main antisemitic organizer in the Kraichgau) in the village of Flehingen. GLAK 357/10035, Gendarmerie Flehingen, 9 March 1892, quoted in DagmarHerzog, 'Anti-Judaism in Intra-Christian Conflict: Catholics and Liberals in Baden in the 1840s', *Central European History*, Vol. 27, No. 3 (1994), p. 298.
38 Ibid., p. 299.
39 'Gewiss nicht zum Segen der Menschheit', *Donaueschinger Wochenblatt*, 17 March 1894.
40 Kauder, *German Politics and the Jews*, p. 154.
41 Grill, *The Nazi Movement in Baden*, pp. 55–8.
42 Heilbronner, *Catholicism, Political Culture, and the Countryside*, pp. 37–8, especially Table 4.
43 Evans, *Coming of the Third Reich*, p. 211.
44 DTA 592, Diary of Heinz Wittmann (Mannheim, 1933), p. 38.
45 Grill, *The Nazi Movement in Baden*, p. 297.
46 Grunwald, 'Die "Vertrauenskrise der Justitz"', p. 179.
47 *Zeitschrift für Kauf- und Warenhäuser*, 3 January 1931.
48 Ibid.
49 Ladwig-Winters and Fischer, *Die Wertheims*, p. 261.
50 *Das Hakenkreuzbanner*, 27 June 1931.
51 Ibid.
52 Ibid.
53 *Handelskammer Baden Jahresbericht* 1931.
54 *Der Führer*, 24 February 1931.
55 Mönninghoff, *Enteignung der Juden*, p. 70.
56 *Der Führer*, 25 June 1931.
57 StadtAF, Freiburg Council Meetings Protocol, 8 January 1932.
58 *Der Führer*, 19 May 1932.

59 Ibid.
60 'Wir haben noch niemals eine so scharfe generische Propaganda gegen uns gehabt wie jetzt.' StAC 31451/449.
61 David, *The Patron*, p. 188.
62 Ladwig-Winters and Fischer, *Die Wertheims*, p. 261.
63 GLAK, *Ständekammer/Badischer Landtag 231 5940 Protokoll Badischer Landtag*, 28 April 1932.
64 *Protokoll Badische Landtag*, 3 May 1932.
65 Ibid.
66 Ibid.
67 Ibid.
68 Ibid.
69 Ibid.
70 Ibid.
71 Ibid.
72 Ibid.
73 Ibid.
74 Lenz, *Karstadt*, p. 168.
75 Eckhard Wandel, *Banken und Versicherungen im 19. und 20. Jahrhundert* (Munich, 1998), p. 100.
76 Ibid., p. 101.
77 Lenz, *Karstadt*, p. 113.
78 Not all of it, however, as after the Second World War, Karstadt was able to expand its network of branches by using land they had not sold before to erect new branches, making it one of the most successful postwar department store chains.
79 StadtAFra S3 R2075, Wronker advertisement (title illegible, unattributed), 29 October 1931.
80 StAC 31451/386.
81 *Zeitschrift für Kauf- und Warenhäuser*, 16 July 1931.
82 StadtMa, *Neue Badische Landeszeitung*, Mannheim, 6 July 1932.
83 StAC 31451/386, notes from Dr Moses.
84 Ibid.
85 Ibid.
86 StAC 31451/386, protocol of a conversation between Dr Lessing of the Dresdner Bank and Salman Schocken, 30 June 1930.
87 StAC 31451/386, protocol of a conversation between Salman Schocken and Dr Lessing of the Dresdner Bank, 14 March 1931.
88 StadtAFra S3 R2075, cuttings, September 1932, all undated and unattributed.
89 Interview with Albrecht Wertheim on 6 October 1988, in Ladwig-Winters and Fischer, *Die Wertheims*, p. 248.

90 Ladwig-Winters and Fischer, *Die Wertheims*, p. 89.
91 Ibid., p. 258; Lenz, *Karstadt*, p. 168.
92 Uwe Spiekermann, *Basis der Konsumgesellschaft: Entstehung und Entwicklung des modernen Kleinhandels in Deutschland 1850–1914* (Munich, 1999), p. 378.
93 Tietz, *Hermann Tietz*, pp. 141–4.
94 *Pforzheimer Freie Presse*, 21 November 1931.
95 Italics added, *Pforzheimer Rundschau*, 21 November 1931.
96 ASDV, 4 April 1931.
97 Italics in original, ASDV, 4 April 1931.
98 ASDV, 4 April 1931.
99 Spiekermann, 'Der Mittelstand stirbt!', in Weiss-Sussex and Zitzelsperger, *Das Berliner Warenhaus*, p. 50.
100 StAC 33309/39, Georg Manasse, 5 April 1932.
101 David, *The Patron*, p. 170.
102 StAC 33309/39, Georg Manasse, 5 April 1932.
103 StAC 31451/386, protocol of a conversation between Dr Lessing of the Dresdner Bank and Salman Schocken, 30 June 1930.
104 StAC 31451/449, 24 August 1931.
105 Ibid.
106 *Pforzheimer Rundschau*, 25 September 1931.
107 Evans, *The Third Reich in Power*, p. 379.
108 This view is very unpopular in Germany as it does not fit in with the prevailing history of the nation in general and the process of Aryanization in particular. A typical erroneous way of reporting this: *Frankfurter Allgemeine*, 7 November 2007 and also Stefan Appelius, 'Lili und die Kaufhauskönige', Einestages Zeitgeschichte auf Spiegel Online, http://einestages.spiegel.de/static/topic albumbackground/589/lili_und_die_kaufhauskoenige.html, last retrieved 23 December 2012.

7 Fall: 1933–9 – 'Two Million Hitler Portraits'

1 *Zeitschrift für Waren- und Kaufhäuser*, January 1933.
2 DTA 1798, 7, p. 28.
3 Ibid., p. 89.
4 Ladwig-Winters and Fischer, *Die Wertheims*, p. 111.
5 Stanislav G. Pugliese, 'Resisting Fascism: The Politics and Literature of Italian Jews, 1922–45', in Berkowitz, Tananbaum and Bloom, *Forging Modern Jewish Identities*, pp. 269–71.
6 *Badische Presse*, 7 March 1933.

7 DTA 19495/II 1-2, Diary of Hedwig Rahmer (Mannheim, 1933), p. 48.
8 Haumann and Schadek, *Geschichte der Stadt Freiburg*, p. 301.
9 Hansmartin Schwarzmeier, 'Der badische Landtag', in Peter Blickle et al. (eds), *Von der Ständeversammlung zum demokratischen Parlament* (Stuttgart, 1982), pp. 236–39. It would not be the only place Nazis and the police colluded, see McElligott, *Contested City*, p. 159.
10 Michael Bock, 'Schmitt, Josef Franz', in *Neue Deutsche Biographie 23* (2007), S. 235–6 [Onlinefassung]; http://www.deutsche-biographie.de/pnd118609262.html.
11 *Badische Presse*, 15 March 1933.
12 McElligott, *Contested City*, p. 212.
13 *Badische Presse*, 13 March 1933.
14 Josef Werner, *Hakenkreuz und Judenstern* (Karlsruhe, 1990), pp. 43–5.
15 Evans, *Coming of the Third Reich*, pp. 97–102.
16 *Badische Presse*, 14 March 1933.
17 *Badische Presse*, 1 April 1933.
18 Ibid.
19 StAF F 202/32, 7030.
20 StadtAK 8/Sts 17/310, Gesprächsprotokoll Wilman Wagemann, 24 June 1987.
21 Ladwig-Winters and Fischer, *Die Wertheims*, p. 267.
22 Das Schwarzbuch, quoted in Ladwig-Winters and Fischer, *Die Wertheims*, p. 268.
23 *Freiburger Tagespost*, 13 March 1933 and also recalled in an interview with Mrs A. Hinzel, Freiburg, 9 March 2010.
24 Gellately, *Backing Hitler*, p. 27. See Illustrations 51–3.
25 *Badische Presse*, 2 April 1933.
26 DTA 592, Diary of Heinz Wittmann (Mannheim, 1933), p. 39; DTA 13,2 Diary of E. C. Halder (Karlsruhe, 1933), p. 17.
27 Lotte Paepcke, *Ein kleiner Händler der mein Vater war* (Baden-Baden, 1989), p. 49; *Freiburger Zeitung*, 3 April 1933 and also the Wertheim store in Berlin. See Ladwig-Winters and Fischer, *Die Wertheims*, p. 162.
28 Fortunately the direct translation of this into English works. Letter from Mrs I. Plfiegensdörfer, Bad Schönborn, 15 February 2011.
29 Kauder, *German Politics and the Jews*, p. 89.
30 Avraham Barkai, *Vom Boykott zur Entjudung, Der wirtschaftliche Existenzkampf der Juden im Dritten Reich 1933–1943* (Frankfurt, 1988), p. 65.
31 Ibid., p. 46; Robert Gellately (ed.), *Social Outsiders in Nazi Germany* (Princeton, 2001), p. 51.
32 These conflicting claims can be found in Norbert Frei, *National Socialist Rule in Germany, The Führer State, 1933–1945* (Oxford, 1933), p. 49 and in Ian Kershaw, *The Nazi Dictatorship, Problems and Perspectives of Interpretation* (London, 2000), p. 87.

33 Christoph Kreutzmüller, *Final Sale in Berlin: The Destruction of Jewish Commercial Activity, 1930–1945* (New York, 2017), p. 7.
34 Kopper, 'Wirtschaftliche Selbstbehauptung im sozialen Ghetto', p. 206.
35 David Schoenbaum, *Hitler's Social Revolution, Class and Status in Nazi Germany 1933–39* (New York, 1980), p. 134.
36 ASDV, possibly by Georg Tippel, early 1954. The ASDV kindly supplied me with a collection of photocopied typed notes on Knopf in Karlsruhe that had been held by Karstadt Karlsruhe, but since lost.
37 *Deutsche Wochenschau*, 4 November 1933.
38 StAC 31451/449, 18 December 1933.
39 Barkai, *Vom Boykott zur Entjudung*, p. 65.
40 Ladwig-Winters and Fischer, *Die Wertheims*, p. 280.
41 Mrs I. Plfiegensdörfer, Bad Schönborn, 15 February 2011.
42 McElligott, *Contested City*, p. 212.
43 *Breisgauer Zeitung/Freiburger Zeitung*, 25 March 1933; *Der Alemanne*, 27 March 1933.
44 NSDAP Gau Baden, Amt für Beamte Letter to the Municipalities (Schocken, Library Jerusalem 115/115/4, p. 21, quoted in Fuchs, *Ein Konzern aus Sachsen*, p. 220.
45 GLAK 480 8049, Nr. 1, EK 8049.
46 *Zeitschrift für Waren- und Kaufhäuser*, 25 March 1933.
47 Schoenbaum, *Hitler's Social Revolution*, p. 133.
48 Ladwig-Winters and Fischer, *Die Wertheims*, pp. 142–4.
49 Evans, *The Third Reich in Power*, p. 380; Schoenbaum, *Hitler's Social Revolution*, p. 135.
50 StAC 31451/449, 19 October 1933.
51 StAC 31451/449, 8 May 1933.
52 Ibid.
53 StAC 33309/39, Georg Manasse, 5 April 1932.
54 Evans, *The Third Reich in Power*, p. 380.
55 Themenabend zur Progrommnacht, Dokumentarfilm Dagmar Christmann and Thomas Tautenberg, 'Ein braunes Band der Sympathie – die Dresdner Bank und das Dritte Reich' First Broadcast ARD Hessen III, 3 November 1997.
56 Busch-Petersen, *Leonhard Tietz*, pp. 80–1.
57 Kopper, 'Wirtschaftliche Selbstbehauptung im sozialen Ghetto', p. 205.
58 Gellately, *Social Outsiders in Nazi Germany*, p. 53.
59 Interview with Mrs A. Hinzel, Freiburg, 9 March 2010.
60 Interviews with Mrs A. Stillhahn, Freiburg, 30 January 2010; Mrs A. Hinzel, Freiburg, 9 March 2010; Mrs G. Nestelberger, Freiburg, 9 March 2010.
61 StAF F196/1 3628/1.

62 Ziefle Collection, Betriebsführer Betriebsordnung 1924 and 1934.
63 Ladwig-Winters and Fischer, *Die Wertheims*, p. 123.
64 Ibid., p. 158.
65 Fuchs, *Ein Konzern aus Sachsen*, p. 198.
66 GLAK 480 8049, Nr. 1 EK 8049.
67 Ibid.
68 StAB DI-REG 5a 4-20-5 (1) 45.
69 StAF 196/1 3628/1.
70 Fuchs, *Ein Konzern aus Sachsen*, p. 210.
71 StAF F196/1 6048.
72 StAF F202/32 7030.
73 Andrea Brucher-Lembach, ... *wie Hunde auf ein Stück Brot* (Bremgarten, 2004), pp. 55–7.
74 Peter Longerich, *Politik der Vernichtung: Eine Gesamtdarstellung der nationalsozialistischen Judenverfolgung* (Munich, 1998), p. 126.
75 StAF F202/32 7030, Letter from the accountant Edwin Urban.
76 ASDV, possibly by Georg Tippel, early 1954 (on the occasion of the takeover of Hölscher KG by the Karstadt AG).
77 GLAK 480 7223.
78 Ibid.
79 Ibid.
80 Kopper, 'Wirtschaftliche Selbstbehauptung im sozialen Ghetto', p. 206.
81 Fuchs, *Ein Konzern aus Sachsen*, p. 228; David, *The Patron*, p. 257.
82 Fuchs, *Ein Konzern aus Sachsen*, p. 232.
83 Ibid., pp. 253–6.
84 David, *The Patron*, p. 281.
85 Evans, *The Third Reich in Power*, p. 381.
86 Kreutzmüller, *Final Sale in Berlin*, p. 192.
87 Ladwig-Winters and Fischer, *Die Wertheims*, p. 284.
88 Ibid., p. 317.
89 Ziefle Collection, 'Dieser Betrieb ab 1. April 1938: Kaufhaus Fritz Richter KG'
90 Evans, *The Third Reich in Power*, p. 387.
91 Information from Wolfgang Ziefle and documents from the Ziefle Collection.
92 Mönninghoff, *Enteignung der Juden*, p. 70.
93 Between 3.41 per cent and 5.29 per cent, between 1935 and 1937, in Ladwig-Winters and Fischer, *Die Wertheims*, pp. 205–6.
94 Interviews with Mrs K. Hipp, Freiburg, 1 and 2 February 2010 and Mrs L. Pauli, Freiburg, 9 March 2010. Customer numbers remained the same at Wertheim too. Ladwig-Winters and Fischer, *Die Wertheims*, p. 207.
95 DTA 1798, 7, p. 111, probably written in December 1937.

96 This amount seems vastly exaggerated but is an indication of how subjectively there seemed to be an awful lot more than was necessary, interview with Mrs A. Hinzel, Freiburg, 9 March 2010.
97 ASDV, possibly by Georg Tippel, early 1954 (on the occasion of the takeover of Hölscher KG by the Karstadt AG); cf. DTA 1798, 7, p. 111; Schoenbaum, *Hitler's Social Revolution*, pp. 142–3.
98 DTA 1798, 7, p. 111.
99 ASDV, possibly by Georg Tippel, early 1954.
100 Ibid.
101 'Brauchbaren Mitgliedern der *Volksgemeinschaft*.' Firma Knopf, *Betriebsordnung der Betriebsgemeinschaft* (30 June 1934), p. 10.
102 Ibid.
103 Ibid., pp. 9–10.
104 Firma Knopf, *Betriebsordnung der Betriebsgemeinschaft* (30 June 1934), p. 1; Ziefle collection.
105 A theory of ethnic nationality, in this case of a racially homogenous hierarchically organized people.
106 Ziefle Collection, Fritz Richter, *Betriebsordnung* (Freiburg, 1937), p. 3.
107 Ibid., p. 11.
108 Ibid., p. 17.
109 Interview with Mrs K. Hipp, Freiburg, 1 and 2 February 2010.
110 Barkai, *Vom Boykott zur Entjudung*, p. 123.
111 Brucher-Lembach, ... *wie Hunde*, p. 21.
112 GLAK 480 7223.
113 David, *The Patron*, pp. 257–61.
114 Ladwig-Winters and Fischer, *Die Wertheims*, p. 325.

Conclusion

1 Rona Wronker, by email, 11 June 2020. Quoted with permission.
2 GLAK, 480 7223.
3 Kreutzmüller, *Final Sale in Berlin*, p. 3.
4 IHK, *Wirtschaftsmagazin Rhein-Neckar* 1/2006.
5 Fuchs, *Ein Konzern aus Sachsen*, pp. 267–73.
6 Ibid., pp. 273–5.
7 StadtAPf, Rj Schoc 14262 2. Ex., p. 26.
8 Petra Ralle, *Konsequenz Abriss, das (un) vermeidbare Ende des Kaufhauses Schocken von Erich Mendelsohn in Stuttgart* (Stuttgart, 2002), p. 85.
9 Cf. Lerner, *The Consuming Temple*, p. 212.

10 The brand Hertie is still owned and traded by investors and an attempt was made in the early twenty-first century to relaunch the department store by converting some of the smaller Karstadt branches. The experiment failed, but the name was sold again and launched in 2014 as an internet-based department store.
11 See Kaplan, 'Friendship in the Margins', p. 477.
12 Kauder, *German Politics and the Jews*, p. 28.

Bibliography

Manuscript sources

References are made, where possible, in the same style as the relevant archive.

Archive of the Südwestdeutsche Druck- & Verlagsgesellschaft GmbH (ASDV)

Karstadt AG Karlsruhe/Warenhaus Knopf.

Deutsches Historisches Museum (DHM)

Handlungsgehilfen Postkarten (1901 and 1904).

Deutsches Tagebuch Archiv, Emmendingen (DTA)

13,2; Halder, E. C.
1641/II 1; Fischer, Rudolf.
1798, 7; Werner, Carl.
19495/II 1–2; Rahmer, Hedwig.
592; Wittmann, Heinz.

Firmenarchiv Karstadt Karlsruhe (KK)

Klopstock, M., Max Knopf als Persönlichkeit, *Zeitschrift für Waren- und Kaufhäuser*, Vol. 29, No. 14 (Berlin, 1931).
Karstadt Magazin, January 1954.

Kantonsarchiv Basel (KA Basel)

DI-REG 5a 4-20-5 (1).

Landesarchiv Baden-Württemberg, Generallandesarchiv Karlsruhe (GLAK)

General-Intendanz Haus Baden 56 13.
Ständekammer/Badischer Landtag 231 5016.
Ständekammer/Badischer Landtag 231 5056.
Ständekammer/Badischer Landtag 231 5068.
Ständekammer/Badischer Landtag 231 5126.
Ständekammer/Badischer Landtag 231 5738.
Ständekammer/Badischer Landtag 231 5940.
Wiedergutmachungsakten 480 7223.

Landesarchiv Baden-Württemberg, Staatsarchiv Freiburg (StAF)

Nachlass Fritz Richter F196/1 Akten Pack 305 Heft 17.
Wiedergutmachung Arthur Knopf F196/1 6048.
Wiedergutmachung Betty Knopf Erben F196/1 3628/2.
Wiedergutmachung Guggenheim & Cie F196/1 14278.
Wiedergutmachung S. Knopf OHG F196/1 14276.
Wiedergutmachung Sally Knopf Witwe F196/1 3628/1.
F202/32, 7030.
A 25/1 300/2.

Leo Baeck Institute (LBI)

Adolf Jandorf Collection AR3144.
Hermann Tietz Collection, AR1943.
Jandorf, Harry, *Erinnerungen an meinen Vater Adolf Jandorf* ME 335.
Lili Wronker Family Collection AR25255.

Private Archive of Donald Levis, United States (Levis Collection)

Private papers of Arthur and Margarete Levis.

Private Archive of Herr Wolfgang Ziefle, Germany (Ziefle Collection)

Die Elegante Dame, Knopf Catalogue (June 1936).
Familienalbum A. Brossmann.
Firma Knopf, *Anleitung für das Selbstkassieren des Verkaufspersonals* (Freiburg,?).
Firma Knopf, *Betriebsordnung der Betriebsgemeinschaft* (22 May 1925).

Firma Knopf, *Betriebsordnung der Betriebsgemeinschaft* (30 June 1934).
Fritz Richter KG, *Betriebsordnung* (Freiburg, 1937).
Poster *Einheits-Preise* (19 September 1928).
Poster *Ostern* (1918).
Poster *Saison Ausverkauf* (18–31 July 1929).
Richter, F., *Die tüchtige Verkäuferin, Aus der Praxis für die Praxis* (Freiburg, before 1925).
Schottlaender & Co. (publishers), *Geschäftskunde* (Berlin, September 1931).
Zeitungsauschnitte (February 1922–December 1933).

Private Archive of the Schleese Family, Canada (Schleese Collection)

Collection of papers regarding the marriage of Hedwig Knopf to Jacob Steilberger (June 1872).
Collection of papers regarding the marriage of Flora and Benno Knopf (June 1897).
Photographs, poems and letters from various other occasions.

Schocken Institute, Jerusalem, Library (SLJ)

111/191.

Schweizer Wirtschaftsarchiv, Basel (SWA)

AC 510.
H III 1 (Warenhäuser Allgemein und Ausland, 1921–32).
H III 1 (Warenhäuser Allgemein und Ausland, bis 1925).
H III 1 (Warenhäuser Schweiz, bis 1978).
H III 1 (Warenhäuser Schweiz, seit 1978).

Staatsarchiv Basel-Stadt (StAB)

DI-REG 5a 4-20-5 (1) 45.
NEG 02218.

Staatsarchiv Chemnitz (StAC)

Georg Manasse 33309/39.
Schocken-Konzern & Nachfolger 31451.

Stadtarchiv Frankfurt (StadtAFra)

Wronker MA S2739 2.
Wronker V51 37.
Wronker W4 252 1.
Zeitungsarchiv Wronker S3 R2075.

Stadtarchiv Freiburg (StadtAF)

Carl Werner K1/139 3b.
Firma C. Werner Blust K1/139 1a (including *100 Jahre C. Werner-Blust*, StadtAF K1/139/2m).
Gewerbe & Handel, Schutz des Einzelhandels K-C4/IX/20/4.
Handel C4/VI/15/5.
Handelserlaubnisse C4/IX/20/5.
Handelskammer Jahresberichte C4/IX/20/1.
Handelskammer, Tätigkeit und Jahresberichte C4/IX/20/1.
Nachlass Leo Blust H18794.
Private Bausachen K-C4 I/26/6.
S. Knopf Katalog M2 Nr. 323 B.
Sonntagsruhe & Ladenschluss im Handel KIX/20/6a 1 & 2.
Sonntagsruhe, Landeschluss und Ruhezeit KIX/20/6 1–3.
Warenhaussteuer KXIV/17/14.

Stadtarchiv Karlsruhe (StadtAK)

1Bauakte Kaiserstraße 1 BOA 3243.
1Bauakte Kaiserstraße BOA 3240.
Plan- und Bildersammlung Kaiserstraße 8/PBS Abt. XIVe Nr. o01088.
Stadtgeschichtliche Sammlung 8/Sts 17/310.
Stadtgeschichtliche Sammlung 8/Sts 28.

Stadtarchiv Mannheim (StadtMa)

Anker Kaufstätte.
Neue Badische Landeszeitung.

Stadtarchiv Pforzheim (StadtAPf)

B64 Westliche Karl-Friedrichstraße.
Rj Schoc 14262 2. Ex.

University Archive Heidelberg (UAH)

Knopf, R., *Die Wirkung der Kartelle der Textil- und Bekleidungsindustrie auf die Abnehmer*, Doctoral Dissertation, University of Heidelberg 1915.
Studentenkartei Knopf, R. HIV 767/9a.

Interviews and letters

Mrs A. Stillhahn, Freiburg, 30 January 2010.
Mrs K. Hipp, Freiburg, 1 and 2 February 2010.
Mrs E. Endele, Freiburg, 2 February 2010.
Mr B. Schillen, Freiburg, 3 February 2010.
Miss C. Gilbert, Freiburg, 8 March 2010.
Mrs G. Nestelberger, Freiburg, 9 March 2010.
Mrs A. Hinzel, Freiburg, 9 March 2010.
Mrs L. Pauli, Freiburg, 9 March 2010.
Mrs L. Unold, Freiburg, 9 March 2010.
Mrs H. Mendez-Rincones, Freiburg, 5 January 2011.
Mr K. Gumbel, Mannheim, 2 February 2011.
Mrs I. Pfliegensdörfer, Bad Schönborn, 15 February 2011.
Mrs U. Hofmann, Mannheim, 17 February 2011.
Mrs E. Pastecki, Mannheim, 17 February 2011.
Mrs H. Abele, Mannheim, 23 February 2011 and 1 April 2011.
Mrs V. Senft, Mannheim, 21 March 2011.
Mrs Schweiger, Ravensburg, 5 April 2011.

Printed primary sources

Bach, Julius, *Die Organisation des gemeinsamen Einkaufs im Warenhaus und Einzelhandel* (Munich, 1934).
Badisches Statistische Landesamt (ed.), *Handel und Verkehr in Baden im Jahre 1925* (Karlsruhe, 1927).
Baum, Marie, *Drei Klassen von Lohnarbeiterinnen in Industrie und Handel der Stadt Karlsruhe, Bericht erstattet und das Großherzoglich Badische Ministerium des Inneren* (Karlsruhe, 1906).
Braun, Lilly, *Die Frauenfrage* (Bremen, 2010), reprint from 1901.
Clouston, R., *Letters from Germany and Belgium by an Autumn Tourist* (London, 1839).
Colze, Leo, *Berliner Warenhauser* (Leipzig, 1908).
Deutsche Waren- and Kaufhausverband (ed.), *Probleme des Warenhauses* (Berlin, 1928).

Dodd, Charles E., *An Autumn Near the Rhine, or, Sketches of Courts, Society, Scenery Etc. in Some German States Bordering on the Rhine* (London, 1818).
Durm, Josef, *Handbuch der Architektur* (Stuttgart, 1902).
Göhre, Peter, 'Das Warenhaus', *Die Gesellschaft* (Frankfurt, 1907), p. 78.
Hirsch, Julius, *Das Warenhaus im Westdeutschland: Seine Organisation und Wirkung* (Leipzig, 1909).
Hirsch, Julius, *Filialbetriebe im Detailhandel* (Bonn, 1913).
Hitler, Adolf, *Mein Kampf* (Munich, 1942).
Howitt, William, *The Rural and Domestic Life of Germany* (London, 1842).
Kramer, Heinz, *Warenhausprobleme der jüngsten Zeit* (Würzburg, 1931).
Laquer, Leopold, *Der Warenhaus-Diebstahl* (Halle, 1907).
Löwenstein, Ruth, *Die soziale Lage der Verkäuferin im Warenhaus: eine sozialstatistische Studie auf Grund von Untersuchungen in einem Züricher Warenhaus* (Basel, 1937).
Lux, Käthe, *Studien über die Entwicklung der Warenhäuser in Deutschland* (Jena, 1910).
Meißinger, Hans, *Die Entwicklung des Detailhandels in Mannheim* (Heidelberg, 1931).
Müller, Martin, *Der Interessenskampf zwischen großkapitalistischen und mittelständischen Einzelhandel* (Freiburg, 1933).
Reif, Josef, *Frauenarbeit im Handel: Was sagen und was antworten unsere Freunde?* (Leipzig, 1907).
Rubens, Werner, *Der Kampf des Spezialgeschäfte gegen das Warenhaus* (Cologne, 1929).
Sartorius von Waltershausen, August, *Deutsche Wirtschaftsgeschichte, 1815–1914* (Jena, 1923).
Stober, Leopold, *Mannheim und seine Bauten* (Mannheim, 1906).
Zola, Emile, *The Ladies' Paradise* (Paris, 1883), translation by Brian Nelson (Oxford, 1995).

Printed primary sources without author

Beilage zum Protokoll der Sitzung der Zweiten Kammer.
Berufszählung. Die berufliche und soziale Gliederung des deutschen Volkes, Band 408 (Berlin, 1931).
Verhandlungen der Ersten Kammer.
Verhandlungen der Stände-Versammlung des Großherzogtums Baden. Protokolle der Zweiten Kammer.
Verhandlungen des Deutschen Reichstags.
Verkaufserfolg durch Menschenkenntnis (Berlin, probably 1920s).

German newspapers

Badische Presse
Berliner Leben
Berliner Tageblatt
Berliner Volkszeitung
Breisgauer Zeitung
Das Hakenkreuzbanner
Der Alemanne
Der Führer
Der Kurier
Deutsche Allgemeine Zeitung
Deutsche Wochenschau
Donaueschinger Wochenblatt
Durlacher Tageblatt
Frankfurter Allgemeine
Frankfurter Zeitung
Freiburger Tagespost
Freiburger Zeitung
General-Anzeiger Mannheim
General-Anzeiger Pforzheim
Intelligenzblatt
Israelisches Gemeindeblatt
Karlsruher Zeitung/Badischer Staatsanzeiger
Oberbadisches Industrie- und Handelsblatt
Oberrheinischer Beobachter
Oberschwäbischer Anzeiger
Pforzheimer Freie Presse
Pforzheimer Kurier
Pforzheimer Rundschau
Rastatter Tageblatt
Sandhofer Anzeiger
Schwarzwälder Tagblatt
Völkischer Beobachter
Volkswacht

Swiss newspapers

Basler Nachrichten
Nationale Zeitung

Other primary sources

Der Konfektionär
Oberbadische Handels- und Wirtschaftszeitung
The Universal Magazine
Zeitschrift für Waren- und Kaufhäuser

Secondary sources

Abelson, Elaine S., *When Ladies Go A-Thieving, Middle-Class Shoplifters in the Victorian Department Store* (Oxford, 1989).
Abrams, Lynn, *Workers' Culture in Imperial Germany, Leisure and Recreation in the Rhineland and Westphalia* (London, 1992).
Adams, Carole E., *Women Clerks in Wilhelmine Germany, Issues of Class and Gender* (Cambridge, 1988).
Applegate, Celia, *A Nation of Provincials, the German Idea of Heimat* (Berkeley, 1990).
Avakin, Armen and Paulus, Franz A., *Die Familie Sternberg* (Bad Kissingen, 2003).
Bavaj, Riccardo, *Die Ambivalenz der Moderne im Nationalsozialismus. Eine Bilanz der Forschung* (Munich, 2003).
Bell, Michael and Gunn, Simon, *Middle Classes, Their Rise and Sprawl* (London, 2002).
Benson, Susan P., *Counter Cultures* (Chicago, 1986).
Berger, Stefan, Donovan, Mark and Passmore, Kevin (eds), *Writing National Histories: Western Europe since 1800* (London, 1999).
Berkowitz, Michael, Tananbaum, Susan L. and Bloom, Sam W. (eds), *Forging Modern Jewish Identities, Public Faces and Private Struggles* (London, 2003).
Berry, Helen, 'Polite Consumption: Shopping in Eighteenth-Century England', *Transactions of the Royal Historical Society*, Sixth Series, Vol. 12 (2002), pp. 375–94.
Blackbourn, David, *Class, Religion, and Local Politics in Wilhelmine Germany: The Centre Party in Württemberg Before 1914* (Connecticut, 1980).
Blackbourn, David and Evans, Richard J., *The German Bourgeoisie. Essays on the Social History of the German Middle Class from the Late Eighteenth to the Early Twentieth Century* (London,1991).
Blackbourn, David, *Populists and Patricians, Essays in Modern German History* (London, 1987).
Blickle, Peter, et al. (eds), *Von der Ständeversammlung zum demokratischen Parlament* (Stuttgart, 1982).
Bloch, Ernst, *Geschichte der Juden von Konstanz im 19. und 20. Jahrhundert* (Konstanz, 1971).
Bollenbeck, Georg, 'German Kultur, the Bildungsbürgertum, and Its Susceptibility to National Socialism', *German Quarterly*, Vol. 73, No. 1 (January 2000), pp. 67–83.

Bräunche, Ernst O. and Nieß, Ulrich, *Geschichte im Plakat 1914–1933, Katalog zur Ausstellung der Stadtarchive Karlsruhe und Mannheim* (Karlsruhe, 2004).
Breckman, Warren G., 'Disciplining Consumption: The Debate about Luxury in Wilhelmine Germany, 1890–1914', *Journal of Social History*, Vol. 24, No. 3 (Spring 1991), pp. 485–505.
Briesen, Detlef, *Warenhaus, Massenkonsum und Sozialmoral – Zur Geschichte der Konsumkritik im 20. Jahrhundert* (Frankfurt, 2001).
Broadberry, Stephen and O'Rourke, Kevin (eds), *The Cambridge Economic History of Modern Europe, Volume 2, 1870 to the Present* (Cambridge, 2010).
Brucher-Lembach, Andrea, *… wie Hunde auf ein Stück Brot* (Bremgarten, 2004).
Busch-Petersen, Nils, *Adolf Jandorf, vom Volkswarenhaus zum KaDeWe* (Berlin, 2008).
Busch-Petersen, Nils, *Leonhard Tietz* (Berlin, 2014).
Busch-Petersen, Nils, *Oscar Tietz* (Berlin, 2004).
Childers, Thomas, 'The Social Language of Politics in Germany. The Sociology of Political Discourse in the Weimar Republic', *American Historical Review*, Vol. 95, No. 2 (April 1990), pp. 331–58.
Cook, David and Walters, David (eds), *Retail Marketing, Theory and Practice* (Hemel Hempstead, 1991).
Cox, Peter, *Spedan's Partnership: The Story of John Lewis and Waitrose* (Cambridge, 2010).
Crossick, Geoffrey and Jaumain, Serge (eds), *Cathedrals of Consumption: The European Department Store, 1850–1939* (Aldershot, 1999).
Cubitt, Geoffrey (ed.), *Imagining Nations* (Manchester, 1998).
Dale, Tim, *Harrods: The Store and the Legend* (London, 1986).
David, Anthony, *The Patron: A Life of Salman Schocken* (New York, 2003).
Dingel, Tina, *Shopping for Masculinity: Constructing the Male Consumer in Germany, 1920s to 1950s* (Limerick, 2008).
Eisendle, Reinhard and Miklautz, Elfie (eds), *Produktkulturen. Dynamik und Bedeutungswandel des Konsums* (Frankfurt/Main, 1992).
Elon, Amos, *The Pity of It All. A Portrait of Jews in Germany 1743–1933* (London, 2004).
Engehausen, Frankm, *Kleine Geschichte des Großherzogtums Baden* (Leinfeld-Echterdingen, 2005).
Evans, Richard J., *The Coming of the Third Reich* (London, 2004).
Evans, Richard J., *The Pursuit of Power: Europe, 1815–1914* (London, 2016).
Evans, Richard J., *The Third Reich in Power* (New York, 2006).
Frei, Helmut, *Tempel der Kauflust* (Leipzig, 1997).
Frei, Norbert, *National Socialist Rule in Germany, The Führer State, 1933–1945* (Oxford, 1933).
Fuchs, Konrad, *Ein Konzern aus Sachsen, Kaufhaus Schocken als Spiegelbild deutscher Wirtschaft und Politik, 1901–1953* (Stuttgart, 1990).
Gaudenzi, Bianca, *Commercial Advertising in Germany and Italy, 1918–1943* (PhD Thesis, Cambridge, 2011).

Gellately, Robert, *Backing Hitler: Consent and Coercion in Nazi Germany* (Oxford, 2001).
Gellately, Robert, *The Politics of Economic Despair. Shopkeepers and German Politics 1890–1914* (London, 1974).
Goggin, Maureen and Tobin, Beth F. (eds), *Material Women, 1750–1950: Consuming Desires and Collecting Practices* (Farnham, 2009).
Grady, Tim, *A Deadly Legacy: Jews and the Great War* (New Haven, 2017).
Green, Nancy, J., 'Art and Industry: The Language of Modernization in the Production of Fashion', *French Studies*, Vol. 18, No. 3 (Spring 1994), pp. 722–48.
Gregor, Neil, *Nazism* (Oxford, 2000).
Grill, Johnpeter H., *The Nazi Movement in Baden 1920–1945* (Chapel Hill, 1983).
Grunsky, Eberhard, 'Das ehemalige Warenhaus Knopf (heute Karstadt) in Karlsruhe', *Denkmalpflege in Baden-Württemberg* (April–June 1979), pp. 57–64.
Grunwald, Henning and Pfister, Manfred (eds), *Krisis! Krisenszenarien, Diagnosen, Diskursstrategien* (Munich, 2007).
Hansen, Hal, 'Rethinking the Role of Artisans in Modern German Development', *Central European History*, Vol. 42, No. 1 (March 2009), pp. 33–64.
Harbordt, Nanni, *Bernhard Sehring – Das Warenhaus Tietz an der Leipziger Strasse* (Ravensburg, 2010).
Haumann, Heinko Schadek, Hans, *Geschichte der Stadt Freiburg*, Volume III (Stuttgart, 1996).
Heilbronner, Oded, 'From Antisemitic Peripheries to Antisemitic Centres: The Place of Antisemitism in Modern German History', *Journal of Contemporary History*, Vol. 35, No. 4 (October 2000), pp. 559–76.
Heilbronner, Oded, *Catholicism, Political Culture, and the Countryside: A Social History of the Nazi Party in South Germany* (Michigan, 1997).
Herzog, Dagmar, 'Anti-Judaism in Intra-Christian Conflict: Catholics and Liberals in Baden in the 1840s', *Central European History*, Vol. 27, No. 3 (1994), pp. 267–81.
Jeffreys, Jeremy B., *Retail Trading in Britain, 1850–1950: A Study of Trends in Retailing with Special Reference to the Development of Co-operative, Multiple Shop and Department Store Methods of Trading* (Cambridge, 1954).
Jenkins, Jennifer, *Provincial Modernity, Local Culture and Liberal Politics in Fin-de-Siècle Hamburg* (London, 2003).
Jerome, Jerome K., *Three Men on the Bummel, Three Men in a Boat and Three Men on the Bummel* (Oxford, 1998).
Kaplan, Marion, 'Friendship on the Margins: Jewish Social Relations in Imperial', *Central European History*, Vol. 34, No. 4 (2001), pp. 471–501.
Kauder, Anthony, *German Politics and the Jews. Düsseldorf and Nuremberg, 1910–1933* (Oxford, 1996).
Kershaw, Ian, *The Nazi Dictatorship, Problems and Perspectives of Interpretation* (London, 2000).
Kocka, Jürgen, *Industrial Culture and Bourgeois Society. Business, Labor and Bureaucracy in Modern Germany* (New York, 1999).

Kocka, Jürgen and Mitchell, Alan (eds), *Bourgeois Society in Nineteenth-Century Europe* (Providence, 1993).

Kreutzmüller, Christoph, *Final Sale in Berlin: The Destruction of Jewish Commercial Activity, 1930–1945* (New York, 2017).

Kroen, Sheryl, 'A Political History of the Consumer', *Historical Journal*, Vol. 47, No. 3 (September 2004), pp. 709–36.

Ladwig-Winters, Simone, *Wertheim – Ein Warenhausunternehmen und seine Eigentümer* (Münster, 1997).

Ladwig-Winters, Simone and Fischer, Erica, *Die Wertheims: Geschichte einer Familie* (Berlin, 2007).

Lancaster, Bill, *The Department Store: A Social History* (Leicester, 1995).

Lange, Martin, *Antisemitic Elements in the Critique of Capitalism in German Culture 1850–1933* (Bern, 2007).

Lebovics, Hermann, 'Reviewed Work: Mittelstand, Demokratie und Nationalsozialismus: Die politische Entwicklung von Handwerk und Kleinhandel in der Weimarer Republik by Heinrich August Winkler', *Journal of Modern History*, Vol. 45, No. 3 (September 1973), pp. 539–40.

Lenz, Rudolf, *Karstadt, Ein deutscher Warenhauskonzern 1920–1950* (Stuttgart, 1995).

Lerner, Paul, 'An All Consuming History? Recent Works on Consumer Culture in Modern Germany', *Central European History*, Vol. 42, No. 3 (September 2009), pp. 509–43.

Lerner, Paul, 'Circulation and Representation: Jews, Department Stores and Cosmopolitan Consumption in Germany, Circa 1880s-1930s', *European Review of History*, Vol. 17, No. 3 (June 2010), pp. 395–413.

Lerner, Paul, *The Consuming Temple: Jews, Department Stores, and the Consumer Revolution in Germany, 1880–1940* (Ithaca, 2015).

Longerich, Peter, *Politik der Vernichtung: Eine Gesamtdarstellung der nationalsozialistischen Judenverfolgung* (Munich, 1998).

Maase, Kaspar and Kaschuba, Wolfgang (eds), *Schund und Schönheit, Populäre Kultur um 1900* (Cologne, 2001).

Madsen, Axel, *The Marshall Fields* (Hoboken, 2002).

McElligott, Anthony, *Contested City. Municipal Politics and the Rise of Nazism in Altona, 1917–1931* (Ann Arbor, 1998).

McElligott, Anthony, *Rethinking the Weimar Republic, Authority and Authoritarianism, 1916–1937* (London, 2014).

Miller, Michael B., *The Bon Marché, Bourgeois Culture and the Department Store, 1869–1920* (London, 1981).

Mommsen, Wolfgang J., *Bürgerliche Kultur und politische Ordnung. Künstler, Schriftsteller und Intellektuelle in der deutschen Geschichte 1830–1933* (Frankfurt, 2000).

Mommsen, Wolfgang J., *Der autoritäre Nationalstaat. Verfassung, Kultur und Gesellschaft im Kaiserreich* (Frankfurt, 1992).

Mommsen, Wolfgang J., *Imperial Germany 1867–1917: Culture and Society in an Authoritarian State* (New York, 1995).

Mönninghoff, Wolfgang, *Enteignung der Juden: Wunder der Wirtschaft, Erbe der Deutschen* (Hamburg, 2001).

Mort, Frank, *Cultures of Consumption, Masculinities and Social Space in Late Twentieth-Century Britain* (New York, 1996).

Mosse, Werner E., *The German-Jewish Economic Elite 1820–1935: A Socio-Cultural Profile* (Oxford, 1989).

Mosse, Werner E., 'Jewish Entrepreneurship in Germany, 1820–1935', *Zeitschrift für Unternehmensgeschichte*, Vol. 64 (1992), pp. 54–66.

Mosse, Werner E. and Pohl, Hans (eds), *Jüdische Unternehmer in Deutschland im 19. Und 20. Jahrhundert* (Stuttgart, 1992), pp. 54–66.

Nieß, Ulrich and Caroli, Michael (eds), *Geschichte der Stadt Mannheim*, Band 2 (Heidelberg, 2010).

Nipperdey, Thomas, *Deutsche Geschichte 1866–1918, Arbeitswelt und Bürgergeist* (Munich, 1990).

Nipperdey, Thomas, *Deutsche Geschichte 1866–1918, Machtstaat vor der Demokratie* (Munich, 1992).

Pasdermadjian, Hrant, *The Department Store. Ist Origins, Evolution and Economics* (London, 1954).

Peal, David, 'Self-Help and the State, Rural Cooperatives in Imperial Germany', *Central European History* Vol. 21, No. 3 (September 1988), pp. 244–66.

Prinz, Michael, *Brot und Dividende, Konsumvereine in Deutschland und England vor 1914* (Göttingen, 1996).

Putzer, Peter, *Jews and the German State* (Oxford, 1992).

Rahden, Till van, 'Jews and the Ambivalences of Civil Society in Germany, 1800–1933: Assessment and Reassessment', *Journal of Modern History*, Vol. 77, No. 4 (December 2005), pp. 1024–47.

Rahden, Till van, *Juden und andere Breslauer. Die Beziehung zwischen Juden, Portestanten und Katholiken in einer deutschen Großstadt 1860–1925* (Göttingen, 2000).

Ralle, Petra, *Konsequenz Abriss, das (un) vermeidbare Ende des Kaufhauses Schocken von Erich Mendelsohn in Stuttgart* (Stuttgart, 2002).

Rappaport, Erica, *Shopping for Pleasure. Women in the Making of London's West End* (Princeton, 2000).

Reich, Karlheinz, *Die Liberalen Parteien in Deutschland 1918–1933* (Osnabrück 1979).

Reinharz, Jehuda and Schatzberg, Walter, *The Jewish Response to German Culture* (London, 1985).

Reuveni, Gideon and Roemer, Nils (eds), *Longing, Belonging, and Making of Jewish Consumer Culture* (Leiden, 2002).

Ritter, Heiner, *Aktion 3. Die Verwertung jüdischen Eigentums in Mannheim. Arisierung von Gegenständen des täglichen Gebrauchs*, Referat 13 January 2005, Arbeitskreis Justiz Mannheim.

Roerkohl, Anna, *Hungerblockade und Heimatfront. Die kommunale Lebensmittelversorgung in Westfalen während des Ersten Weltkrieges* (Stuttgart, 1991).
Rooch, Alarich, *Zwischen Museum und Warenhaus. Ästhetisierungsprozesse und sozialkommunikative Raumaneignung des Bürgertums* (Bremen, 2000).
Rüegg, Walter and Neuloh, Otto (eds), *Zur soziologischen Theorie und Analyse des 19. Jahrhunderts* (Göttingen, 1971).
Saldern, Adelheid von, *Mittelstand im Dritten Reich. Handwerk – Einzelhändler – Bauern* (Frankfurt, 1979).
Schmitt, Heinz, *Juden in Karlsruhe* (Karlsruhe, 1988).
Schoenbaum, David, *Hitler's Social Revolution, Class and Status in Nazi Germany 1933–39* (New York, 1980).
Schulze, Hagen, 'Is There a German History?', *The 1987 Annual Lecture of the German Historical Institute* (London, 1987).
Schwarz, Jürgen, *Architektur und Kommerz: Studien zur deutschen Kauf- und Warenhausarchitektur vor dem Ersten Weltkrieg am Beispiel der Frankfurter Zeil* (Frankfurt, 1995).
Schwarzmaier, Hansmartin (ed.), *Handbuch der baden-württembergischen Geschichte*. Volume 5: Wirtschafts- und Sozialgeschichte seit 1918. Übersicht und Materialien. Gesamtregister (Stuttgart, 2007).
Seifert, Annatina, *Der Nahrungsmittelkonzern Maggi: Auswirkungen des Ersten Weltkriegs auf ein schweizerisches Unternehmen*, Dissertation Universität Zürich (Zürich, 2006).
Seiffert, Hans, *In Argentinien gerettet – in Auschwitz ermordet* (Konstanz, 2010).
Siry, J., *Carson Pirie Scott, Louis Sullivan and the Chicago Department Store* (Chicago, 2012).
Spiekermann, Uwe, *Basis der Konsumgesellschaft: Entstehung und Entwicklung des modernen Kleinhandels in Deutschland 1850-1914* (Munich, 1999).
Spiekermann, Uwe, *Warenhaussteuer in Deutschland, Mittelstandsbewegung, Kapitalismus und Rechtstaat im späten Kaiserreich* (Frankfurt, 1994).
Tietz, Georg, *Hermann Tietz – Geschichte einer Familie und ihrer Warenhäuser* (Stuttgart, 1965).
Trentmann, Frank, 'Beyond Consumerism: New Historical Perspectives on Consumption', *Journal of Contemporary History*, Vol. 39, No. 3 (July 2004), pp. 373–404.
Trost, Oskar 'Abschied vom alten Marktplatz', *Lebendige Vergangenheit*, Heft 11 (February 1962).
Ugolini, Laura, *Men and Menswear, Sartorial Consumption in Britain 1880–1939* (Aldershot, 2007).
Unterstell, Rembert, *Mittelstand in der Weimarer Republik. Die soziale Entwicklung und politische Orientierung von Handwerk, Kleinhandel und Hausbesit 19–1933* (Frankfurt, 1989).
Vaupel, Elizabeth, 'Gewürze aus der Retorte', *Kultur & Technick*, Vol. 2 (2010), pp. 44–50.

Vogel, R., *Ein Stück von uns: Deutsche Juden in deutschen Armeen, 1813–1976* (Mainz, 1977).
Walker, Philip, *Zola* (London, 1985).
Wandel, Eckhard, *Banken und Versicherungen im 19. Und 20. Jahrhundert* (Munich, 1998).
Wehler, Hans-Ulrich, *Deutsche Gesellschaftsgeschichte Band 3. Von der Deutschen Doppelrevolution bis zum Beginn des Ersten Weltkrieges, 1849–1914* (Munich, 2007).
Wehler, Hans-Ulrich, *Deutsche Gesellschaftsgeschichte Band 4. Vom Beginn des Ersten Weltkriegs bis zur Gründung der beiden deutschen Staaten, 1914–1949* (Munich, 2008).
Weiss-Sussex, Godela and Zitzelsperger, Ulrike (eds), *Das Berliner Warenhaus: Gesichte und Diskurse* (The Berlin Department Store: History and Discourse) (Frankfurt, 2013).
Weitz, Eric D., *Weimar Germany: Promise and Tragedy* (Princeton, 2007).
Werner, Josef, *Hakenkreuz und Judenstern* (Karlsruhe, 1990).
Winkler, Heinrich A., *Mittelstand, Demokratie und Nationalsozialismus: Die politische Entwicklung von Handwerk und Kleinhandel in der Weimarer Republik* (Cologne, 1972).
Zang, Georg, *Konstanz in der Großherzoglichen Zeit* (Constance, 1994).
Ziegler, Dieter (ed.), *Großbürger und Unternehmer: Die deutsche Wirtschaftselite im 20. Jahrhundert*, Bürgertum Vol. 17 (Göttingen, 2000).

Other secondary sources

Appelius, Stefan, 'Lili und die Kaufhauskönige', Einestages Zeitgeschichte auf Spiegel Online, http://einestages.spiegel.de/static/topicalbumbackground/589/lili_und_die_kaufhauskoenige.html, last retrieved 23 December 2012.
Der Fächer, a pamphlet published by the Karstadt AG to celebrate the gutting and extension of the store at Karlsruhe (1990).
IHK, *Wirtschaftsmagazin Rhein-Neckar* 1/2006.
Neue Deutsche Biographie 23 (2007), S. 235–6 [Onlinefassung]; http://www.deutsche-biographie.de/pnd118609262.html.

Index

Note: *Cursive* script indicates an illustration.

advertising
  appeal to children 56
  criticism of 59, 61, 109, 149
  decline of, 122
  of the departure of Jewish managers and owners, 176, 178
  growth of 51–3
  role of Staff in 78, 84
  role at Schocken stores 134–6
Althoff, Theodor, Company 125–6
Anti-Department Store Movement 3, 6, 150, 153
  and the Mittelstand 4, 61, 63–7, 73, 109–12, 151
antisemitism 6–7, 12–13, 67, 127, *142*, *144*, *145*, 163, 189–90
  change of character of 112–13, 178
  lack of cohesion of, 100–1, 113, 123–4, 147–8
  origins of 5, 20, 49, 188
  during the First World War 119
architecture
  see Bauhaus, Gothic, Mendelsohn, Messel and Olbrich
Aryanization 167, 170–1, 176–8, 191–2
AWAG 175, 183

Baden 17, 30–3, 43, 59–64, 84, 95, 109–12, 143, 164
Basel 181–2, 187
Bauhaus Architecture 133–4
Berlin 5, 9, 35–6, 87, 93, 106, 108–9, 121–2, 129, 144, 182
Birnbaum (Międzychód) 23, 27, 48, 120
Blust, Leo *see* Werner-Blust, Company
Bon Marché 2, 63
Brossmann, Albert *176*, 177
brownshirts 150, 163–6, 191

Cadinen 44, 101–2
Chemnitz 134, 157
children as customers 56, 109
colonialism 50
consumer cooperatives 42–3, 149

department store tax *see* tax
Deutsche Demokratische Republik *see* German Democratic Republic

Ehape or EPA (Einheitspreisgeschäft) 127
electric lighting 78–9, 82
elevators *see* lifts
Emden, Jakob 35
Emden Söhne Hamburger En Gros Lager, M.I., Company 35–6, 132
Emperor Wilhelm II 44, 49–50, *88*, 100–2, 106, *116*, 117, 120, 124, 126, 174–5

First World War 115–19
Frankfurt 28, 98, 105, 129–30
Freiburg 33, 104–5, 131, 143, 145–6, 150, 164, 171–3, 178, 181–2

German Democratic Republic (DDR) viii, 187
German Federation of Department Stores (*Verband Deutscher Waren- und Kaufhäuser*) 15–16, 148, 161
gothic architecture 2, 33, 97, 131
Guggenheim & Cie 41

Hamburg 8–9, 35–6, 123, 169
Heimat 45, 166
heraldic quality of goods 8
Hertie 171, 186 *see also* Tietz, Hermann
Herzl, Theodore 101–2
Hitler, Adolf 2, 123–4, 161–8, *162*, 175

imperialism *see* colonialism

Jandorf, Adolf 34, 35–6, 106, 118–19, 132
Jandorf, Company, 35–6, 98, 106, *107*, 156
  and the KaDeWe 108, *108*, 118,
  156, 170
Jewish *see also* antisemitism
  faith 2, 48
  places of worship 48, 104, 106, 182

KaDeWe (Kaufhaus des Westens) *see*
  Jandorf, Company
Kaiser Wilhelm II *see* Emperor
Karlsruhe 29–31, 43, 71–82, 93–8, 121,
  143, 157, 164–5
Karstadt, Rudolph 36
Karstadt, Rudolph, Company 36, 44, *125*,
  129, 132, 170
  finances of 125–7, 153, 155–6, 187
kleptomania 3, 93, 11, 100
Knopf, Geschwister, Company 28–34, *70*,
  94, 98, 117, 129, 142, 174
Knopf, Margarete *see* Levis, Margarete
Knopf, Max 28, *30*, 33, *78*, 92–3, 95, 118,
  138, 156–7
Knopf, Sally 33, 104–5, 127
Knopf, Sally, Company 28–34, *78*, *119*,
  130, 131, 165, 172, *176*, 177, *179*
Knopf, Simon *see* Knopf, Sally

Ladies' Paradise (Aux Bonheur des
  Dames) *see* Zola, Edmund
Landtag of Baden 61–5, 84, 109–12,
  146–8, 151–2
Leipzig 38, 44, 126
Levis, Arthur *32*, 104–5, 132, 182, 185
Levis, Margarete *32*, 104–5, 132, 174,
  182, 185
Lewis, John, Company 2
lifts 96, 129

Manasse, George 38, 56, 84, 96, 103, 146
manufacturing 18–19, 39–41, 43–5, 52,
  59, 109, 118
men
  shopping habits of 55–6
Mendelsohn, Erich 133–4, 158, 182, 187
Mein Kampf 2, 123–4, 161 *see also*
  Hitler, Adolf

Merkur 174–6, 186
Messel, Alfred 93, 97, 101
Mittelstand 6–7, 60–7, 63, 124, 146, 189
  membership of Jews of 58, 104
modernism 133–4
Munich 27, 58, 106, 123

National Socialist Party (NSDAP)
  123, 148–50
  and anti-department store rhetoric
  148, 150–1
  and infringement of department stores
  168, 178
  polling results 147–8, 159, 163
  violence against stores 150–1
Nazi *see* National Socialist Party
Nuremberg 133–4, 157, 172
  laws of 170, 173

Oelsnitz 38
Olbrich, Joseph 91–2
orders, honours and decorations received
  102, 107–8, 118–19, 124, 189

Palestine 101–2, 113, 182
parliament *see* Landtag and Reichstag
Pforzheim 43, 91–3, 156, 158
Posen (Poznan) *see* Birnbaum

Raiffeisen *see* consumer cooperative
refreshment rooms 96, 98–9, 169, 178
Reichstag 59–65, 93–5, 100, 109, 112, 121,
  124, 147, 159, 163
Richter, Fritz 74, 172–3, 176, 178,
  180–1, 186

SA (Sturmabteilung) *see* Brownshirts
Sassleben 103, 183
Saxony 7, 38, 58, 61
Schmoller, Hermann 31
Schmoller, Hermann, Company 31, 52,
  56–9, 84, 129, 137, 149, 166, 176
Schocken Söhne, I. *see* Schocken,
  Company
Schocken, Company 8, 56, 58, 71, 75–6,
  80, 84–5, 129, *133*, 157–8, 174
Schocken, Salman 8, *37*, 38–9, 74, 103–4,
  133–8, 150, 155, 168–9, 182
Schocken, Simon 38, 104, 138

Schöndorff, Hermann 126, 129, 170
shopgirls *see* employment of women
shoplifting *see* kleptomania
Social Democratic Party of Germany (SPD), formerly Socialist Workers' Party of Germany 18, 64–5, 109–10, 120–1, 143, 147–8, 151–2
Stralsund 21–3, 25
Stuttgart 134, 157

taxing department stores 60–7, 109–12, 122, 127–8, 150–3, 169
Tietz, Chaskel 23–5, 27–8
Tietz, Flora 25
Tietz, Georg 27, 64, 106, 109, 117, 121, 132, 156, 167, 170, 182
Tietz, Hermann 25, 56
Tietz, Hermann, Company 25–7, 42, *50*, *57*, 58, 64, 186
  architecture of 97
  finances of 156, 170–1
Tietz, Leonhard 23–5, *24*
Tietz, Leonhard, Company 23–5, 80, *81*, *90*, 91–2, 98, 127, 170–1
Tietz, Oscar *16*, 23, 25–7, *26*, 58, 64, 76, 83, 102, 106, 109, 117–18, 132

Ury, Company 38–9

Weimar 121
Werner, Carl 120, 127, 145, 150, 161, 178
Werner-Blust, C., Company 40–1
Wertheim, Abraham 21
Wertheim, Abraham, Company 21–3, 97, *99* 100–1, 106, 118, *128*, 153, 156, 166, 175
  architecture of 93–4
Wertheim, Georg 22, *22*, 101–3, *102*, 150, 165, 168, 183
Wilhelm II *see* Emperor
women
  shopping habits of 9, 51–8
Woolworths (Wohlwert) 104, 127, 151, 152
World War, First *see* First World War
Wronker, Company 27–8, 82, 91–2, 129, *154*, 158, 171, 176–7
  finances of 155–6
Wronker, Hermann 27–8, *28*, 84, 103, 105, 129–30, 182
Wronker, Ida 27–8, *28*, 155–6, 182
Wronker, Max *28*, 109, 119, 132

Zionism 101–2, 104, 182
Zola, Emile 3, 188
Zwickau 38–9, 58, 71, 103, 158

www.ingramcontent.com/pod-product-compliance
Lightning Source LLC
Chambersburg PA
CBHW062141300426
44115CB00012BA/1995